D103 SOCIETY AND SOCIAL SCIENCE: A FOUNDATION COURSE

BLOCK 4
POLITICS AND POWER

THE OPEN UNIVERSITY

D103 PRODUCTION TEAM

John Allen
James Anderson (Chairperson)
Robert Bocock
Peter Bradshaw
Vivienne Brown
Linda Clark (Course Secretary)
David Coates
Allan Cochrane
Jeremy Cooper (BBC)
Neil Costello
Clare Falkner (BBC)
Stuart Hall
Susan Himmelweit
Jack Leathem (BBC)
Richard Maidment
Doreen Massey
Gregor McLennan
Andrew Northedge
Kay Pole
Marilyn Ricci (Course Manager)
Paul Smith
Richard Stevens
Elaine Storkey
Kenneth Thompson
Diane Watson
Margaret Wetherell

External Consultants
Tom Burden
David Deacon
David Denver
Caroline Dumonteil
Owen Hartley
Tom Hulley
Robert Looker
Angela Phillips
Colm Regan
Richard Sanders
Neil Thompson
Patrick Wright

Tutor Assessors
Alan Brown
Lyn Brennan
Mona Clark
Ian Crosher
Donna Dickenson
Brian Graham
Philip Markey
Norma Sherratt
Jan Vance

Tom Hunter, Chris Wooldridge, David Wilson, Robert Cookson, Nigel Draper, David Scott-Macnab (Editors); Paul Smith (Librarian); Alison George (Graphic Artist); Jane Sheppard (Designer); Sue Rippon and Mollie Hancock (Project Control); Robin Thornton (Summer School Manager); John Hunt (IT for Summer School); John Bennett and others.

External Academic Assessors
Professor Anthony Giddens, Cambridge University (Overall Course Assessor)
Dr Geoffrey Harcourt, Cambridge University (Block III)
Dr Patrick Dunleavy, London School of Economics and Political Science (Block IV)
Dr Halla Beloff, Edinburgh University (Block V)
Professor Brian Robson, Manchester University (Block VI)

The Open University,
Walton Hall,
Milton Keynes, MK7 6AA

First published 1991; Second Edition 1995

© 1995 The Open University

Edited, designed and typeset by The Open University.

Printed in the United Kingdom by The Alden Press, Oxford.

ISBN 0 7492 0183 5

This text forms part of an Open University Foundation Level Course D103 *Society and Social Science: a Foundation Course*. If you would like a copy of *Studying with the Open University*, please write to the Central Enquiry Service, PO Box 200, The Open University, Walton Hall, Milton Keynes, MK7 6YZ, United Kingdom.

2.1

BLOCK INTRODUCTION AND STUDY GUIDE

Prepared for the Course Team by Richard Maidment

Welcome to Block IV. In this block, the course will focus on the political dimension of the unfolding story of the making of the modern United Kingdom. The five units in the block will examine several of the most important issues of British politics in the 1990s, and also will introduce you to some of the key concepts that political scientists use in their study of the political and governmental processes. The fact that Block IV is primarily concerned with politics, does not mean that politics has been absent from the course until this point. Indeed, the issue of food in Block I and the range of economic considerations that you explored in Block III, for instance, are very highly charged politically. So this block will build on and develop your earlier introduction to the arena of politics.

Each of the five units of the block have their own particular story to tell, but they also have several concerns in common. The most significant unifying thread in all the units is the notion of *power*. This is a notion that is immediately familiar to most of us; it is present in all aspects of our lives. It is present in our domestic life and at work, nor is it absent from our leisure or social life. Although it does have a particular meaning and particular implications for the study of politics, the concept of power as it is applied in this block will not be strikingly different from its usage in everyday life. The concept will be explained and discussed in detail in Unit 15, though each of the units will be concerned directly or indirectly with it as it is a particularly important concept in the discipline of politics.

Unit 14 will deal with power and sovereignty at the international level and examine the position of the United Kingdom in the global and European arena. It seeks to discover the degree and the extent to which the UK has been able to shape its own destiny within the configuration of power that exists in the world. Unit 15 is concerned with power at the national level. It will explore the making of public policy and the differential impact of the various interests that operate within British society. Unit 16 also looks at power in relation to the concept of democracy. To what extent do 'the people' control the political process that is supposedly theirs? What should be the scope of democratic rule? Which people should rule? The unit explores the answers to these questions, which in turn raises issues over the subject of democracy. Unit 17 is concerned with the power of ideas and the influence and impact of those ideas, which shape the way we construct the world. Unit 18, which is the half-unit of this block, will reflect on the main points that have arisen from the preceeding four units, particularly some of their theoretical content. It will specifically address the inter-relationships between theories and evidence.

There are three Reader chapters associated with the block, and they too address the concept of power. The first is by Steven Lukes (Chapter 12), and is to be read during your study of Unit 15. The Lukes piece directly examines the ideas that lie behind the concept of power, and it offers us a particular and distinctive view of it. The second of the Reader chapters is by April Carter (Chapter 13), and is also attached to Unit 15. It provides an illustration of the changing patterns of power in UK society, through an examination of two important pieces of equal opportunity legislation. The third chapter, by John Dearlove and Peter Saunders (Chapter 14), which should be read with Unit 16, examines the relationship between, and compatibility of, capitalism and democracy, and the issue of power has an important role in the discussion.

The television programmes attached to the block are closely integrated with the units and will develop and elaborate on the material in them. TV07, which will be broadcast in the same week as you read Unit 14, looks at the responses of nations other than the United Kingdom, to membership of the European Union. Do they believe that the EU threatens their national sovereignty? TV08 explores the issue of equal opportunities, and examines how the political agenda of the UK has been altered on this issue over the course of the past few decades. TV09 explores the role of ideas in the mass media investigating news and current affairs programmes and soap opera on television.

The course themes are present in all the units of the block, although each of the units primarily focuses on one of them. The theme of *Local and Global* is central to the concerns of Unit 14, while *Public and Private* is the more important theme in Units 15 and 16. Unit 17 develops the theme of *Representation and Reality*.

With Unit 14 you should read *The Good Study Guide,* Chapter 5, Sections 3 and 4, and Chapter 6, Sections 1 and 2; with Unit 16 read Chapter 6, Section 5.

In the course of the block, you will note connections to all four traditions of social thought. You will be asked when studying Unit 15 to read about social reformism in Chapter 22, Section 2.3 of the Reader. In Unit 17 you will be asked to read Section 4 of the same chapter, and Section 1 with Unit 18.

This block also includes two radio programmes. The first of these will examine the developments and changes in the international arena, while the other will be a programme relating to TMA04. There is, in addition, an audio-cassette to help you with the Lukes chapter in the Reader and to help with Unit 16. Side B is taken up with a review of how the course themes have been used in Blocks I to IV.

BLOCK IV STUDY GUIDE

The following study guide will enable you to plan roughly what proportion of your available time to devote to each component.

Block components	Approximate study time (hours)
Block Introduction and Study Guide	$\frac{1}{2}$
Unit 14: The sovereignty of the United Kingdom	$5\frac{1}{2}$
The Good Study Guide: Chapter 5, Sections 3 and 4; Chapter 6, Sections 1 and 2	3
TV07: 'Questions of sovereignty'	2
Total	11
Unit 15: Power and the state	6
Reader: Chapters 12 and 13	$1\frac{1}{2}$
Reader: 'Social reformism' in Chapter 22, Section 2.3	$1\frac{1}{2}$
Radio 07	$\frac{1}{2}$
Audio-cassette 4	$\frac{1}{2}$
Total	10
Unit 16: Power and the people	6
Reader: Chapter 14	1
The Good Study Guide, Chapter 6, Section 5	1
Audio-cassette 4	$\frac{1}{2}$
TV08: 'The politics of equal opportunity'	2
Total	$10\frac{1}{2}$
Unit 17: The power of ideology	6
Reader: Chapter 22, Section 4	1
Radio 08	$\frac{1}{2}$
Audio-cassette 4	$\frac{1}{2}$
Total	8
Unit 18: Theories and evidence	3
Reader: Chapter 22, Section 1	$\frac{1}{2}$
TV09: 'Television: propaganda or critical forum?'	2
TMA 04	6
Total	$11\frac{1}{2}$

UNIT 14   THE SOVEREIGNTY OF THE UNITED KINGDOM

Prepared for the Course Team by Richard Maidment

CONTENTS

1   INTRODUCTION

The question of whether the United Kingdom possesses the ability to control its own destiny has been raised in previous blocks. You will have already noted, from Blocks I and III in particular, the striking degree of interdependence that exists in the world. The web of relationships that have been formed globally, transcends the boundaries of any individual state. This density of transnational relationships and connections strongly suggests that the ability of individual nations to control their own affairs has been substantially impaired. Critical decisions, as you will have noted in Unit 12, are not only taken by national governments, but also by other institutions both public and private that are located outside the frontiers of the UK. Unit 15 will be returning to this theme in some detail, but this position is evident from even a cursory examination of some of the news that appears in our newspapers and on our television screens.

Global influences appear to be particularly significant in understanding the working of the British economy. UK companies are bought and sold by foreign corporations. Decisions to invest, or not to invest, in the UK are made not only in the boardrooms of Manchester and Birmingham, but also in the headquarters of multinational corporations located in, for example, Tokyo, Frankfurt and Los Angeles. The foreign exchange rate of sterling or the level of interest rates are determined not only in London, but also by the markets in Hong Kong, Paris and New York and so on. The run on the pound has become a far too familiar occurrence for anyone in the UK to believe that such matters are determined solely by British institutions. The sheer volume of money that is traded across the world's foreign exchanges has made it all but impossible for the UK government to retain control or even to claim that it controls these matters. A whole host of players, private and public, British and foreign, effect, and to an increasing extent determine, the outcomes which have a profound impact on the economy of the UK.

But these global influences are not solely limited to the economy, they are evident in virtually every area of our daily lives from food, as chronicled in Unit 1, to the television programmes that we watch. It is difficult to believe that only a few decades ago the television service both in ownership and in content was almost exclusively British. The portrait of the television service in the 1990s is very different. There are an increasing number of channels, delivered by cable and satellite, broadcasting a vast range of non-UK programmes, with a significant percentage of ownership in the hands of multinational corporations. The television service which had always appeared to be so quintessentially British has undergone a fundamental change and the process of change will continue. The environment offers a further example. Decisions taken in a variety of locations and institutions around the globe will have a profound impact on the environment for those of us who live in the UK. The list could be easily extended but the point is made. We live in an interdependent world and the degree of that interdependence appears to increase annually.

The factors that fuel and encourage this globalization appear to be inexorable. Companies develop global strategies. Automobile companies do not design and manufacture cars only for the UK. If they are to be successful they have to develop a car which will be attractive to consumers in every nation. This is true for most products and services. Environmental issues cannot be dealt with successfully at the national level. The problems of pollution spill over national boundaries. They need to be handled at least regionally, and for some of them, globally. So one major consequence of the impact of globalization is the apparent reduction in the control that we in the UK can exercise over our lives.

Decisions are made, and in a sense have to be taken, beyond the shores of the UK. We have less autonomy. So what are we to make of it and what does it tell us about our independence and sovereignty? It is to these issues that we now turn.

This unit is concerned centrally with the concept of sovereignty and will explore the degree to which this concept is helpful in understanding the position of the United Kingdom in the world. So in this unit we will:

1   examine the concept of sovereignty;

2   look at the real-world implications of sovereignty, primarily, through the relationship between the UK and the European Union (EU);

3   reflect on the development of the relationship between the UK and the EU over the past decades;

4   consider the factors that are likely to affect this relationship until the end of the decade;

5   consider the value of the concept of sovereignty in the conditions that face a state, such as the UK, in the world at the end of the twentieth century; and

6   provide you with a perspective for examining the most recent developments in the global arena.

Although this unit deals with the recent past, what it cannot attempt to do is to offer you an up-to-the minute account of the location of the UK in the world. If it sought to do so, it would date very rapidly. The unit was written during a period of quite extraordinary change in the world. Just a partial list of what has happened in the preceding decade will remind you of the momentous nature of these events:

1   the end of the Cold War;

2   the disintegration of the Soviet Union and the attempt by several of the nation-states that emerged to introduce both a democratic polity and a market economy;

3   the reunification of Germany after it had appeared to be diplomatically and politically unachievable for several decades;

4   the revolutions that swept through Eastern Europe during 1989 and the collapse of several of these states, notably Yugoslavia;

5   the increasing integration and expansion of the European Union;

6   the paradox of the United States which appears to be in a state of relative economic decline but which is now the only superpower in the world;

7   the emergence of the Asian Pacific as an important, if not the most important, economic region in the world.

These are just some, albeit the most important, of the developments, that are in the process of altering radically the global order. It is all but impossible to predict the outcomes and the impact of these developments and it would be unwise of me to do so. However, this unit will attempt to provide you with the ability to consider the consequences for the UK as these events and others unfold in the global arena.

2   SOVEREIGNTY

What does sovereignty mean and why is it important to our understanding of the issues that are of concern to this block?

——————————— ACTIVITY 1 ———————————

You will find it useful and interesting to make a list of the main characteristics that you associate with the word 'sovereignty'. Although, as you will see, sovereignty does have a particular meaning that is specific to the study of politics, it also has a wider usage. You will have noticed over the past few years that the debates over the European Union have been dominated by the sovereignty of the UK. Interestingly few of the participants defined the concept but, for some, it has been an imperative for the UK to retain it while for others sovereignty has been a less than pressing consideration. So with that in mind, write your list and then consider it again when you have finished reading this section.

Sovereignty is both a legal and a political concept, with a long history that can be traced back to the writers and philosophers of the Roman Empire. However, the origins, development and evolution of the concept over several centuries need not concern us here. Our concern is with the meaning and operation of sovereignty in the modern world. For most of the past two centuries, it has been understood broadly to mean, that a state, which is independent, possesses the exclusive and sole authority over a specific people and territory. The government of this state exercises the final and ultimate, or sovereign, authority within its borders.

The notion of sovereignty requires all independent states to accept and recognize the jurisdictions of each other. States must recognize and respect each other's claim to exercise the final and ultimate authority within certain specified borders and over a designated population. In this sense, all independent states are sovereign and are accepted as being sovereign by other states. The power of this concept is reflected in one of the striking characteristics of the twentieth century, namely the successful claims for independence and sovereignty of countries in Africa, Asia, the Caribbean and elsewhere, which had hitherto been part of the European colonial empires. Sovereignty was and is important to these countries and indeed to all states, because it establishes their legitimate authority over a designated jurisdiction of a particular area and population. Moreover, sovereignty in this global context also implies an equality among states at least at a legal level.

The relationships between states, however, are affected by numerous considerations, and sovereignty is only one of them. One of the most important considerations is power, and power and influence are not equally distributed throughout the globe. Nevertheless, within the very complex web of relationships — diplomatic, economic and military — that exist in the global arena, there is one important sense in which all states are equal. They are equal because they are all sovereign states, and there is a mutual and legal recognition of this sovereignty. Indeed, this legal recognition is a very important dimension of the theory of sovereignty. The most powerful countries accept the legal authority of the least powerful state and its government to rule within its designated borders. The disparities in their economies or in the size of their military establishments does not affect their mutual recognition of sovereignty.

So the concept of sovereignty, as far as it concerns us, is characterized firstly by the claim to exclusive jurisdiction over people and territory (a claim which is legally recognized by other states), and secondly by what can be referred to as the sovereign equality of states.

ACTIVITY 2

Now I am sure that you can immediately detect some problems or limitations with the concept of sovereignty as it has been defined above. Briefly, you should make a list of some of these problems and questions and how sovereignty relates to the real world.

The principal problem that immediately arises for me, is that sovereignty does not appear to relate to the real world. Let me explain by raising some issues and questions. The ones that immediately come to mind are:

1   How meaningful is it to declare that states operate on a basis of a legal equality within the global arena when in terms of power and influence, be it economic, military or diplomatic, countries are not equally endowed?

2   Is not legal equality undermined by the unequal distribution of power?

3   If power is unequally distributed, do not the less powerful states, in particular, effectively lose control of the populations and territory over which they have sovereign jurisdiction?

4   Even the most powerful states are not in control of all aspects of their society, polity and economy. They do not possess a great deal of autonomy.

5   Is there a distinction to be made between the nation and the state?

There are several responses to these questions and observations. Let me take the last point and deal with it first, as we tend to assume that the words nation and state are almost interchangeable and that both have strong claims to sovereignty. There are several examples of nations co-existing happily within a state; it is of course the state that possesses sovereignty and not the individual nations, who accept this position. However, there are many other states where the possession of sovereignty has been contested, for example in Canada by the Francophones and in Spain by the Catalonians and the Basques. The most dramatic manifestations of contested sovereignty, of course, have been in Eastern Europe in recent years. It is also a major issue in Britain. The location of Northern Ireland and to a lesser extent Scotland within the United Kingdom has been and continues to be an issue of central political importance and profound source of division. So, at the very least, we have to be aware of the distinctions between nation and state.

Turning to the implications of sovereignty in the global context, is it a concept that is merely a legal fiction? There have always been more and less powerful countries. In the real world the more powerful have constantly intervened in the affairs of those who had less power and influence, regardless of sovereignty. They, in effect, have violated the sovereignty of other states. In this century alone there is an abundance of examples, but a few instances drawn from the post-Second World War period will suffice to make the point. The invasions by the Soviet Union of Hungary in 1956 and Czechoslovakia in 1968 are both instances when the sovereignty of these two nations did not prevent the incursion of a foreign army. The invasion by the United States of the Caribbean island of Grenada in 1982 and of Panama in 1989, or the American bombing of

Libya in 1985 similarly flouted the mutual recognition of sovereignty. The invasion of Kuwait by Iraq in 1990 is a further example. So what benefit was conferred on Czechoslovakia, Kuwait and Grenada by their possession of sovereignty? The history of the globe over the past fifty years suggests that there is a very real tension between sovereignty on the one hand and the realities of global power on the other and generally the imperatives of power have prevailed.

Yet this is not the whole story for I have a further response which, in a sense, is the obverse of the one above. If power and influence are the sole determinants of what matters in the global arena, why has the issue of sovereignty lingered? If sovereignty is merely a legal fiction, why have so many states been anxious to maintain or assert their sovereignty? Why do they see it as a vital attribute of their existence as states? In 1982, the dispute between Argentina and the UK over which state had sovereignty of the Falkland Islands led to a brief but bloody war. In the debate over the ratification of the Treaty of Maastricht, British sovereignty and the extent to which it was being ceded was at the very heart of the argument and it raised powerful and intense emotions. So, sovereignty and its possession has been, and continues to be, an important and central component of the political consciousness of the United Kingdom and most other states. It cannot be dismissed or ignored; its presence is significant, and critical to the belief of being an independent state. In the remainder of this unit we will attempt to deal with this apparent paradox — that power and influence appear at one level to make sovereignty a legal fiction, and yet the desire for independence and sovereignty remains a powerful force in the politics of the international arena.

A further response which applies to all states, regardless of their relative power, is that they are not in control of their own destinies. This point has been made earlier in the unit. The government of the United States, the most powerful sovereign state, has to accept that there are a range of matters and issues, several of which are critical to the well being of the country, that are decided by a host of institutions American and foreign, public and private. Issues which are nominally under the control of the American government, such as interest rates or the foreign exchange level of the dollar are in reality determined by the world financial markets. The United States is a sovereign country but it is not autonomous. In other words sovereignty and autonomy are not synonymous. There is a very important distinction to be made between the legal authority to make and pass laws, to be in legal and constitutional control over a country's affairs on the one hand, and the ability to have effective — real world — control over these matters on the other. This is the distinction between sovereignty and autonomy. The possession of sovereignty does not guarantee autonomy. The authority to take decisions does not guarantee the power to make them effective.

In fact there may well be a further dimension to this paradox. This is the ability of a state to assert power or influence in the world, and to establish greater control or autonomy over its own affairs, paradoxically, may be enhanced only through a diminution of its sovereignty. Let me explain. Since the end of the Second World War, the UK has joined numerous multinational organizations and institutions, political, military and economic, the membership of which has imposed both obligations and restrictions on successive British governments. Perhaps the most significant of these has been the European Union (EU) which was joined, in part, to enhance British power and influence in a world increasingly dominated by economic and military superpowers. Whether joining these organizations fulfilled the objective of bolstering the British position in the international arena is a question that continues to arouse debate, but undoubtedly one of the effects of membership has been an impact on the sovereignty of the UK.

Those who support British membership of these organizations have argued that any loss of sovereignty is more than compensated for. Firstly, these organizations, by virtue of their multinational membership, have a far greater impact in the global arena than any single state (particularly a state such as the UK which is no longer in the first rank either militarily or economically) and so can influence events more substantially. Secondly, by working from within these organizations, the UK can obtain far greater control or autonomy over its own affairs than if it was a non-member, buffeted by events and developments outside its control. Of course, this view has not been universally accepted, but most British governments since the end of the Second World War have tended to endorse it, though with a considerable degree of unease. They have been anxious to assert the power and influence of the UK, establish greater control over British affairs, and have accepted the notion that these objectives are best achieved through membership of multinational organizations, but they have been very uneasy about the ceding of British sovereignty. This tension over control or autonomy on the one hand and sovereignty on the other has constantly surfaced over the past fifty years. Conservative and Labour governments alike have grappled with it. In the remainder of this unit, we shall explore this tension and the consequences for British sovereignty by looking at the relationship between the UK and the European Union.

––––––––––––––––––––––––––––––– ACTIVITY 3 –––––––––––––––––––––––––––––––

Look back at the list you made at the start of this section and consider it in the light of what you have just read. Has your understanding of sovereignty changed? Would you now identify a different set of characteristics with the notion of sovereignty? You may find it useful to construct a new list of the key features of sovereignty and then contrast it with your first list. It will indicate the differences, and also the shared assumptions, between the general and popular meaning of the word on the one hand and the academic usage of the term on the other.

SUMMARY

- Sovereignty is a legal and a political concept.
- It is characterized firstly by the claim to exclusive jurisdiction over both people and territory and, secondly, by what is known as the sovereign equality of states.
- There is a tension between the notion of sovereignty and the realities of global power. Sovereignty, nevertheless, is an important component element of a nation's political consciousness.
- Paradoxically, the enhancement of a country's autonomy or control of its own affairs may well be improved by the diminution of its sovereignty.

3   THE UK AND THE GLOBAL ORDER SINCE 1945

Before we begin to discuss the relationship between the UK and the European Union it may be helpful to consider briefly the broad background to these events — the background which established the context within which successive British governments have had to operate over the past fifty years. The years since the end of the Second World War, on the whole, have been difficult for all British governments. The easy and assured assumption that existed before 1939 that the country was a great power, a major player in deciding the destiny of the world, gradually and painfully evaporated in the decades after 1945. The loss of an empire on which the sun never set, the relatively poor performance of the economy in the post-war years, documented in Block III, and the concomitant decline in the size and relative importance of Britain's military forces, combined to create a rather dramatic erosion in British power

THE BIG THREE

American preponderance in Suez policy.
Source: *Punch*, 26 September 1956. Reproduced by permission.

and influence throughout the world. Moreover, the aftermath of the Second World War saw the rise of the two superpowers — further confirmation, if confirmation was required, that Britain was no longer one of the nations which had great global influence. The emergence and pre-eminence of the United States and the Soviet Union on the world stage diminished and overshadowed the comparative position of the UK within the international arena. What then were the consequences of this very substantial change in the circumstances of the UK?

No British government since 1945 has been able to ignore these developments, at least for any sustained period of time, although there have been a few occasions, most notably during the 1950s and the crisis over the Suez Canal, when some governments succumbed to the temptation to ignore the new global configuration of power, only to discover that the past could not be reinstated. Inevitably, the process of adjustment and accommodation to these new and very different circumstances was not smooth and untroubled. Both Conservative and Labour governments found the transition from being a world power to a nation with more modest preoccupations, fraught with difficulty. In particular, the retreat from empire was a painful one. The process of disengagement was complex and troubled, frequently involving the deployment of troops in bitter military conflicts in several parts of the world including Malaya, Kenya, Aden, Cyprus and, during the 1980s, the Falklands. The politics of decline, to put it bluntly, have not been easy.

In a remark, made in 1962, but quoted very frequently since, a former Secretary of State of the United States observed, 'Great Britain has lost an empire and has not yet found a role'. It is this sense of a lost past and an unsure future, of transition, and of uncertainty over the place of the UK in the world order that developed after 1945 which provides the context for this unit and also for the whole block. The lack of confidence has been evident. Successive governments have been hesitant about whether to secure a future for the United Kingdom within the Commonwealth, develop the 'special relationship' with the United States or look to Europe for Britain's destiny. Of the three alternatives, the Commonwealth was the least viable option. It had a powerful sentimental appeal but it was far too diverse a collection of states and had no real prospect of being a significant global organization. It was also soon apparent that the nations who had just secured their independence from the United Kingdom were unwilling to let the Commonwealth be anything more than a very loose association of nations with the shared historical experience of British rule.

A close relationship with the United States, however, offered a very different prospect. The United States was clearly the dominant power in the post-1945 world and an association with it was attractive. Moreover the UK had forged a very close and successful working partnership with the USA during the Second World War. In addition, the ties of history, culture and language encouraged most of the British political class to view the connection with the United States as central to the UK's role in the world. The UK through its connection with the United States could play a vital global role. Leading British politicians, of all parties, have been, and to some extent still are, anxious to proclaim this 'special relationship' between the UK and the United States, which would distinguish and elevate the position of Britain from that of any other American ally. Historically there were good reasons to take this view. The links between the two governments have been particularly close. Winston Churchill and Franklin Roosevelt cultivated a striking relationship during the Second World War and so to a lesser extent did Harold Macmillan and John Kennedy in the 1960s. In the 1980s Ronald Reagan and Margaret Thatcher clearly developed an empathy. The level of cooperation and information sharing on intelligence matters between the two nations is unique and reflects a degree of trust that spans the entire governmental structure of both countries. Nevertheless, it is very noticeable that the 'special relationship' is referred to far more frequently on this side of the Atlantic. The United States with its global concerns and activities has cultivated several 'special relationships' — with several of the nations of Latin America, with Japan, and with Germany amongst others — while the UK has tended to emphasize only this one. The United States does have interests and concerns other than the UK to satisfy. Consequently there have been several occasions over the past fifty years when British governments have felt less than pleased by American decisions. Perhaps the most notable of these crises in Anglo/American relations occurred during the Suez crisis in 1956, when Britain and France, in the face of the clear opposition of the US administration invaded Egypt to maintain control of the Suez Canal. Likewise, the US invasion of Grenada, a member of the Commonwealth, in 1982 did not please the British government. More recently President Clinton's decision in 1994 to allow Gerry Adams, the leader of Sinn Fein, to visit the United States caused a great deal of British disquiet. These episodes and several others encouraged a sense of unhappiness about the 'special relationship' in the UK. It became apparent to many that the 'special relationship' could not be the rock on which the UK could base its role in the world. The growing imbalance in power and the different national interests between a global superpower and a

Sheep in wolf's clothing — Eden's Middle East 'venture'
Source: *Punch*, 7 November 1956. Reproduced by permission.

nation with more modest concerns suggested that the UK had to look elsewhere to discover its role. For an increasing number of people in Britain, Europe provided a solution to this problem. However, the European option had its own set of difficulties, the most important one being sovereignty.

British membership of the European Economic Community (EEC), which became the European Community (EC) and finally the European Union (EU) has always had its supporters in the UK which spanned the party spectrum. However, there also has been consistent opposition to British membership, an opposition which also crossed the party divide. The source of the opposition has focused on the issue of sovereignty, for unlike any other organization that the UK has joined, membership of the EU has involved a loss of sovereignty.

SUMMARY

- At the end of the Second World War, the UK was no longer one of the world's superpowers.

- The UK was confronted with a choice of finding a role for itself within the Commonwealth, developing the 'special relationship' with the United States or looking to Europe.

- The 'special relationship' was a very attractive option to many in the British political class, but the very real differences between the national interests of the UK and the United States made it an inappropriate base for Britain's role in the world.

- Europe provided the remaining alternative although equally difficult issues, principally sovereignty, characterized this relationship.

4   EVOLUTION OF THE EUROPEAN UNION

The UK entered the European Union, or as it was then known the European Economic Community, in 1973. The EU had been in existence since 1957, albeit in a different form. The UK had the opportunity to be a founder member of the Union, but the Conservative government at the time decided that it did not wish the UK to join the EU along with Belgium, the Federal Republic of Germany (the former West Germany), France, Italy, Luxembourg and the Netherlands. Indeed this absence of enthusiasm for European involvements also led the first post-war Labour government to stay aloof from negotiations to form the European Coal and Steel Community (ECSC). The ECSC came into operation in 1952, and in many ways was the predecessor of the EU. In that year, the then Conservative Prime Minister, Winston Churchill made a remark that reflected the British disdain for this new institution, by dismissing the formation of the ECSC as an organization of states which were not on a par with the UK: 'I love France and Belgium, but we must not allow ourselves to be pulled down to that level'.

Such a lack of enthusiasm has been a striking and continuing feature of British attitudes towards the EU. It has not always been determinative, but it has never been far from the surface. During the 1950s, the reservations of succeeding governments over the EU, in part, stemmed from a sense that Britain continued to have interests and concerns that were far wider than Europe. Britain saw itself not only as a European power but as a global power. The connections with the United States were seen as more important to Britain than relationships with, say, France and Germany. The Commonwealth and the remnants of the Empire were an arena which continued to absorb the energy of some British politicians. The assertion of British power and influence, in the view of those politicians in office, was more appropriately deployed outside the EU. The prevailing assumption was that the UK's interests and British autonomy would not be enhanced by membership of the EU. But in addition to these geo-political considerations, the doubts over the EU focused on the question of sovereignty.

The hesitation that many British politicians had over the EU, as opposed to some other forms of association at either the European or global level, derived from a sense that membership of the EU involved a diminution of the legal and formal control of the UK Parliament. The Treaty of Rome, the document signed in 1957, by the six founding members of the Community, created the structure and institutions of the EU (the principal institutions of the EU are described in the box below). This Treaty did envisage a transfer of authority, albeit modest, from national governments to these new European organizations. Initially, the ability of the European organization to impose its collective will on the member states was heavily circumscribed. The Council of Ministers, composed of representatives of each state, had the power of veto over any legislation or regulations that emerged from either the European Commission or the European Parliament.

THE PRINCIPAL INSTITUTIONS AND TREATIES OF THE EUROPEAN UNION

The Commission: The Commission is the executive institution of the Community. It is perhaps the most important and certainly the most visible of the European institutions. The President of the Commission is increasingly seen as the person who speaks on behalf of the European Union. It has the obligation to implement the Treaty of Rome and administer the decisions made by the Council of Ministers, although it also has the specific right to put proposals before the Council. Currently the Commission is composed of seventeen members, of which two are allocated to each of the five larger states, France, Italy, West Germany, Spain and the UK. The visibility of the Commission has led to the belief that the Community is overly bureaucratic.

The Council of Ministers: If the Commission is the most visible of the European institutions, the Council is the most powerful. It is composed of representatives from each member state. There is no permanent representative from each member state. The representation is entirely dependent on the nature of the particular subject under discussion. The Council has been in effect the legislature of the Community, although this position is increasingly challenged by the European Parliament, since the introduction of direct elections. Community legislation, which is known as Directives or Regulations, in most cases have to be adopted or approved by the Council of Ministers. The Council usually worked on the principle that most decisions are taken unanimously, although majority voting is now applied to a growing number of issues and the practice looks likely to increase.

The European Parliament: There are currently over 500 Members of the European Parliament (MEPs). Since 1979, MEPs have been directly elected, but this change in the electoral arrangements has not altered the powers of the Parliament. They are not substantially different from the predecessor institution, the Assembly, whose members were appointed. This has resulted in a considerable degree of frustration for MEPs, who have wanted to exercise their democratic authority; a desire which has resulted in a continuing conflict with the Council of Ministers, who see the MEPs as a competitor for power. The Parliament has only an advisory role in legislative matters, although its powers have been strengthened by the Single European Act. Nevertheless, it continues to be less important in the legislative process than the Council. The Parliament has budgetary powers, which ensure that no budget can be approved without its agreement. The Parliament also has supervisory powers over both the Commission and the Council, and possesses the authority to dismiss the Commission. To date this authority has not been exercised.

The Court of Justice: The task of ensuring that the law is uniformly applied throughout the Community in accordance with the provisions of the treaties is the responsibility of the European Court of Justice based in Luxembourg. In 1994 there were thirteen judges, one from each member state plus one other. There are in addition six advocates-general, who assist the judges in reaching their judgements. There are six broad categories of cases that come before the Court, including disputes between the member states. Perhaps the most significant of these categories, however, are the cases that are referred to the European Court by the national courts. These cases ensure that the Court is able to monitor the application of Community law in the member countries.

The European Council: This is the formal title given to the heads of government meetings which take place three times a year. It possesses no special power and in effect has the same status as a meeting of the Council of Ministers.

The Treaty of Rome: The Treaty of Rome was signed in 1957, by the six original members, Belgium, France, the Federal Republic of Germany, Italy, Luxembourg, and the Netherlands. It provides the ultimate authority for the European Union, its institutions and its activities.

The Single European Act: The Single European Act was signed in 1986. The objective was to create a unified and single market in order to provide producers of goods and services in the Union with the same advantages as their competitors in the United States and Japan. In order to achieve this objective, the Act expanded majority voting in the Council of Ministers and restricted the requirement for unanimity among the member countries. The Act also extended the powers of the central institutions over the individual countries. In addition, it also increased the powers of the European Parliament.

The Treaty of Maastricht: The Treaty on European Union was signed in Maastricht in February 1992. The process of ratifying the Treaty in several of the member countries proved to be both difficult and prolonged, although each nation finally did so. This Treaty, like the Single European Act, established objectives for the Union, including a common European currency by 1999. The Treaty on Union further bolstered the powers of the European Parliament, and also enhanced the powers of the European institutions at the expense of the individual member countries. The Treaty established the goal of a common security and foreign policies. Together with the Single European Act, this Treaty substantially increased the integration and centralization of the Union.

Any one member could prevent the introduction of a development of which it did not approve. On several occasions during the late 1950s and 1960s, the French government all but brought the operation of the EC to a halt by imposing its veto on proposals of which it disapproved, but which were supported by the other members. However, this position has been, and continues to be, modified. The power of the national veto is no longer absolute. The influence of the Union institutions has grown. The range of Union activities has vastly increased. The authority of the European Parliament has been enhanced by the introduction of direct elections from 1979. Consequently, the individual member states do not find it quite so easy to resist the collective will of the Community.

This developing integration has been both the source of concern and the attraction of the European Union. Certainly those who were associated with the founding of the Union had a vision, in the late 1940s, of a continent that would be able to transcend the national antagonisms that had led to two world wars. They wanted to create a political organization that would defuse the tensions of inter-European rivalries; that would lock those nations, particularly France and Germany, who were traditionally wary of, and hostile to, one another into a structure of a powerful set of institutions, which would require their effective cooperation. The Treaty of Rome was just a beginning down this long road. Those who shared this view, realized that it would require a far greater degree of integration and a willingness to surrender a greater degree of national sovereignty than was agreed in 1957. National parliaments would have to accept the supremacy of European law. A federal European state, perhaps even a United States of Europe, was envisaged by some advocates of an integrated Community. Of course, this has not come about to date, nor would it be accurate to say that the EU is irrevocably heading along the road to a federal state. But it is this concern over sovereignty that has been at the centre of the debates; firstly, over whether the UK should join the EU and secondly, after 1973, over the future development and structure of the Community.

4.1   JOINING THE UNION

In the UK, this concern has not been confined to either of the major political parties, and enthusiasm for the EC is to be found in both the Labour and Conservative parties. Nevertheless, the two full applications to join the Community occurred during periods of Conservative rule. In the early 1960s, the government of Harold Macmillan decided that, despite the concern over sovereignty, the balance of advantage lay with British membership and applied to join. The concerns of sovereignty were subordinated to the judgement that Britain's interests would be more effectively safeguarded and promoted within the Community. The view of Britain as a global power was far more difficult to sustain by the end of the 1950s. The UK simply was not in the same league militarily as that of the United States or the Soviet Union. The British economy, while growing rapidly in terms of its own historic levels, was not as large as that of the United States nor as dynamic as those in Europe, particularly West Germany. The sense of superiority evident in the sentiments of Churchill was a reflection of the recent past and was not rooted in the emerging realities of global economic and military power. To an increasing number of politicians, in both the Conservative and Labour parties, the European Union offered a solution to the decline of British power. To such supporters of British membership, the loss of sovereignty was not a difficulty. It was merely the consequence of joining an organization, which was the only effective avenue for the UK to enhance its power, influence and autonomy in a world which was increasingly inhospitable to those states which were not superpowers.

RUSSIAN ROULETTE

"It's not fair — mine isn't loaded!"

Macmillan's insistence on an independent deterrent
Source: *Punch*, 19 December 1962. Reproduced by permission.

However, the British application for entry in 1963 was unsuccessful. It was vetoed by the French government, which, ironically, viewed the UK as a Trojan horse for the United States. The French veto did not diminish the enthusiasm and support of those who wished to see British membership. Finally in 1972, the negotiations started by another Conservative government, under the leadership of Edward Heath, resulted in the UK's admission to what was known then as the European Economic Community. But the issue of British membership was not settled finally until 1975 when a referendum, which was unprecedented in British constitutional history, was held. The result endorsed British membership, by a very substantial majority, and those who had supported the campaign for the UK to join the Community over the previous decades believed that they had finally and definitively settled the issue. In one sense they had, although there are voices who continue to advocate that the UK should leave. However, the same concerns over sovereignty continued to emerge, albeit in a different form.

─────────── ACTIVITY 4 ───────────

Tony Benn was a member of the Cabinet in the Labour governments between 1974 and 1979 which organized the referendum and was one of the most implacable opponents of British membership. He claims that the European Communities Act of 1972 which gave authority to British membership of the EC was the 'most important constitutional document in our history, because laws can now be made and apply in Britain without any Parliamentary approval'. How do you respond to this view? Is this loss of legislative control as significant as Benn suggests?

───

My response to Benn's remark would be to reflect on the issue of British sovereignty in relationship to the European Community. What loss of sovereignty took place in 1973? Certainly the notion of parliamentary sovereignty, which is central to British constitutional theory, was abridged. In theory until 1973, all persons and institutions were subordinate to Parliament. The established view was that Parliament at Westminster possessed the authority to pass any law that it desired. It could not be overruled and it could overrule any

" Now try to read the small type "

The hidden dangers of UK entry into the Common Market.
Source: *Punch*, 15 August 1962. Reproduced by permission.

other institution whenever it chose to. Of course, in practice this authority was circumscribed by the realities of the political world, but, nevertheless, Parliament was the supreme institution of British governance. But when Britain signed the Treaty of Rome and Parliament gave effect to it by passing The European Communities Act in 1972, it ceded a degree of sovereignty. Parliament accepted that it was no longer the supreme law-making body for the UK. Laws, regulations and legal judgements that emerged from the institutions of the Community, over certain issues, could not be amended by Parliament. After 1972, there were areas of policy making where the British Parliament could be overruled. It was no longer supreme. In other words it was no longer sovereign. It was no longer sovereign in the sense that it had lost possession of that formal and legal authority to make any law and regulation that it should choose. For instance, when the European Court decides that an Act of Parliament does not conform with European Law, Parliament is compelled, as a result of this judicial ruling, to amend it in accordance with the judgement. Nevertheless, the extent of this transfer of sovereignty in 1972 was limited. The areas where European institutions and law were supreme were relatively few. The range of majority decisions was not extensive. The loss of sovereignty, in principle, might have been substantial but, in practice, was not that significant. However, the question of sovereignty did not disappear from the agenda, because of the increasing movement towards integration within the EU.

SUMMARY

- A central intention behind the Treaty of Rome, which was signed in 1957, was to end the decades of war and antagonism that had divided Europe. In particular it sought to bind France and Germany within one organization which could see the development of a common set of interests, rather than a conflicting set of national interests.

- The UK chose not to be a founder signatory of the Treaty of Rome, because it was believed that Britain continued to have global interests and influence.

- The growing realization that this was no longer the case convinced a broad coalition of opinion, which crossed party lines, that the UK should join the EU and an unsuccessful application to be a member was submitted by a Conservative government in the early 1960s.

- A further application was made by a Conservative government under Edward Heath. Negotiations were successful and the UK joined in 1973.

- The issue of sovereignty, nevertheless, remained an issue, particularly with opponents of British membership.

- Membership has resulted in a loss of sovereignty.

The Widening and Deepening of the European Union

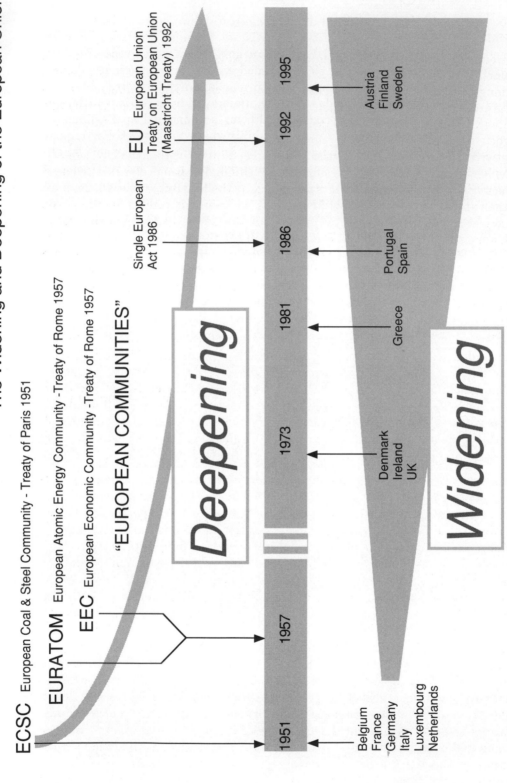

ECSC   European Coal & Steel Community - Treaty of Paris 1951

EURATOM   European Atomic Energy Community - Treaty of Rome 1957

EEC   European Economic Community - Treaty of Rome 1957

"EUROPEAN COMMUNITIES"

Deepening

Single European Act 1986

EU   European Union Treaty on European Union (Maastricht Treaty) 1992

1951   1957   1973   1981   1986   1992   1995

Belgium
France
Germany
Italy
Luxembourg
Netherlands

Denmark
Ireland
UK

Greece

Portugal
Spain

Austria
Finland
Sweden

Widening

Figure 1

5   THE MOVE TO INTEGRATION: I. THE SINGLE MARKET

Circumstances and conditions have altered very considerably since the UK joined the European Union in 1972. Indeed they are in a process of constant change and the Union has sought to respond to them. The EU has not been a static organization. It has both deepened in the sense of becoming increasingly integrated and it has widened geographically (see Figure 1, which traces both types of developments). For some observers there is a potential tension between these two characteristics and it is certainly true that the UK, which is the least enthusiastic integrationist in the Union, has been consistently one of the most enthusiastic supporters for enlarging the EU. But, on the whole, most other states do not believe that there is an inherent conflict in these two processes and membership by the end of the 1980s had grown to twelve. Denmark and the Republic of Ireland joined the Community at the same time as the UK. Greece joined in 1981 and in 1986 the Union was further enlarged by the admission of Spain and Portugal. All of these nations, apart from Denmark, had appreciably lower levels of income than the EU average, which altered the sense of the Union as an association of the wealthier nations of Northern Europe. In 1990 the former East Germany became a part of the Union when it merged with West Germany. By 1994, the EU successfully concluded negotiations with four prosperous nations Austria, Finland, Norway and Sweden. However there are several other countries anxious to join the Union including a number in Eastern Europe which, should they be admitted, will again have a significant effect on the character of the EU. Although the importance of this expansion in the Union's membership cannot be diminished, perhaps the most significant development throughout the 1980s was the drive to make the EU a more cohesive and integrated entity.

Most member countries endorsed this movement. France and Germany, perhaps the two most influential nations, felt that the future success of the Community required the further integration of the national economies. In the UK, however, the Conservative governments of the 1980s and early 1990s under Margaret Thatcher and then John Major were far from enthusiastic. Most notably on several occasions Mrs Thatcher declared her opposition to what she saw as the integrative and centralizing tendencies of the Union. However the Conservatives did not resist all the moves in this direction and the British government was active in supporting one of the most significant developments, the passage of the Single European Act which was signed in 1986 by Mrs Thatcher, although the potential consequences of the Act for UK sovereignty may not have been fully appreciated. The object behind the formation of a single market was to provide European manufacturing and service industries with the conditions that their counterparts in the United States and Japan already possess. It was believed that the absence of such a market placed Europeans at a significant disadvantage. Although restrictions on internal trade had been removed by the early 1980s, it was evident that the member states of the EU did not collectively provide a single market. A welter of national regulations, differential tax rates and a desire to protect national industries, prevented the emergence of a unified European market and cost every worker in the Union, according to a report submitted to the European Parliament, the equivalent of a week's earnings every year. In 1985, the decision was taken, in principle, to move to a single market and in order to do so, the Single European Act, an act of the European Community, was passed to come into effect in 1987. It was given effect in the UK by the European Communities (Amendment) Bill 1986.

A White Paper, prepared by the European Commission, identified three types of barriers to a single market and proposals for their removal. Firstly, there were physical barriers, such as frontier controls, which were to be entirely removed. Secondly, there were technical barriers, created by different national standards and regulations. Thirdly, fiscal barriers were identified as preventing the development of a single market. The identification of these three types of barriers and their removal absorbed a considerable degree of political energy within the Community. Some of the proposals in the White Paper were controversial and are unlikely to be implemented fully, but the movement towards the single market was all but irresistible. By early 1993, over 500 measures to bring about the market had been agreed. Over 95 per cent of the measures in the White Paper had been, or were about to be, implemented. The key object of the single market was to ensure the four freedoms of movement. Three of these freedoms, of goods, services and capital had been achieved by 1993. The final freedom, that of movement of people, is still to be implemented. The Single European Act was in place.

A great deal of attention has focused on the economic dimension and understandably so, as the emergence of the single market in the EU is likely to have a very substantial impact on the national economies of the member states and indeed on the entire global economy. Projections made in 1988 indicated that the introduction of the single market would increase the GNP of the EU countries by approximately 5 per cent. Moreover, a single market of approximately 320 million people will almost certainly have a very major effect on global investment and trade patterns. But perhaps the excitement of these unfolding economic developments has overshadowed the political dimension of the single market.

To achieve the four freedoms, the Single European Act moved the EU down a different track. The most significant modification was that it extended the role of majority voting in the Council of Ministers. It expanded the range of issues, delineated in the Treaty of Rome, which could be decided by majority voting. The issues over which majority voting now applied included the abolition of border controls, taxation and certain aspects of employment law, all of which were sensitive and potentially highly politically charged. This development further diminished the sovereignty of the member nations since certain types of regulation seen as necessary to bring about the single market can be issued by the Union and do not require the consent or permission of the British Parliament. So the initial list of policy areas where the British Parliament had lost its legal authority and supremacy under the Treaty of Rome was extended under the Single European Act. The British government was prepared to accept this position, although there is a view that members of the British Parliament were not fully aware of the consequences and impact of what they were signing away to the EU under the Single European Act.

The Act also increased the powers of the European Parliament in the decision-making process, which has implications for the sovereignty of member nations. The standard complaint of British politicians over the years has been directed at what they believed were the excesses of the bureaucrats in Brussels. It is easier for member nations to complain about, and then resist, the 'bureaucratic' institutions of the Union. It is far more difficult to oppose those institutions which possess a measure of democratic legitimacy. The strengthening of the Parliament will be of increasing importance in defining the relationships within the Union and the views of the Parliament will be less easy to resist. Apart from providing the Parliament with a greater role, the Act also enlarged the scope of concerns to the environment, research and technology and certain elements of energy policy. So the Act brought in its train a substantial increase in the reach and powers of the Union with all the concomitant implications for national sovereignty.

The issue of the single European market highlights the tension between sovereignty and autonomy, independence and the assertion of power. The rationale for the single market lies with economies of scale. The manufacturing and service industries in the United States and Japan benefit from their access to a large unified market with a national regulatory regime. Japanese or American automobile manufacturers, computer companies and so on, have advantages, for example, in terms of costs and product development, because of the large market they service. These are benefits which their French or British counterparts, who do not have access to a similar large and unified market, do not possess. Consequently, they operate at a substantial disadvantage, which France and the UK cannot rectify by themselves, because at a national level they are unable to provide a comparable economic base of operations. Only the European Union collectively can provide a comparable base. So the rewards of such an internal market will only be available to the UK through its membership of the EU and this effectively means a further diminution of national sovereignty, but an increase in the profile and importance of British companies in the global market. But the sheer complexity of delivering a single market by 1992 required a further transfer of decision making to the Community institutions and away from the national capitals; a further increase in the issues, such as aspects of taxation, over which the UK Parliament was no longer supreme. In the judgement of the British government it was a worthwhile exchange. Community control for economic growth; sovereignty for power, in this case economic power; independence for a greater ability to compete in the global economy. But although the British government was prepared to make this trade over the single market, it has not been prepared to endorse proposals which extend this loss of sovereignty to a further range of issues, which would emerge in the Treaty of Union that was signed at Maastricht.

—————————————— ACTIVITY 5 ——————————————

The single market brings into focus the trade off between sovereignty and economic advantage. There are benefits from being a part of a large internal market. However there are costs as well. Make a list of both the costs and the benefits.

SUMMARY

- There are substantial economic advantages associated with the creation of the single market.
- However the development of the single European market has further reduced British sovereignty.
- The British government believed this trade of sovereignty for economic benefit to be worthwhile.
- The full implications for British sovereignty, however were not fully absorbed.

6 THE MOVE TO INTEGRATION:
2. THE TREATY ON UNION (MAASTRICHT)

The desire to deepen and strengthen the EU did not end with the single market. Most members, notably France and Germany, wanted the process to continue. The vision of the French and German governments and of several others was of an ever closer union. It was a vision that was not shared by the UK. In 1988 the British Prime Minister, Margaret Thatcher, delivered a speech to the College of Europe at Bruges which laid bare the differences between Britain and the other major European countries. It revealed a profoundly contrasting set of attitudes and instincts, which spoke for a broad spectrum of British opinion. The central focus of her speech was the primacy of national sovereignty. The development of Europe could only take place on the 'willing and active cooperation between independent and sovereign states'. The preservation of nationhood was vital and it should not be suppressed in order to 'concentrate power at the centre of a European conglomerate'. The power of Brussels was another of her central concerns. The needs of Europe did 'not require power to be centralized in Brussels to be taken by an appointed bureaucracy'. She argued that her government had not successfully 'rolled back the frontiers of the state ... only to see them reimposed at a European level, with a European super-state exercising a new dominance in Brussels. Unity was needed in Europe but it had to be achieved in a manner that preserves the different traditions, Parliamentary powers and sense of national pride in one's own country'. The Bruges speech was seen as offering an alternative view of Europe's future. It had a very important impact particularly in the UK.

Although the speech did not command unanimous support, even in the Conservative party, it was, in several important respects, emblematic of the British approach to Europe. British governments, almost regardless of party and with the exception of that led by Edward Heath in 1970–1974, have been reluctant Europeans. Their instinct has always been one of wariness, occasionally bordering on hostility. In the words of one observer of the EU, the UK has always been 'an awkward partner'. UK attitudes have almost invariably been characterized by the assumption that British interests are unlikely to be shared by the other members of the EU and indeed are more likely to be opposed. Consequently it was important to retain a British voice and even more important for the UK to continue to possess the capacity to resist the other members of the EU. In order to do so, the Westminster Parliament had to retain as much legal authority or sovereignty. This, then, was the heart of the British vision for Europe; a relatively loose coalition of independent sovereign states, where each nation could veto any development that was against its national interest.

There were, however, several difficulties with this vision. Firstly, by 1988, the UK already had travelled some considerable distance down the integrationist road. The Treaty of Rome and the Single European Act had limited and reduced the sovereignty of the Westminster Parliament. The Bruges speech appeared to be reopening a debate that most had taken to have been closed for some years. Secondly, the speech also suggested a reopening of the debate over Britain's role. Did it lie in Europe or with the USA? During the 1980s Anglo-American relations were going through a particularly strong phase and there is little doubt where Mrs Thatcher's preferences lay. She clearly enjoyed her relationship with President Reagan and then subsequently with President Bush and she also relished her role on the world's stage that was in part due to her closeness with both Presidents. Europe, by contrast, had been difficult for her as it had been characterized by the acrimony over the UK's contribution to the EU budget. She clearly had far less rapport with the leaders of the other members of the EU. But this sense that Britain must choose between Europe on the one hand and the USA on the other would not have to be brought to a head if the British vision for Europe commanded some support with the other nations. This was not the case and, to a large extent, was the source of the problems with the Treaty of Union which was signed at Maastricht.

The central difficulty for the British government was not so much that other governments disagreed with it but, with the possible exception of Denmark, they perceived the issues in a very different manner. For most of the other countries the development of the EU had been, and continues to be, a political project of the first order. Those Europeans, such as Jean Monnet, who had set in train the movement that led to the creation of the EU, had been driven by a desire to end the divisions that had wracked the continent of Europe during the twentieth century. In particular, they wanted to bring about the reconciliation of France and Germany. They wanted these two nations to have a sense of common interests and destiny, which they believed could only be attained through the formation of a European organization of some power and authority. The precise vision of Monnet and others need not concern us here, but it is important to note that, for them, the objectives were primarily political and these aims were of central importance to the countries on mainland Europe. For the UK, by contrast, membership of the EU has been primarily an economic project. Even those who have made the case for British membership have done so in the language of economic advantage. The UK needed the markets in Europe, or British trade was increasingly skewed towards Europe, have been the type of arguments deployed for the UK joining and then for staying within the EU. Political themes such as sovereignty have usually been developed by those who have been hostile either to membership of the EU or to what they see as the centralizing and integrationist tendencies of the Union. The UK joined the EU for a set of reasons that were different and, perhaps of even greater significance, the European project has not played a similar role in the British political consciousness.

Because of the different histories, the other members of the EU are not quite so concerned about the strengthening of the powers of the EU institutions. Clearly all the member states have a sense of their own national interest and are equally conscious of their respective national identities. Moreover, there is no reason to believe that they feel any less passionately about these matters than successive governments in the UK. However, they do not believe, in the words of the Single European Act, that an 'ever closer union of the peoples of Europe' threatened their interests or their identity. Indeed, and quite to the contrary, most governments believe that a more integrated organization with greater centralization is in their national interests. Their loss of sovereignty was not perceived as a problem, but seen as vital to the development which would increase the power and influence of Europe. These very different perspectives surfaced yet again in the preparation of the Maastricht Treaty.

The Single European Act required all the member countries to examine the state of play about Economic and Monetary Union (EMU) and, in 1988, just before Mrs Thatcher's speech in Bruges, a committee under the President of the European Commission, Jacques Delors, was created to examine the steps to bring about EMU. Delors suggested a number of measures, which included a common monetary policy and the linking of all the national currencies in a fixed relationship. On the basis of the Delors report, a majority of the nations, which did not include the UK, decided to call a conference on EMU. But at the same time that EMU was being considered events were taking place at an almost bewildering pace in Eastern Europe and in the former Soviet Union. The historic importance of these developments led President Mitterand of France and Chancellor Kohl of Germany to call for a move towards European

Political Union (EPU). So, by 1991 the impetus towards both political, as well as economic and monetary union, was in motion.

The Treaty on European Union was signed in Maastricht on February 7 1992. The principal features of the Treaty in respect of political union were:

* Enhanced powers for the European Parliament.

* Wider powers and range of issues over which the European institutions had control such as telecommunications and transport.

* The development of a foreign and security policy common to all member states.

* The creation of European citizenship.

* The development of a social policy across the EU. Any measures taken by the EU will not apply to Britain. The UK government obtained an 'opt out' from the Social Chapter because, in its view, the EU was likely to adopt policies that would adversely affect the global economic competitiveness of Europe by increasing the social costs of employment. The UK government believed that by 'opting out' of the Social Chapter, the UK would be the most attractive location of all the EU nations for foreign, primarily Japanese and US, investors.

The principal features for Economic and Monetary Union were:

* The development of a common currency by 1999.

* Strict criteria for development of the Union were established. Standards had to be met before member nations would be allowed to join. For instance, only those states which had achieved a rate of inflation that was not more than 1.5 per cent higher than the average inflation rate of the three members with the lowest rate of inflation.

* If most members met all the criteria laid down by the end of 1996, then a date could be set for the final stage of monetary union. The date did not require unanimity but could be set by a majority vote, as long as it was no later than the end of 1999.

* The establishment of a European Central Bank.

* The United Kingdom and Denmark were not committed by a majority decision of the other states. They reserved the right to decide at a later date whether they wished to join the final stages of the Monetary Union.

It is clear that the Treaty of Union signed at Maastricht extended the process of the further and closer integration of the member states. Since the Treaty of Rome there has been a continuous strengthening of the powers of the Union institutions and the Maastricht Treaty was yet another step in this direction. Once again, the sovereignty of the individual member state was eroded and once again the UK found itself almost the sole defender of national sovereignty, although on this occasion it had a degree of support from Denmark. The thirteen countries were ceding to the Union very important powers over a wide range of issues. The most important of these were in the realm of the economy, an area which is of central political importance. The British reservations were not trivial but they did not find a resonance on the mainland of Europe, at least at the governmental level. There were some indications that the electorates were not quite so enthusiastic as their leaders.

6.1 THE RATIFICATION OF THE TREATY OF UNION

The process of ratification of the Treaty was far more controversial than was anticipated during the Maastricht Conference in December 1991. The prevailing view was that adequate support existed for the Treaty in each of the member nations, including the UK, where all three major parties supported it. Indeed, the main criticism made by the Labour and Liberal Democratic parties was directed at the British 'opt-outs' over monetary union and social policy that had been negotiated by the Prime Minister John Major. It was assumed that the Treaty would be comfortably passed by both Houses of Parliament at Westminster. This did not prove to be the case.

The ratification of the Treaty took place at a time when Europe was mired in a severe recession. It was a difficult period for virtually all of the governments and they were unpopular with their respective electorates. The economies throughout Europe were suffering and the prospects of recovery were bleak. Popular dissatisfaction with the economic policies of national governments became linked rather curiously with opposition to the Maastricht Treaty. A sense of general malaise which was perceptible in most of the countries found expression in antagonism to the integration of the European Union. In early June 1992, the Danish electorate rejected the Treaty in a referendum. As the Treaty required the approval of every state, the Danish referendum technically killed the Treaty. If it was going to be revived there would need to be a second referendum in Denmark which would have to reverse the result. A further consequence of the Danish referendum was that it encouraged opponents of the Treaty throughout Europe. In France, where the government had been an enthusiastic proponent of the Treaty, a referendum produced a majority of barely 2 per cent in favour of Maastricht. In the UK the opposition increased sharply with such events helping to strengthen their position.

A series of crises in the foreign currency markets in 1992 raised doubts over the prospect of economic and monetary union. The Exchange Rate Mechanism (ERM) was a device created to maintain a degree of stability in value between the currencies of the member nations of the EU, or at least those members that wished to join. Broadly the intention of the ERM was to ensure that the value of any single currency would not fluctuate more than 2.5 per cent — although in the case of some currencies 6 per cent was permitted — against a carefully weighted basket of all the EU currencies. When the system came into operation in 1980, the ERM operated with considerable flexibility. It was accepted that the national economies would perform differentially and adjustments in the relative values of the currencies inevitably would occur. Consequently rates were adjusted reasonably frequently usually because of the comparative strength of the Mark and the German economy. So the ERM provided periods of relative stability combined with moments of currency realignment. However from 1988, the points of adjustment became increasingly infrequent and the ERM appeared to provide a set of fixed relationships between the currencies. The UK initially did not join the ERM, but in 1990 after a great deal of debate within the government and against the opposition of the Prime Minister, Mrs Thatcher, Sterling entered.

By 1992 the divergence between the economies of the EU nations had begun to place a very considerable strain on the ERM. Notably, the UK economy had gone into both a prolonged and deep recession, while Germany was still benefitting from the result of unification. Indeed, there were several signs that the German economy was growing too rapidly and overheating while the British economy needed some stimulus to end the recession. Most observers believed that while the German economy required higher interest rates, the British economy needed the precise opposite. The dominant view of the financial markets was that sooner or later, and most probably sooner, both of these developments were going to take place. Because the markets believed that German interest rates had to rise, the Mark became a comparatively more attractive currency. Accordingly, there were many more purchasers of the Mark than sellers and consequently the price of the Mark started to rise against the traditionally vulnerable currencies, Sterling and the Italian Lira but also some others, and began to threaten the ERM. The initial response of the governments was to maintain the existing ERM values but the sheer volume of money that was prepared to buy Marks and sell the other ERM currencies resulted in a series of devaluations. The devaluation of Sterling in September 1992 was particularly dramatic and politically damaging to the British government. In addition, British opponents of the Maastricht Treaty used the turmoil surrounding the ERM against the notion of Monetary Union, in particular, and the entire integrationist ethic of the Treaty. It was claimed that the Treaty was too federalist, diminished British institutions and so on. Indeed there was almost an implicit sense in some of the arguments that the UK should never have joined what was then the EEC. Whatever the intellectual force of these arguments the government felt it had to respond, if not to the precise claims, then at least to the general concern that the Treaty of Union would transfer too much power and control from London and hand it to Brussels. Sovereignty once again was at the heart of the British debate about Europe.

The response of the government was to distance itself to some extent from the Treaty and wait on events. It had a plausible reason for doing so. The Treaty was nominally dead until a second referendum in Denmark, and before that could be organized, the Danish government wanted certain modifications at least as the Treaty affected Denmark. A meeting of all the heads of government late in 1992 offered Denmark some of these modifications that provided the basis for the second referendum, which resulted in a Danish vote in favour of the Treaty. The meeting also attempted to diminish British fears of encroachment by the institutions of Europe. The form of words issued at the end of the meeting were sufficient at least for the British government to proceed with the ratification of the Treaty in the Westminster Parliament. The process of ratification was slow and very difficult and the Parliamentary debate provided a further indication of the depth of division over Britain's role in Europe and the intensity of emotions that this issue continued to generate. The Treaty was finally ratified in May 1993.

--------------------------------- ACTIVITY 6 ---------------------------------

Let us return to the issue of sovereignty and autonomy. The argument deployed by those who have opposed British membership of the EU, and continue to oppose the movements toward integration within the Community, is focused on *sovereignty*. By contrast those who supported membership and support integration have emphasized *autonomy*. How do you evaluate the competing claims? Has membership of the EU increased the autonomy of the UK? Is the loss of sovereignty unimportant?

SUMMARY

- In 1988, Margaret Thatcher, in a speech at Bruges, offered a distinctively British view of how the EU should develop. Her vision emphasized the importance of national sovereignty.

- This view did not strike a chord with the other members of the EU. By 1991 the move towards both political, as well as economic and monetary, union was well established.

- The Treaty on Union which was signed at Maastricht in 1992 broadly continued the process and direction of the Single European Act.

- The Maastricht Treaty gave increased powers to the institutions of the Union. It also widened the scope of their authority. It also established a timetable for economic and monetary union. In general, the Treaty took a different direction from that which was advocated by Margaret Thatcher.

- The process of ratifying the Treaty in several of the member states was far more difficult and long drawn out than was initially anticipated.

7   THE UK AND THE EUROPEAN UNION: THE FUTURE

It is difficult to predict the future. This unit was written in early 1994 and, if the past decade is a guide, it seems rather unwise to look into a crystal ball. In any case, it is not my intention to provide you with detailed predictions of future events in this section, but rather to indicate very broadly how the relationship between the United Kingdom and the European Union may develop.

It is fairly clear from the preceding sections that, in my view, the relationship between the EU and the UK has, over the past twenty years, been dominated by the question of sovereignty. On the British side there has been a profound degree of discomfort over the fact that sovereignty has been ceded to the European Union. It is evident that a significant degree of opinion in the UK has not been reconciled to the loss of sovereignty that has already occurred and continues to resist any further transfer of legal authority to the EU. Every development which involves such a transfer is converted into a major issue of fundamental political principle within the UK. There are many examples but one will suffice.

In early 1994, the proposed admission of four new countries, Austria, Finland, Norway and Sweden brought the question of sovereignty to the fore once again. In this particular instance, it involved the system of qualified majority voting in the Council of Ministers. Under the rules that were in operation in 1994, each nation was allocated a designated number of votes, with the most populous members such as the UK and Germany possessing 10 votes while the smaller countries had 3 votes. Under a qualified majority voting system, a majority of 70 per cent was required to pass a measure, while 30 per cent or 23 votes could block it. The admission of a further four small nations would increase the number required to block a measure to 27, if the 30 per cent rule was to continue. This increase in the number needed to block became an issue of considerable political importance in the UK. The opposition to its introduction was centred on the view that the change in the voting mechanism was a further step in the inexorable movement of power, control and sovereignty from Westminster to Brussels. There are some interesting points to note from this episode.

Firstly, no other member of the EU saw the problem in quite the same terms. Spain the only other nation that opposed the change, did so for material and pragmatic reasons of interest which primarily concerned the protection of

Mediterranean agriculture. Secondly, and closely related, virtually all the other members were surprised that the amendments to the voting system had become an issue at all and were certainly taken aback by the intensity and vehemence of the emotions that it aroused amongst British politicians. Thirdly, for the members of the EU, bar the UK, the change in voting was a matter of procedure or process not an issue of principle. This is an indication of the very substantial gap in attitudes to the EU that exists between the UK on the one hand and its partners on the other. If this gap persists then the remainder of the decade will see a continuation of a difficult relationship and some issues that are already on the agenda will almost certainly be contentious. The most notable of these issues involve monetary union, and critical decisions about this will have to be taken in 1996.

SUMMARY

- There is every indication that the difficult relationship between the UK and the other members of the EU is set to continue.

- The heated debate over majority voting in the Council of Ministers that occurred in 1994 suggests that the differences in perception have not dissipated.

- Key and contentious decisions on monetary union will need to be taken in 1996.

---

8   THE SOVEREIGNTY OF THE UK

At the start of this unit, I provided a brief account of how the concept of sovereignty is understood. I suggested some of the principle characteristics of this concept and it may be helpful to remind you of them:

1   Sovereignty is characterized by the claim to exclusive jurisdiction over people and territory; a claim which is legally recognized by other states.

2   It is characterized by the notion of the sovereign equality of states.

I also suggested that if these were characteristics that defined sovereignty, then there might be some problems with the concept when we began to consider the sovereignty of the UK. The difficulty was that the UK no longer retains *exclusive* jurisdiction over people and territory, but has ceded formal control over certain issues to the institutions of the EU, although the degree and extent of this diminution of sovereignty was not extensive when Britain joined the Community in 1972. However, the Single European Act and the Treaty of Union signed at Maastricht have substantially increased the number of issues that are not within the power and authority of the Westminster Parliament to resolve. Moreover, the EU is not a static organization and the desire for the further integration of the organization has not noticeably diminished and, consequently, either the erosion of sovereignty will continue or the UK will have to consider its position within the EU. The alternatives appear to be both straightforward and clear. This is not a situation that any other member of the EU has to confront.

Throughout this unit, I have repeatedly noted the position taken by the British government of the period and contrasted it with the views expressed by most of the other member states. In part, I have suggested that the differing viewpoints were a consequence of the centrality of the development of the EU to most of the nations on the mainland of Europe. Whereas, for Britain, membership of the EU has been a reluctant option and, by and large, it has been presented to the people of the UK as an organization that should be helpful to the British economy. British politicians, on the whole, have not presented the political case for membership of the EU. Accordingly, electoral support for the EU has never been particularly strongly or deeply felt, even when it has commanded a majority in the opinion polls. Indeed, the EU is frequently portrayed in the British media as posing a threat to various aspects of life in these islands, from the content of sausages to whether beer can be served in a pint glass. Of course, the most serious of these threats is to the sovereignty of the UK.

Those who argue that membership of the EU has had an enormous impact on the sovereignty of the UK are entirely correct. Prior to 1972, the UK was a sovereign nation. Parliament possessed the absolute authority to pass legislation and establish the rules for all areas of public policy. This power was absolute and there was no legal or formal limitation over Parliament's authority. However, since the UK joined the Union, this authority has been curtailed. From 1972 onwards the power of the British Parliament has not been supreme or absolute. The Treaty of Rome established the supremacy of European institutions in certain areas of public policy and both the Single European Act and the Maastricht Treaty expanded these areas significantly. The UK is no longer sovereign in the sense that it was before it joined the EU in 1972. Of course, this is true for the other member countries so why does the issue appear to have a much higher profile in Britain?

The answer, in part, lies in the historical differences and experiences of the UK and her European partners. Sovereignty and all that it implies has a slightly different meaning and context in the UK. The doctrine of Parliamentary supremacy has been established in Britain for several centuries. This supremacy has traditionally been viewed as absolute and seamless. There were no exceptions to this supremacy and it was seen as central to the fabric of British constitutional and political practice. Parliament possessed the authority to enact any law, however foolish or misconceived. No other institution, the courts or local government for instance, within the UK could challenge this authority. However, since 1972, this doctrine has been riddled with exceptions. The European Court, the Council of Ministers and the European Parliament can all make rules which the UK Parliament is unable to amend. The doctrine of absolute Parliamentary supremacy can no longer exist because that supremacy no longer operates. An institution cannot have absolute authority but only in part. Membership of the EU has changed radically the basis of British constitutional assumptions. The impact on the countries of mainland Europe has not been quite so substantial. They too have had to cede authority to the institutions of Europe, but the effect has not been so dramatic, because very few of these nations have developed constitutional doctrines comparable to that of the UK. In most of these countries, at least in recent history, power and authority constitutionally has been dispersed. It has rarely been vested in just one institution which has exercised total constitutional supremacy. The more common practice has been to disperse power and authority between written constitutions, courts, and national legislatures. In addition, in several European countries regional and local governments have independent powers which are guaranteed by national constitutions. In this context, it has been easier to accommodate the power and authority of the institutions of the EU. No fundamental assumptions have been undermined, at least, to the same extent as in the UK. The consequence of these different constitutional traditions is that membership of the EU has not been quite so traumatic as it has been for the UK, nor has it posed a challenge, in quite the same way, to a set of historically established understandings. Moreover, it is not an issue which can be disguised or ignored because it will continually resurface if, as seems likely, the EU becomes increasingly integrated and centralized.

The problem for the UK is that the number of exceptions to Parliamentary supremacy and national sovereignty is likely to expand. The move to economic and monetary union will clearly absorb the attention of the EU over the coming years. The timetable for economic and monetary union has been established although the UK and Denmark have reserved the right over whether to join. This decision will inevitably raise the question of sovereignty and correctly so, because national governments will be losing power over central aspects of economic policy including control over their own currency. Few issues will bring national sovereignty into clearer focus. However, for many, this will not be a particularly significant question because they will argue that it raises a combination of theoretical as well as legal and formal issues. Legal sovereignty, it will be argued, is only meaningful if it is matched by commensurate power, and this the UK lacks. The legal entitlement to be in control of your own economic policy is not meaningful if, in practice, the British authorities have no effective discretion but are merely following the lead of the more powerful economies in the world. Economic and monetary union, on the other hand, would give the UK an effective voice in the EU over these matters. For instance, the British government would no longer be in the position of being closely constrained by the decisions of the Bundesbank, but would be a participant in the decision-making process of the appropriate EU institution, the European Central Bank. So where does this leave the evaluation of the UK's sovereignty?

A constant and present theme in this unit has been the tension between sovereignty and power, independence and autonomy. Sovereignty, in the case of the UK's relationship with the EU, apparently can be obtained at the expense of effective control, but effective control, in turn, can only be bought at a cost to the UK's sovereignty. It is a quandary that has been at the centre of debates in the UK over Britain's role in the EU. Because of the UK's diminished role in the global order, a very substantial element in both the major political parties over the past three decades, with varying degrees of enthusiasm, have sought the protection that the EU can offer in an unfriendly global environment. Nevertheless, the loss of sovereignty that this protection has entailed has been resented. The European Union has offered British politicians, over the past decades, a fairly stark choice — greater political control or sovereignty. Sovereignty can be relatively easily retained but autonomy may well suffer the consequences.

The assertion of sovereignty contains the assumption that a state is in sole control of a people and territory, while the relationships of influence and power in the globe, to some extent, subvert it, does not suggest to me that sovereignty is an irrelevant concept. It does suggest that the concept of sovereignty is both an important explanatory concept and a consequential factor in understanding the location and role of the UK in the world, but that it is not the only factor. There is a discrepancy, as you will have observed, between the legal status and claims of sovereignty and the ability of a state to achieve these claims. In other words, there is an important distinction to be made between these two characteristics: between sovereignty and the capacity of the state to achieve it. While the UK's sovereignty has been altered radically by its admission to the EU, its ability to control its own destiny has been limited to a far greater extent by the diminution of its autonomy. Indeed, membership of the EU has, if anything, been helpful in exercising control over the nation's affairs.

The post-war global order has placed restrictions on the boundaries within which successive British governments have had to operate. This global context has had a profound impact on the politics of the UK. Indeed politics, the 'local' politics of the UK, cannot be understood outside of this global context. The issues that have dominated British politics over the past few decades have been shaped and structured to a significant extent by the pattern of events and developments beyond the frontiers of the UK. The economic and military power of the United States, the demise of the Soviet Union, the rise of the new economic giants of the Far East, the globalization of the financial markets and, indeed, of business in general have constrained and limited the options of the British authorities. The greatest impact of this global order has been felt on the autonomy of the UK, which has been diminished significantly. Membership of the EU, if anything, has provided a greater degree of control over these forces than the UK could exercise by itself. Because the EU is one of the major players in the globe, the UK is able to participate in a manner that would not be available if it was not a member. However, this enhancement of autonomy has been purchased at the cost of sovereignty. Of course the concept of sovereignty is concerned with jurisdiction, legitimacy, legality and authority, but the notion of autonomy is concerned with power. It is to the concept of power that we will turn in the next unit.

=== THE GOOD STUDY GUIDE ===

To continue work on your essay writing skills, now read Sections 3 and 4 of Chapter 5 and Sections 1 and 2 of Chapter 6 of *The Good Study Guide*.

REFERENCES AND SELECTED SOURCES

Bulmer, S., George, S. and Scott, A. (eds) (1992), *The United Kingdom and EC Membership Evaluated,* London, Pinter.

George, S. (1990) *An Awkward Partner, Britain in the European Community,* Oxford, Oxford University Press.

Hinsley, F.H. (1986) *Sovereignty* (2nd edn), Cambridge, Cambridge University Press.

Kennedy, P. (1988) *The Rise and Fall of the Great Powers*, London, Unwin Hyman.

Laslett, P. (1965) *John Locke: Two Treatises of Government,* New York, Mentor.

McAllister, R. (1992) *The European Community: an historical and political survey,* Hemel Hempstead, Harvester Wheatsheaf.

Swann, D. (ed) (1992) *The Single European Market and Beyond,* London, Pinter.

ACKNOWLEDGEMENTS

Grateful acknowledgement is made to the following sources for permission to reproduce material in this unit:

Cartoons

pp.14, 16, 21, 22: Punch.

UNIT 15   POWER AND THE STATE

Prepared for the Course Team by David Coates

CONTENTS

INTRODUCTION

Unit 14 was concerned with the question of sovereignty. Unit 15 is concerned with the related question of power. In Unit 14 we looked at the relationship of UK governments to certain important European and *global* institutions and processes, and traced the impact of that relationship on the effectiveness of the UK state on the world stage. It is time now to look at how effectively UK governments can achieve their objectives at home, partly by continuing this analysis of global institutions and processes, but primarily by examining their relationship to certain important *local* institutions and processes.

So in this unit we shall:

1   examine the meaning of the term 'power';

2   discuss the different ways in which power can be measured;

3   look at the way power is exercised, both by public bodies and private groups, in two important areas of contemporary political life: the making of economic policy, and legislation on equal opportunities;

4   come to some preliminary view on where power lies in the contemporary UK, and prepare the ground for the theoretical debate on that issue which we will meet more fully in Unit 18;

1   POWER

The exact meaning of the term 'power' is extremely difficult to specify. 'Power is one of those things, like gravity and electricity, which makes its existence apparent to us through its effects, and hence it has always been found much easier to describe its consequences than to identify its nature' (Barnes, 1988, p.ix). Power is difficult to isolate and define precisely because it is everywhere, it is part of everything around us. It is like the air. How do you capture it? One way, of course, is to capture it in a definition; and lots of people have tried. So why don't we?

 ACTIVITY 1

Before you read on, write down the words, phrases, and sentences that come to mind when the term 'power' is used.

Preliminary definition of 'power':

For me, the term 'power' brings two sets of images to mind. One is an image of different sorts of people all sharing a common ability to make others do certain things. It is an image of people able to impose their will on others: by the strength of their personalities, or by the strength of their arguments, or by the strength of their arms. This notion of power seems to suggest a distinction between two sorts of people: those who can effect what they want (the powerful) and those who can't (the powerless). It also seems to suggest the existence of a relationship between the powerful and the powerless, a sense that there is some fixed sum of power: that some people have power only because others don't.

So there is one image of power — 'power over'. But the other image that springs to mind when the word is used is that of electricity — the power industry — of things being done because we have the capacity to do them. This is less strong an image for me; and yet I am conscious that options can widen — things can be done that couldn't be done before — when the stock of knowledge is increased, and when individuals come together and cooperate on the basis of that knowledge. We now have the knowledge (and hence the power) to eradicate certain illnesses that our predecessors did not; and we have the organizational structures to implement that knowledge — structures which again, long ago, were not there. More prosaically we can say that this foundation course exists only because a lot of people worked together. Collectively we had the power to produce it; individually we did not. So there is in my mind a second, if weaker, image of power — of power as capacity: the power to do something. The term 'power' brings to mind the recognition that the way cooperation is organized socially seems to make it easier to get some things done rather than others.

This complexity of associations with the term 'power' is well captured in the range of definitions of the term available in the scholarly literature. As we saw in Block II, understanding the world requires precise conceptualization; and around key social processes, disagreements tend to exist about which conceptualization is best. Power, as a basic feature of social life, cannot escape this dispute. It is a 'contested' concept. Scholars disagree with each other about how to define 'power', and in their disagreement are led to understand the world differently.

Consider, for example, these definitions of power from the philosophers Bertrand Russell and Hannah Arendt, the sociologists Max Weber and Talcott Parsons, and the political scientists Robert Dahl and Nicos Poulantzas:

RUSSELL: power is — 'the production of intended effects'

WEBER: power is 'the probability that an actor in a social relationship will be a position to carry out his own will despite resistance'

DAHL: his 'intuitive idea of power is that A has power over B to the extent that he can get B to do something that B would otherwise not do'

ARENDT: power 'is not the property of an individual', it 'corresponds to the human ability not just to act but to act in concert'

PARSONS: power is 'a generalised facility or resource in the society, analogous to money, which enables the achievement of collective goals through the agreement of members of a society to legitimate leadership positions whose incumbents further the goals of the system'

POULANTZAS: power is 'the capacity of a class to realise its specific objective interests'

Source: Lukes, 1986, pp.1–4

──────────────────────── ACTIVITY 2 ────────────────────────

Think about each of these definitions in turn. Then go back to your original listing of words and sentences about power and see if there is anything that you wish to add.

Supplementary definition of power:

Steven Lukes, who first put together the six definitions listed above, was keen to emphasize that none of them was adequate on its own. Instead, what each did was to draw attention to an important facet of the nature of power. As he said:

> Each does say something true and relevant ... Affecting behaviour is certainly a centrally important form of power ... The co-operative and communicative aspect of empowerment certainly requires attention, as do the ways in which power maintains social systems and advances conflicting collective interests within them.
>
> (*ibid.*, p.4)

But of course we can't study power in all its forms all at once. We need a way in, a strategy for moving from the simple to the complex. We need some common starting point on which to build our understanding of basic processes, and to which later we can add any necessary complexities. That starting point can be found by probing deeper still, by going beneath the competing definitions of the concept to locate what is common to and underlies them all. For though they disagree on the level at which power relationships are to be examined (whether it should be between individuals, or at the level of society), and they certainly differ in their sense of power as constraining or enabling, they do at least share a common sense that *to possess power is to possess the ability to shape action.*

So as a way of starting our analysis of power, we can at least say that individuals have power if they can shape the action of other individuals; and that, likewise, institutions can be said to have power if they have the ability to prescribe the activities of those subject to their will. Indeed we experience the presence of power in society in at least these two senses: facing individuals who possess the ability to make us act in particular ways, and facing institutions whose rules we are expected to obey.

It is possible to analyse power relationships purely at the level of the interplay between individuals, to ask why it is that some individuals exercise more power than others. If we are to answer that question, we shall need to make an assessment of the different kinds and scale of political resources that individuals enjoy. We shall have to look in particular at their physical prowess and ability to coerce, at their personal charm (even charisma), and at their possession of the things valued in the society as a whole (their command of status, wealth, beauty, qualifications and so on). We shall need to determine whether the individuals concerned are male or female, white or black, young or old, and to see how their possession of one of those attributes rather than the other gives them advantages in a society which prioritizes a certain gender, colour of skin, and degree of maturity. We shall also have to look at the positions they occupy in rule-making institutions: to see, for example, if they are bank managers able to advance or deny credit, employers able to provide or take away employment, even course tutors able to award or deny grades.

As soon as we do that, we shall be in a position to recognize that so much of what looks like individually-generated power is in fact nothing of the kind. Rather it is power which derives — *not* from any personal attribute individually possessed and socially prized — but from the position occupied by particular individuals in key institutions. We shall see, that is, that much of what looks like the power of individuals is in fact the power of the institutions into which those individuals are temporarily inserted. Individuals will come and go, but the power to shape action will remain, locked in the institution, and exercised on the institution's behalf by the individual office-holders within it.

———————————— ACTIVITY 3 ————————————

We live surrounded by rule-making institutions. The rules they make, and the decisions they take, shape our actions in a myriad of ways. So now, look beyond the individuals you know, to the institutions which lie behind them. Go beyond the father, to see the structure of the family that gives the father his power. Go beyond the bank managers, to the financial institutions which empower them, and for whom they act as agents. Ask yourself what are the main rules which shape *your* action, and which are the main places in society from which they emerge. Then fill in the boxes below. (I have put an example in to help you begin).

Rules that constrain you as an individual	Source of rules	Sanctions against rule-breakers
Moral code	Church, family, school	Social disapproval …

To track down all those who constrain us, and all the rules to which we are subject, would take forever. There are parents, teachers, the adult(s) with whom we live, friends, employers, police officers and so on. There are rules at work, rules at church, rules when driving, and rules about property. There are rules too of a very general kind, that specify what is and isn't 'on' when at home, when dealing with friends, when coming into new situations, and so on. In other words, there are moral codes, social conventions, club rules, employment contracts, and legal prohibitions. My list came out something like this:

Rules	Sources	Sanctions
Moral code	Church, family, school	Social disapproval in this life, hell-fire in the next
Social norms	Family, peers	Social ostracism
Club rules	Voluntary organizations	Expulsion
Work rules	Employer	Dismissal
Law	Government	Fines and imprisonment

Your list will probably not be the quite the same as mine: there are many ways of cataloguing the rules, and the institutions which make and enforce them. But I hope that your list will throw into relief two features of the catalogue that are of particular importance for the argument to follow:

1   The first is that there are both public and private sources of rules. The government, as a *public* body, makes rules which apply across the society, to all *private* institutions (from workplaces, through clubs, to informal groups and family units). Governments decide, for example, what statutory rights workers will have in factories, at what age children will go to school, under what conditions marriages can be annulled, and so on. In each of these private areas, and in many others, governments exercise their power to make and enforce rules. Yet there are also extensive private rule-making processes evident in the catalogue; private rule-making processes which reflect, and reproduce, private relationships of power. This is very clear in the sphere of relationships between men and women. The dominant assumptions in the social code about the division of labour and authority within the family, the rules employers make for their employees (on hours, promotion, or pay), and the way voluntary organizations (like trade unions and churches) regulate their internal behaviour (the timing of union meetings or the ordination of priests) — all these things profoundly affect the capacity of women to achieve a set of life experiences as wide as that available to men.

This distinction between the public and the private is a persistent theme in D103, and is more complex a business than might at first appear. Indeed it is quite easy to be confused by the different ways in which the distinction can be drawn. In D103, the distinction is normally drawn in two ways: as one dividing a private sphere of home and family from a public one of paid work and politics; or as one differentiating a public sector of state provision from a private one in which the state plays no direct role. If the emphasis of the first distinction is on the gap between home and society, the focus of the second is often on the interplay of the economy and the state.

The danger of confusion lies in the way in which what is 'public' in the first distinction (the wider society) is itself divided into public and private spheres (the state and the economy) in the second. But of course that is how the terms are used in general conversation. Sometimes the 'private' refers to the individual or the family. We all speak of 'the privacy of our own homes' from which we 'go out' to participate 'in the public domain', not least by working in the economy. But on other occasions we refer to large parts of that economy as something that is also to be labelled as 'private', to distinguish it from areas of social and economic life provided by public bodies; that is, by the state. We cannot abolish this ambiguity of terminology from popular use, nor indeed from our own ways of thinking. We just need to be clear on each occasion how we are using the distinction and what we mean by it.

In this unit, when I talk of the public and the private, I really have in mind the second way of handling the distinction. The focus of much of what follows will be on the way the state (as a public body) exercises power over the economy (as an area of private activity). That will be true even of the second case study (on equal opportunities legislation) and the television programme associated with it (TV 08). The focus of much equal opportunities legislation is on the public regulation of employment practices in the private economy. But the need for that legislation reflects the presence — within the private practices of the economy — of the way power is distributed in the other public–private divide: that between the family and the wider world.

Private rule making within the family is much more difficult to spot than the very public activities of governments, but it goes on none the less. We can presumably all recognize power relationships within a factory, or in a classroom; but the power relationships between adults within a family are often less visible. That is why the insistence by the women's movement in the 1970s that 'the personal is political' was so important: it offered a way of recognizing that many of the tensions experienced by women in their personal relationships derived from the uneven distribution of power within the family unit, an unevenness which was itself rooted in the wider inequalities of power between men and women in the society as a whole.

2 This set of observations on the complexity of the division between the private and the public brings me to the second feature of my catalogue of rules, sources and sanctions. It is not just that there are both private and public sources of rules in this society. It is also that private and public rule-making processes are intimately related. The moral code informs the law, the law sets limits on what voluntary organizations can prescribe, and so on. Indeed it is possible to discuss which are the *dominant* rules in our society.

——————————— ACTIVITY 4 ———————————

Which do you find are the most important/potent set of rules from my list above?

I think that the choice lies between the *law* and the *moral code*. Certainly work rules operate within the constraints fixed by each; and though governments are able to change laws in ways which suggest that they are the ultimate source of rules, I suspect that those who head the government are just as moulded by basic moral codes as the rest of us.

It also seems to me that governments have an important freedom here: to decide which private rule-making processes to constrain and to shape, and which to leave alone. In that way, governments can change or bolster private patterns of power both by what they do and by what they choose not to do. In other words, private rules make private power; and governments then reinforce or undermine these inequalities of private power by the extent to which their public rules either challenge and forbid these private practices, or support and sanction them. And, in this way too, private power can be preserved by what is *kept off* the political agenda of governments, as well as by what is included.

SUMMARY

- Power is a difficult concept to define; and many definitions exist. They share a sense of power as the ability to shape action.

- Individuals exercise power. So too do institutions. Much of the power exercised by individuals derives from the roles they play within key social institutions.

- Both public and private institutions exercise power by making and enforcing rules. Patterns of private power are affected by the extent and the nature of public regulation.

2 THE MEASUREMENT OF POWER

It is with this relationship of private power to public power that the rest of this unit and its associated television programme (TV 08) are concerned. Our focus will be on public power — on the power of governments. But our concern will not be so much with the procedures through which governments make and pass laws as with the interplay of governments with the societies they govern. We want to know *how powerful governments are, or can be, in their dealings with key centres of private power; and we want to know too how easy or difficult it is for those without private power to use government to redress their private grievances*. Later in the unit both these questions will be explored through case studies: on government relationships with private economic institutions; and on the use of legislation to strengthen the position of women in the world of paid work. But before we turn to these case studies, and begin to measure the power of government there, we need to establish some way of recognizing and measuring power itself. This is our task in this second section of the unit.

The question of how to recognize and measure power has preoccupied many political scientists in the post-war period, and part of the debate between them is surveyed in the Reader article by Steven Lukes (Chapter 12). There Lukes refers to a much-cited study of local politics in the United States — a study of New Haven in Connecticut by Robert Dahl, called *Who Governs?* — and to an equally cited critique of Dahl's work by two other American political scientists, Peter Bachrach and Morton Baratz. The exchange between them, and Lukes's comments upon it, will help to extend our understanding of contemporary power relationships in the UK.

=== **READER AND AUDIO CASSETTE** ===

Read the 'one-dimensional view' section of the Lukes article, 'Power: a radical view'. To help you, I will use part of the audio-cassette for Block IV to take you through each section of the Lukes article in turn. So listen to the first part of segment one on side A of the cassette for Block IV as you read this section of the article.

The Dahl method emphasized in the 'one-dimensional view' section of the article is available for use by us too. We can begin to decide how powerful the government is by looking at the way government policy is formulated and implemented — at the way issues are resolved in the political arena. According to this approach to the recognition and measurement of power, we need to look at government policy on one day (to see what ministers intend to do) and then look again on another (to see what they have achieved). In some cases, ministers will have formulated legislative proposals, successfully steered these proposals through Parliament unamended, and seen them implemented without difficulty. In those cases we can say that the power of ministers is high. But on other issues, where the degree of resistance is greater, ministers will have had more difficulty steering their legislation through or seeing it successfully implemented. Then we can say that their power is limited. But either way, the charting of the effectiveness of government initiatives will give us one measure of the degree of power enjoyed by the senior politicians and administrators who formally control the state.

This approach to the recognition and measurement of power is what Steven Lukes calls 'a one-dimensional view of power'. It is a way into the complexities of political power which focuses on the surface detail of political life. It even offers us a way of assessing the relative power of key interest groups, and not just the government itself. If, for example, the CBI wants government policy to include wage restraint, and the TUC wants wage restraint eased, then we can draw a model of their interaction with the government — by treating government policy as a ball, as shown in Figure 1, and the CBI and TUC as pressures operating upon it. If government policy rolls to the right, rather than to the left, then the power of the TUC on this issue seems larger than that of the CBI. If it rolls to the left, then the CBI seems ahead of the TUC in influence; and so on.

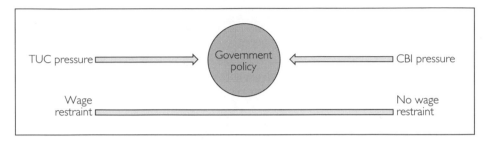

Figure 1

I say 'seems larger' and 'seems ahead' because in reality this measure of power only touches the surface of the relationships we are seeking to measure. The detail of political life is important, but it is only the top layer of the phenomenon we need to examine. The example we have just cited could have used the analogy of a hockey or football match to measure movement on the 'playing pitch' of wage restraint. But we need to know too why it was that pitch on which the game was being played. Why weren't the CBI, the TUC and the government discussing and contesting public ownership, levels of investment, industrial democracy, maternity and paternity leave, job sharing, equal opportunities and so on? For the distribution of political power affects not only the *outcomes* of political debate, but also the *agenda* around which that debate is organized.

============= READER AND AUDIO CASSETTE =============

Now read the section in Lukes's article on 'the two-dimensional view' of power, and listen to the second part of the first segment of side A of the audio-cassette for Block IV in which this is discussed.

As we shall see in the second case study, the biggest problem with equal opportunities legislation was not getting the laws passed and implemented. That was (and remains) difficult enough. The real problem was one of having the issue of equal opportunities discussed seriously at all in political circles. For years such discussion was effectively blocked out of politics; and this blocking is a second face of power. To measure power in this second sense, we need to know how easy it is for the government to fix its own agenda. We need to know the ability of key interest groups to get their concerns considered by the government, and have them considered on their own terms. We need to know about the ability of politicians and private groups to keep items out of public life, or to set very restricted terms for their public discussion. The fixing of the political agenda is a dimension of power which the measurement of surface effects never touches. A full analysis of the distribution of power requires us to know, that is, where the match is being played as well as who is winning. We need to have a clear sense of *where the football or hockey pitch is*, and who or what put it there, as well as knowing to which end of the pitch the ball is actually being hit.

Finally there is a 'third dimension of power', a dimension that touches the question of social process. Stay with the image of the hockey pitch and the TUC–CBI struggle for influence upon it. We can draw this as shown in Figure 2.

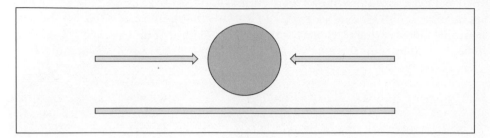

Figure 2

But actually we need to know the gradient of the ground as well. Perhaps it ought to be drawn as shown in Figure 3.

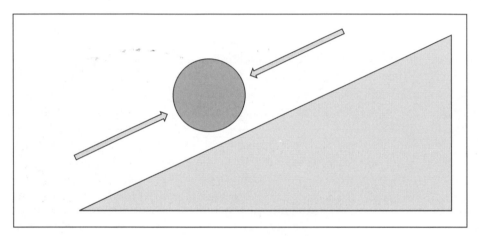

Figure 3

Various factors seem to fix the gradient on which power relationships around the government are played out: factors such as property rights, market forces, economic conditions, legal systems, patterns of social division, general cultural variables. These factors are easier to illustrate than to quantify. So, for example, it is more difficult to obtain better maternity rights if economic competition is tight and sexist attitudes are unchallenged than it is if neither of these conditions apply. It is easier for the TUC to influence the government when employment is high than when it is low, when the culture favours collective over individual goals, and when the legal constraints on picketing and striking are easier. It is more difficult for private industry to obtain state aid if the ruling orthodoxies of economic life are monetarist rather than Keynesian, and so on.

=========================   READER AND AUDIO CASSETTE   =========================

To round out your understanding of this third face of power, read Lukes on 'the three-dimensional view' and listen to the third part of segment one on side A of the tape.

Lukes talks of 'the bias of the system' being sustained by what he calls 'socially structured and culturally patterned ... practices of institutions'. This is a very important notion, but also one which is particularly hard to grasp. Again an example might help. In 1977 the Labour government was running a wage policy, with an income norm of 10 per cent. That wage policy was challenged by an official strike of firemen — firemen who were seeking a 30 per cent pay rise (some £900 a year) to supplement their basic annual salary of £3,000. The firemen had to strike for eleven weeks to win a better offer, one that still fell far short of the £900 they sought. Yet, at the same time, the Labour government implemented the recommendations of its review body on the salaries of senior officials in the public sector, awarding the head of the then publicly owned British Steel an extra 10 per cent in line with the policy. Sir Charles Villier's salary then rose by £3,000, to £33,000, and did so without industrial action by him (he didn't have to go on strike). His pay rise came easily, and did so in response to the logic of market forces which might otherwise draw senior figures out of the public sector into the private. One man got as a pre-tax rise what others had as their total pre-tax salary; and did so because of the particular constellation of salary structures, market forces and general cultural attitudes surrounding the making of state policy. The gradient ran with Sir Charles, and ran against the firemen.

This is just an example of power relationships in Lukes's third sense. Perhaps there are other very different examples that spring to mind. But let's stay with trade unionism for a minute, because it will help to take us into the discussion of the general distribution of power in a complex industrial society like the UK. The *visibility* of union strike action often creates the impression of trade union power. Thus, on the first dimension of power, trade union action suggests potency. Unions strike, wage settlements rise, the 'ball' shifts in the direction that the trade unions require. But think a while. Why strike if things are going your way? Trade unions strike because (and when) the agenda of decision making (in the state sector, or in industry generally) goes against them. They strike because they cannot fix the agenda: they are relatively powerless at the second level of power — and, beneath that, at the third. Strikes, if successful, can then recapture part of the ground lost by the slope of the hill: but they touch neither the placing of the pitch nor the slope of the hill on which it sits.

We can illustrate that by drawing our gradient picture again, and by listing the things that tilt the gradient either for or against easy wage settlements; see Figure 4.

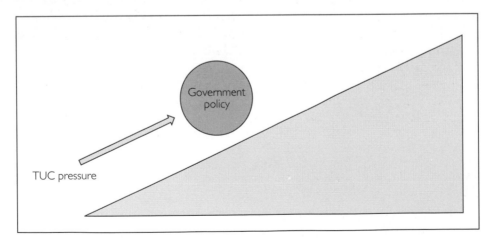

Figure 4

—————————————— ACTIVITY 5 ——————————————

Before you read on, make a list of what you think those factors might be.

I would put it this way. The basic asymmetry in the distribution of power in an industrial society like the UK dominates both unions and their members. The individual worker faces an employer who is armed with immensely superior sanctions (that is why unionism arose in the first place) and that asymmetry of power does not go away because of the union's presence. Without unionism, workers are vulnerable to dismissal and loss of wages, sanctions that are necessarily traumatic for them but are only marginal to the costs of the employer. Even when unionized, work groups still face an authority structure in industry that is mainly in private hands, in which managerial policy is implemented automatically unless unions act quickly to stop it. So even at the level of the individual firm, union power is often necessarily negative and reactive, no matter how easy the conditions of bargaining happen to be; and in the broader social context, union power is still frequently of that kind. That is, it is still engaged in attempting to shape and reverse policies initiated else-where, ones that are carried through quite automatically by market forces and private managerial structures unless the unions are strong enough to block them.

So as far as I can tell the forces stacking the gradient against effective union power seem to include such things as: (1) the private ownership of industry and commerce, and the right to manage which that ownership brings; (2) the pressure of market forces in a competitively-exposed economy; (3) the general framework of laws which limit trade union activity, and the disposition of senior civil servants to work more closely with management than with unions; and (4) the general political climate of ideas — those that treat unionism as a problem and undesirable. It is these which ensure that unions are invariably obliged to push the ball up a hill down which, left to itself, it would roll automatically. The tide of power runs with the gradient of market forces. That of the unions does not; and as a result unions have to work very hard indeed to move government policy in their direction, and to keep it there, once moved; see Figure 5.

Now to stop there would be to give a very one-sided view of union power. Clearly there are factors which ease the gradient, or even tip it in the unions' favour. The gradient eases with full employment, favourable labour law, the spread of radical ideas, and so on. If they appear, and appear simultaneously, then the incline of the hill would have to be drawn very differently from the way it appears in Figure 5. But Figure 5 seems the right way to draw it now — to me at least — because these 'gradient-easing' factors are largely absent as this unit is being written.

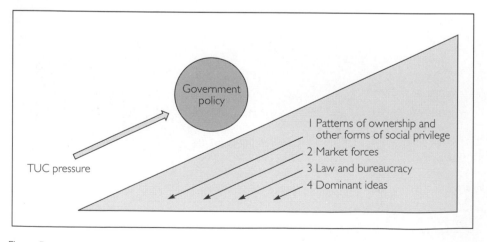

Figure 5

—————————— ACTIVITY 6 ——————————

Try the exercise yourself, not on trade unions this time, but on the struggle to obtain equal opportunities for women, and for people regardless of ethnic origin, discussed in the television programme (TV 08). There again the gradient seems set against any easy achievement of such a policy outcome. Why? What is the equivalent — when considering equal opportunities policies for women — to the 'patterns of ownership and other forms of social privilege' listed in Figure 5 as a constraint on trade union power? Is the notion of 'social privilege' there to be replaced by one of 'male privilege'? What dominant ideas make the policy difficult to achieve? Sexist ideas? What about the pressures of a patriarchal family structure fitting here, as the pressure of market forces did for the union case. Fill in your own factors in Figure 6; and see if it helps you to grasp why it is so difficult to legislate effectively in this area. I think it helps enormously, and I hope you do too (and you will be in a better position to check it again after doing more work on equal opportunities later in this unit).

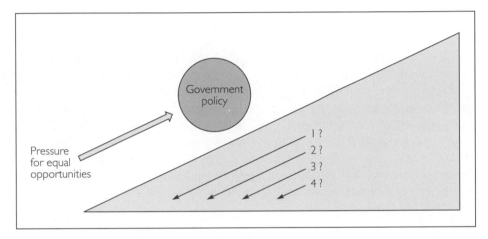

Figure 6

—————————————————————————————————————

SUMMARY

- Power can be measured, in its most obvious sense, by charting the ability of individuals, groups and institutions directly to influence the decisions that are made.

- Power can be measured, in its second dimension, by charting the ability of individuals, group and institutions to control the issues that enter decision-making processes, and to set the terms on which they are discussed there.

- Power can be measured, in its third dimension, by isolating biases in the way society is organized, that make it easier for some individuals, groups and institutions (and harder for others) to see the things they desire actually come to fruition.

3   TWO CASE STUDIES

Let's now apply this three-dimensional understanding of the nature of power to two case studies: first, to the making of economic policy discussed in Block III; and then to the policy on equal opportunities which is examined in more detail in the television programme associated with this unit (TV 08). In each case, as you read on, ask yourself:

1   Which individuals, groups or institutions directly *influence* the decisions that are made?

2   Who/what is setting the political *agenda*?

3   Who is running with, and who against, the *gradient* (of dominant market forces, social practices, belief systems and patterns of privilege)?

Watch for *influence*, *agenda* and *gradient* in order to decide where power lies in each case study.

3.1   THE MAKING OF ECONOMIC POLICY

If you look back to Unit 12, you will see that the Labour government of 1974, and the Conservative governments of the 1980s, had similar economic goals but very different sets of policies to achieve them. Both sets of governments sought economic growth, long-term high employment, price stability and a sound balance of payments. But they sought those things in very different ways. Labour sought them by trying to share power in industry between itself, employers and unions; the Conservatives preferred instead to restrict their own role, to let management manage, and to encourage market forces to operate more freely. Labour attempted to increase the role of the public sector. The Conservatives tried to reduce it.

So Labour came into office in 1974 proposing:

- to extend worker and trade union rights (with new labour laws, extensions of industrial democracy, and a big role for union leaders — in the making of economic policy, and as executive directors of new interventionist economic agencies covering safety at work, arbitration and the management of publicly owned firms);

- to extend the government's powers over industry (including an extension of public ownership, and the creation of a system of planning agreements, by which large private firms had to agree their investment plans with the government and the unions);

- to increase pensions, apply price controls and tax the rich.

The Conservatives came in with a very different agenda:

- to curb trade union power, and to close down Labour's interventionist economic agencies;

- 'to roll back the state': by curbing spending, privatizing publicly owned firms and industries, and removing controls on the free movement of capital;

- to lower direct taxes on high incomes and reduce and redirect welfare payments (to encourage initiative and effort).

—————————— ACTIVITY 7 ——————————

Go back to the graph in Figure 1 in Unit 12, and re-examine the movement of economic growth, inflation, unemployment and the balance of payments under the two governments. That will give you a first rough indication of how successful these policy packages were.

As we discussed more fully in Unit 12, the graph shows modest but sustained economic growth under Labour in the 1970s, with unemployment levels rising but still low in comparison to the 1980s. However, inflation and the balance of payments look much less impressive under Labour. It was the Conservatives who brought inflation down, and eventually produced economic growth again; at the cost of high unemployment early in the decade, and a large deficit on the balance of payments by the end. So the impact of each package looks patchy. Let's see what happened in each case.

The *Labour government* entered office just as the world economy went into severe recession in the wake of the 1973 oil crisis. Labour arrived in government with a set of policies it had agreed with the TUC, policies which reflected union leaders' concerns with labour law, pensions, and industrial planning. In effect, Labour offered the unions a 'social contract': new worker/union rights, and social reform, in return for wage restraint and union cooperation in industrial restructuring. The Labour government began with a pro-union Industrial Relations Act. It created new interventionist agencies. It nationalized companies. It raised pensions, and even — in 1974 — froze rents and some prices. But wage settlements remained high, inflation touched almost 30 per cent in May 1975, and there was a major run on sterling: to all of which the government responded with a tight incomes policy — one that lasted for the remaining four years it was in office.

Yet in spite of widespread popular support for the introduction of an incomes policy, the money markets remained nervous of Labour in power. They were nervous partly because of the radicalism of bits of Labour's programme, and partly because the economy's balance of payments remained in deficit. The economy just wasn't sufficiently competitive to earn enough foreign currency, or to attract enough foreign investment to balance its overseas account. Instead the deficit grew so large, and unease among financial institutions remained so intense, that speculation against sterling continued unabated: to the point at which, by the autumn of 1976, the Labour government was forced to go to the International Monetary Fund for a loan to cover the economy's foreign debts. That loan was given only on condition that planned welfare spending was curtailed and wage restraint continued. In other words, the terms of the loan set real limits on the implementation of the radical parts of

Denis Healey, Labour Chancellor of the Exchequer, 1976, acknowledging cheers at the Labour Party Conference after defending his defence of sterling and negotiations with the IMF

Labour's programme. By then, in any case, this radicalism was in retreat in the face of the strong opposition of private industry to power-sharing. In the event, only two planning agreements were ever signed, and the CBI led so vociferous a campaign against Labour proposals on industrial democracy that they were never implemented.

So instead of extending union power in industry, the Labour government found that its relationship with union leaders and union members deteriorated over time. Early union influence on the political agenda slipped away. Union leaders were still regularly consulted, and their presence in the 'corridors of power' helped to keep alive an image of influence. But the reality of power was different. After 1975, union leaders could only keep up a rearguard action, affecting the detail of policy — on such things as incomes or employment — while the main thrust of policy moved in directions they disliked. Unemployment rose, wage restraint remained tight, and industrial output in 1979 still lay below its 1974 level. Only the strike figures revived, and Labour fell to electoral defeat after a 'winter of discontent' which showed only too clearly the gap that had emerged between government policy and union requirements. The pattern of strikes under governments of different political persuasions is evident in Figure 7.

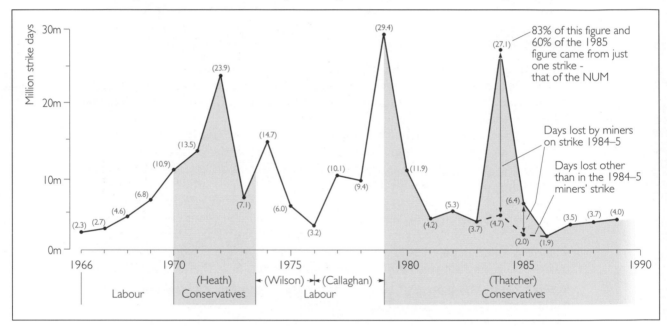

Figure 7   Strike days, 1966–89   Source: *Department of Employment Gazette*

SUMMARY

- The Labour government's economic policy between 1974 and 1979 involved a significant increase in public ownership and control of industry, new rights for trade unions and workers, and extensive social reform. Much of that policy was designed in negotiation with national trade union leaders.
- These policies met opposition from significant sections of private industry, made financial institutions uneasy, and eventually alienated certain groups of workers. Even the majority of national trade union leaders in the end came to oppose voluntary wage restraint.
- The Labour government was eventually obliged to shed the radical parts of its programme, and to tolerate higher levels of unemployment than it had initially desired. It found no way to increase significantly the competitiveness of UK- based manufacturing firms.

The *Conservative governments* that followed had a very different experience. They closed down or downgraded Labour's interventionist agencies; and by their second term they were selling back large numbers of publicly owned firms and industries to private buyers. The Conservatives didn't try to run the economy through extensive consultation. Instead, initially, they kept tight control on the amount of money in circulation by restricting public spending and allowing the unrestrained export of capital. The short-term effect of this was a severe recession. The volume of industrial production fell by 15 per cent in 1980 alone; and one in five of the manufacturing jobs in existence in 1979 had been lost by 1981. Economic growth then returned, but industrial production did not reach its 1979 levels again until 1988; and by then the initial preoccupation with money supply had given way to a more general concern to curb inflation — using variations in interest rates and tight controls on government spending as the main levers of control. Policy towards the unions remained more consistent. The government tightened labour laws in a series of Acts, to make illegal the mass picketing and sympathy action that had troubled the Conservative government under Edward Heath between 1970 and 1974. The Conservative governments endured a series of public sector strikes — from steel workers, teachers, nurses, civil servants and the miners — in each case emerging in a position to impose the wage settlements and restructuring programmes that they (and the senior managers in each public sector industry concerned) required. So, by 1986, strike figures were at a post-war low; though it should be noted that they had risen again by 1989 when the Conservatives — after a decade in power — ran into their own mini-'summer of discontent' with strikes by railwaymen, dockers and local government workers.

In general, relationships between the government and the representative bodies of industry and finance were close and harmonious. The CBI periodically registered its dislike of high interest rates — and on one occasion even promised a 'bare knuckle fight' with the government if they did not come down. But that outburst was the exception. Normally, Conservative governments do not govern under the hail of public criticism from industrial and financial bodies which Labour governments periodically experience; and in the late 1980s City institutions tolerated a much higher balance of payments deficit from the Conservative government than they had from Labour in the 1970s.

That toleration reflected in part the extent to which even the Conservatives had to tailor their policies to avoid sterling crises. In 1984, for example, the pound fell rapidly against the dollar, coming close to parity with it at one point; and this obliged the government to increase interest rates to attract foreign speculative capital. Again in 1988, after income tax had been cut to 25p in the pound, the resulting rapid rise in consumer spending produced an unexpectedly large balance of payments deficit; and interest rates had to rise. Indeed in that year the bank base rate rose repeatedly in half-point stages from $7\frac{1}{2}$ per cent to 12 per cent in just four months — months which culminated in the economy's worst ever monthly balance of trade figures. The government was obliged to put interest rates up for two connected but distinct reasons. Interest rates rose first in an attempt to stem the rise in consumer spending and slow the rate of inflation (particularly in house prices) caused by this excess demand. They also rose in an attempt to stabilize the currency, and reassure the money markets, by keeping interest rates here so high relative to major competitors abroad that the inflow of foreign investment would offset the outflow of payments on the trade imbalance.

No doubt other policy options might have done this too. The government was still free to choose how to respond to unease in the money markets caused by the trade imbalance. But it was not free to ignore the problem. It had to make some response, and had to address that response primarily to the preoccupations of the money markets. For Conservative governments, no less than their predecessors, operated under constraints of a financial kind. They just seemed able to do so without the levels of high drama associated with Labour's 'winters of discontent' and negotiations with the IMF.

SUMMARY

- Conservative governments entered office determined to control the money supply, curb trade unions, reduce the scale of government activity, and expose UK industry to greater competition.
- They met opposition from sections of the trade union movement, but not from City or industrial interests in anything like the degree experienced by Labour in power between 1974 and 1979.
- They held to the broad lines of their policy over a decade; but found that they could not control the money supply as first intended, nor avoid having to alter policy to appease fears in the City, nor prevent the emergence of a large deficit on the balance of payments.

──────────────── ACTIVITY 8 ────────────────

Go back through the case study and list:

1   any individuals, groups or institutions shaping economic policy;

2   any individuals, groups or institutions shaping the agenda of politics;

3   any information on factors affecting the 'gradient' on which policy is made.

Then keep that list by you, to check against mine later in the unit.

3.2   EQUAL OPPORTUNITIES

The case study you have just worked through was about the shaping of government activity in an already established area of policy making. This case study is very different. It is the story of the struggle to have policy made in the first place, in an area in which government had hitherto been inactive. It is the story of a sustained attempt to use the public power of the state to redress an imbalance of power in the private world of men and women. To use the imagery of Section 2 again: if the previous case study was about the battle of power on an established pitch, this case study is about the attempt to have the pitch moved.

This case study fits closely with the subject matter of TV 08. The range of equal opportunity initiatives considered in that programme stretches out to encompass questions of ethnicity and gender. Here I want to look at gender alone. I want to look at the origin of two Acts which extended the formal rights of women: the *Equal Pay Act* (1970) which established the principle of equal pay for the same or broadly similar work; and the *Sex Discrimination Act* (1975) which made both direct and indirect discrimination on the grounds of gender illegal in a number of spheres of public life — in education, training, employment, housing and the provision of public services.

──────────────── READER ────────────────

Let's approach this case study in a slightly different way. Turn now to Chapter 13 of the Reader, and read April Carter's history of those Acts, 'The politics of women's rights'.

In April Carter's account, we see a quite different pattern of politics and power from our first case study. Much of the first case study was about politics in Lukes's 'one-dimensional' sense — about the interplay of political actors around a public policy. Much of this second case study is really about Lukes's second dimension of power — about the control of the political agenda. The first imperative of campaigners for women's rights was to have their problem recognized, discussed and eventually acted upon by the politicians. The Conservative Party, as late as the early 1960s, was still declining to do this, insisting that the question of equal pay was a matter for employers and unions alone. It took sustained and prolonged pressure to break that resistance down, and to force women's issues on to the national political agenda.

Who were the key individuals and institutions who maintained that pressure? April Carter suggests a list of key activists here: women trade unionists lobbying their unions, a national male trade union leadership reluctantly galvanized into action, the Women's Advisory Committee of the TUC, women in the Labour Party, women on strike at Fords, sympathetic MPs, and eventually Barbara Castle. They at least were the active forces pushing equal pay on to the agenda of a Labour government. On sex discrimination, April Carter gives them less of a role, stressing instead the more generalized impact on public opinion of 'feminist ideas and feminist activism'.

TUC Women's Day March, May 1975, London

──────────────── ACTIVITY 9 ────────────────

Can you find much material in the April Carter account that is concerned with Lukes's first dimension of power — much on the actual people shaping the legislation as it emerges?

───

There is not much, as that is not April Carter's prime concern. She rather leaps over the detail of the legislative process, though she does give us a few cryptic clues when she talks of Barbara Castle accepting compromises 'under pressure', and refusing on her own initiative to extend the bill to cover recruitment and training. There is also some mention of employer opposition to the Sex Discrimination Act, because of worries about its impact on industrial costs.

─────────── ACTIVITY 10 ───────────

What then of the gradient? What is there in the account that gives weight to wider questions of economic life, cultural practices, dominant belief systems and so on?

CHRONOLOGY OF THE STRUGGLE

1888: First resolution passed by TUC in favour of equal pay.
1911: National Insurance introduced. Women retired at 60, men at 65, so women lose 5 years' earning capacity.
1942: TUC pledges itself to principle of equal pay.
1946: Royal Commission on Equal Pay recommends equal pay for women teachers, local government officers and civil servants.
1953: Equal pay for women teachers accepted.
1955: Equal pay for women civil servants accepted.
1967: Joyce Butler MP fails to push through Private Member's Bill making discrimination on grounds of sex illegal.
1970: Equal Pay Act becomes law. Employers given five years to put their house in order.
1975: Act comes into force. Equal Opportunities Commission (EOC) established as enforcer.
Early 1980s: Most employers observe the Act, but increasingly the EOC relies on European law to win cases, because the Act does not recognize the principle of equal pay for work of equal value.
1984: Government finally accepts this principle in an amendment to the Act.

WINNERS AND LOSERS IN THE COURTS

Banking staff: In March 1981, Susan Worringham and Margaret Humphreys lost an equal pay claim against Lloyd's Bank. The bank argued that men, unlike women, had to contribute the 5 per cent in question to the company's pension scheme. But they won the appeal when the European Court of Justice decided that employers' pension contributions count as 'pay'.
Canteen cook: In May 1988, the Law Lords ruled that Julie Hayward, a shipyard canteen cook from Merseyside, was entitled to the same basic rate of pay as male painters, joiners and thermal insulation engineers in the same company.
Warehouse packers: In June 1988, after four years, Irene Pickstone and other mail order checkers won the right to bring a claim for equal pay with men unloading goods from vans. The case continues.
Nursery nurse: In December 1988, Marion Leverton, a nursery nurse employed by the Clwyd County Council, lost a claim for 'equal pay for work of equal value', when compared with a clerk. The council successfully argued that the nursery nurse worked shorter hours and was entitled to longer holidays.

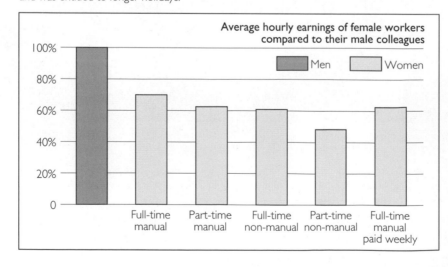

Figure 8   Chronology of the struggle

Source: *The Independent*, 2 March 1990, p.21

In April Carter's view, the biggest single obstacle to the introduction of equal pay 'was the widespread assumption that women's issues were unimportant, at least in the political arena'. The gradient of public opinion was so steep against the campaigners for women's rights that they couldn't even start the ball rolling up the hill until there was a 'change in attitudes to women's rights by the press, radio and television and among many of the public'. Only then did we see 'a marked increase in sympathy and interest among MPs in that period'.

Both the first and third dimension of power have continued to shape the life of these pieces of legislation long *after* they became law. Serious difficulties of enforcement remain. At the first level of power, those opposed to equal pay remain very active (particularly employers regrading jobs or denying similarity of tasks), whilst the enforcement agencies (especially the Equal Opportunities Commission) remain insufficiently strong and active to overcome all the back-sliding that goes on. And the gradient of popular culture and social organization remains set against any easy and rapid equalization of opportunities for men and women. Sexism hasn't vanished. Women still carry prime responsibility for children and the servicing of the adults in the family. The hill is still not level: and that is something to which we shall return later in the unit. (A summary of the struggle for equal opportunities for women is given in Figure 8.)

4   ANALYSIS OF THE CASE STUDIES

We have already begun to analyse the three dimensions of power shaping the creation and implementation of equal opportunity policies. It is now time to extend that analysis to cover the case studies as a whole, in order to answer the two questions with which Section 2 began, namely: how powerful are governments, or can they be, in their dealings with key centres of private power?; and how easy or difficult is it for those without private power to use government to redress their private grievances?

4.1   LEVEL 1: ACTORS AND ISSUES

We said earlier (when talking of a 'one-dimensional' understanding of power) that 'power can be measured, in its most obvious sense, by charting the ability of individuals, groups and institutions directly to influence the decisions that are made'. So let's see who/what was doing the influencing in the two case studies.

The key initial actors in both cases seem to be the *senior figures in the major political parties*. Legislation on equal pay depended on the support of the Labour government, and particularly on the personal commitment of Barbara Castle. Economic policy in the first case study varied with the political party in power; and in both case studies ministers were uniquely placed to shape the detail of legislation. Indeed, as the first case study made clear, the story of UK politics either side of 1979 was different in tone and content because of the programmes of the political parties who were in government. No other institution or group was as central to the story as the parties themselves.

However, even on the surface of political life, political parties are not the only actors in play. It is easy to be misled by the appearance of things, and to see political parties as powerful bodies in their own right. In reality they are not. A government and its immediate parliamentary supporters are normally less than 450 people, who draft legislation, talk about it in public, and vote on it. That legislation is in no way self-enforcing, although of course it enjoys an immense authority (because of the way in which it was made) and it is buttressed by the administrative and coercive apparatus of the state, which also helps to give it force. But governments have found on many occasions that they cannot rely on the automatic and full cooperation of the civil service and the judiciary. They have found too that, even when public servants have been entirely loyal and pliant, the complexity and resources of the private centres of power that they face mean that no government is in a position to coerce all its citizens into submission to its will on all issues. This is particularly true in liberal democracies such as ours, where governments do not enjoy the freedom to use coercion on a scale and in the manner of more authoritarian regimes. The governments to which we are directly subject are obliged instead to canvass support, and to mobilize coalitions of self-interested groups, if they wish to see their policies implemented. To help them do this, such governments have many resources at their disposal — but as we saw in the first case study, these are never extensive enough to remove entirely the need to negotiate and to cajole.

———————————————— ACTIVITY 11 ————————————————

Look back to the first case study, and compare the list you made in Activity 8 (of the institutions, groups and individuals shaping economic policy and the political agenda) with my list below of trade unions, manufacturing firms, and financial institutions.

TRADE UNIONS

Other institutions — outside the state — can exercise influence upon the making of policy by their willingness to cooperate with government, and by their ability to indicate the terms on which that cooperation will be forthcoming. In the first case study we examined, the *trade unions* appeared initially to be the key private institution playing that role. With employment levels high, industrial militancy already underway, and a government elected which had long and close connections with trade union officialdom, the unions were in a good position to influence policy. Even when that influence waned, the very fact that the Labour government was keen to achieve voluntary wage restraint meant that the unions were continually consulted — not just on the detail of incomes policy, but on other things too. In fact it is possible to map the range of political concerns that trade unions have pursued, as shown in Figure 9.

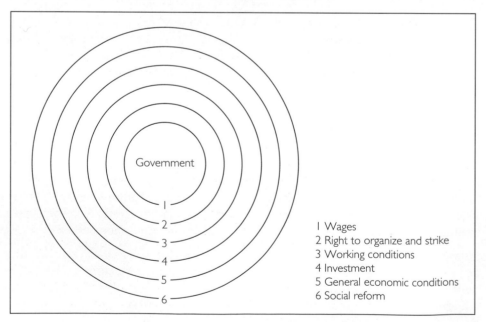

Figure 9

The diagram is drawn with wages at the centre, to show the unions' historic preoccupation with that topic. The case study makes clear that — even with a sympathetic government in power — trade union influence diminished on issues, the further those issues were from the centre of its concerns. It was also clear that, even on the unions' central concerns, their influence between 1974 and 1979 diminished quickly, as more powerful pressures came into play; and that after 1979 their influence fell away entirely. Indeed the case study suggests the following points about trade union political power since 1974.

SUMMARY

- Trade union influence is highest on wages, lowest on social reform, an higher under Labour than under the Conservatives

- In the 1970s trade union influence waned even under a Labour government as more powerful forces came into play.

- Trade union influence since 1979 has beren curbed by new labour laws, by higher unemployment, and by government antipathy to strong trade unionism.

Nurses from Merseyside and Yorkshire demonstrating in Downing Street in support of their campaign for more money, May 1974

MANUFACTURING FIRMS

When governments were making economic policy in our first case study, or pushing equal opportunities policy on industry in our second, they faced a manufacturing sector dominated by large companies. In twenty of the twenty-two industrial sectors listed by the Department of Employment, six firms or fewer are now responsible for over half the sector's output; and indeed as long ago as 1970 half of the UK's total manufacturing output came from just 140 firms. Many of these, of course, operate on a world-scale, and many are partly or wholly foreign owned.

We didn't see much direct evidence of their political power at work in either case study; but the visibility of power is not always the best guide to its existence. Multinational companies in particular have very powerful sanctions which they can deploy against governments whose policies they dislike. They can choose to place their investments elsewhere than in the UK. They can move their reserves of foreign currency out of London; and since at least 20 per cent of foreign trade entering and leaving the UK is now trade *within* big companies (say from Ford of Britain to Ford in Germany) they can even directly affect the balance of payments by the way they do their own internal accounting. The prices levied by one section of the company to another are, as far as the company is concerned, merely an internal bookkeeping device: but of course if Ford UK is selling under cost to Ford of Germany, the foreign earnings of the UK economy are thereby impaired.

This control of foreign currency, and the capacity to redirect investment on the world scale, gives multinational companies very potent sanctions against left-wing governments, or even against Conservative governments insufficiently tough with trade unions. But they are sanctions normally deployed, if they are deployed at all, in the quiet of private rooms, not in the full glare of publicity — as union strikes have to be. So we get glimpses of them, rather than regular and quantifiable evidence. Henry Ford, for example, flew in to make such a threat on the redeployment of investment when Edward Heath was Prime Minister in the early 1970s. But these public manifestations of corporate power are the exception, not the norm. More normally, governments have to operate 'with a pistol to the head' as Harold Wilson said of his dealings with the Chrysler Motor Company in the 1970s — aware, that is, that if policy is seen as unsympathetic to private enterprise, investment will be redeployed. The law of anticipated reactions is often enough to give multinational companies their leverage here: the knowledge that economic success will come only if the conditions for private capital accumulation are seen to be better in the UK than elsewhere in the international capitalist world. Governments of the left tend to court trade unions. Governments of the right tend to legislate against them. But it takes a very tough left-wing government to legislate against multinational firms. Such firms tend rather to be courted, attracted in with loans and grants, at most cajoled rather than bullied — and they tend to be handled in this way by governments of all political persuasions.

It is not all one-way, of course. Governments do possess very powerful sanctions against individual firms, even against whole industries. They are the major purchasers of the products of some industries (defence ones particularly), and bulk consumers of the products of others. They are able to fix levels of corporate taxation, and the kind and quantity of industrial aid. They negotiate on behalf of industry with other governments — winning entry into their markets and so on; and of course they can influence levels of consumer spending in the economy as a whole. These are powerful levers of influence, and small firms are particularly vulnerable to them. For the smaller the firm, the more dependent it is on the home market, and the less it has access to overseas funds. It is large firms which governments find difficult to control. Small businesses, like the unions, can in the end normally be tamed.

SUMMARY

- UK governments face an industrial sector divided into a large number of small and medium size firms and a smaller number of large (and often) multinational companies who dominate production in their particular sectors.

- Multinational companies have powerful sanctions to use against recalcitrant governments. These include the export of capital, the transfer of resources out of the country through their own internal financial arrangements, and the ability to speculate against the currency.

- Governments have resources too, which are particularly effective against smaller companies. These include the ability to tax, withdraw industrial aid, alter general levels of consumer demand, and negotiate on industry's behalf with representatives of other governments and international agencies.

FINANCIAL INSTITUTIONS

The money markets of the City of London played a very big part in the first of our case studies. This is partly because City institutions now command enormous resources (in 1981 they had 'at their disposal a massive treasury of £562 billion, or just over £10,000 per head of the 1981 population' (Coakley and Harris, 1983). It is also because close connections exist between the government and the main financial institutions of the City, not least between the Treasury and the Bank of England. Governments needing to borrow money have to go to the City to get it. Governments wanting to offset a trade deficit by invisible earnings have to make sure that the City is able to attract those earnings. Governments wanting to maintain a stable currency need to persuade the money markets not to move out of sterling. Those markets are now heavily international. Flows of currency can be attracted and retained only if conditions here are more acceptable to holders of speculative funds than are conditions elsewhere. So profit levels and growth rates have to be higher, or interest rates have to be differentially attractive: and if they are not, as we saw repeatedly in the first case study, the capacity of the City to bring a government into line is quite remarkable.

The equity dealing floor at the City of London headquarters of an international bank

Then finally, the state is surrounded by a series of key *foreign-based institutions*. We have already mentioned multinational companies and foreign holders of sterling. There are also central bankers working in close cooperation with each other, and each central bank liaises with international banking institutions such as the IMF. We have already seen the impact which the IMF can have on the policy of governments driven to borrow from it; and its influence is of course wider even than that, as the need to avoid a visit to the IMF can shape policy even in the economies of the strong.

SUMMARY

- UK governments face strong financial institutions with immense assets and extensive international connections.
- Governments depend on the cooperation of big City institutions for the financing of their own programmes and for their management of capital imports.
- Big international bankers meet regularly, and the international nature of contemporary money markets obliges governments to keep interest rates here internationally competitive.

Headquarters of the International Monetary Fund, Washington, USA

So governments have to operate within a variety of constraints established by the distribution of power in the private society that surrounds them. Policy is established only in complex processes of negotiation with key private groups, and always with a sense of how key institutions are likely to respond, even when not consulted. In fact it is possible to capture that level of constraint, map that distribution of power, and see the limited potency of the state even with power defined only in its first dimension. Visualize the state for the moment as a pebble dropped into a still pond. Each ripple that runs off the pebble can be thought of as a circle of constraint, each outer one more powerful than the ones within, locking the state into a complex and interconnected system of private power. Figure 10 shows how I would draw the circles. See if your placing of key institutions is similar to, or different from, mine.

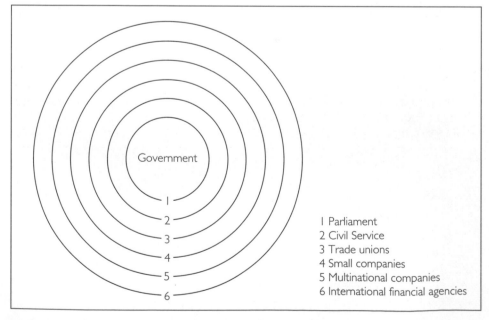

Figure 10

—————————————— ACTIVITY 12 ——————————————

To consolidate your understanding of the argument up to this point, try to fill in the boxes below: list the sanctions governments are able to use against key interest groups, and the sanctions interest groups are able to use against government. Don't be surprised if some boxes are fuller than others.

	Government sanctions	Interest group sanctions
Trade unions		
Small companies		
Multinational companies		
City institutions		
Foreign banks and governments		

—————————————— ACTIVITY 12 ——————————————

4.2   LEVEL 2: AGENDA SETTING

So to understand the experience of politicians in office it is necessary to grasp the power — the power to resist, the power to block and the power to circumvent — which is enjoyed in a society like ours by significantly placed private institutions. But the mapping of those institutions is only the first stage in our analysis of the distribution of power around the contemporary UK state. We also need to explore that distribution of power in its second and third dimensions too. We need to look at agenda setting as well as at policy resolution. We need to ask: 'Who or what fixes the issues which occupy the policy makers? Who or what is in a position to keep issues off the political agenda?' The 'who' in those questions is reasonably straightforward, the 'what' is less so, as we shall see.

WHO FIXES THE AGENDA?

Let us handle the 'who' question as a series of points.

1   The political parties are themselves key agenda setters. They initiate issues in their own right.

2   They are also a vital channel for initiation by others. That was very clear in the case study on equal opportunities. Women organized *inside* the political parties, and inside the trade unions; and used that insider position to put equal pay on to the political agenda. Activity inside the trade unions made sense here because of the close relationship between the unions and the Labour Party. In both case studies, the trade unions used their positions within the decision-making structures of the Labour Party (their block votes at conference, their membership of the party's National Executive) to ensure that their concerns also became party concerns. Likewise, though no doubt in a far less public and direct way, the companies that fund the Conservative Party normally expect the party to express views and concerns which they hold dear. To a degree at least, 'he who pays the piper calls the tune' — though, in each case, the 'calling' is in practice more limited and more subtle than a simple counting of block votes or corporate cheques might initially suggest.

Labour Party Conference, Brighton, 1979

3 Key interest groups have other channels of access too. Their relationship with sponsoring departments of government is often vital to them, as a way of influencing the agenda of politics. Teachers will lobby the Department of Education and Science, private firms will contact the Department of Trade and Industry, environmental groups will approach the Department of the Environment. Indeed there are *insider* and *outsider* interest groups at play here. Groups favoured by the politicians and the civil servants will find it easier to influence the agenda, as well as the outcome, of the policy-making process than will others who are less favoured. Indeed the more 'inside' you are as an interest group, the less visible will be your exercise of influence. So groups marching in the streets, going on strike, writing to MPs and so on are the ones without the influence. As any reading of the memoirs of leading politicians makes abundantly clear, those who just ring up, meet the Permanent Secretary for lunch, or sit on the departmental committees are in the key positions. The trade unions enjoyed this sort of 'insider' status under Labour, and lost it after 1979. To a degree, the CBI had the reverse experience: and of course the publicly owned Bank of England has a seemingly permanent insider status, through its relationship to the Treasury and the ease of access to the Prime Minister enjoyed by the Governor of the Bank. This is how Harold Wilson described one of those moments of access in his autobiography:

> The Governor was in his gloomiest mood and clearly felt that the financial end of the world was near. More speculation, more trouble for the pound could only mean the collapse of the world monetary system. The dollar would be engulfed: it might even go first ... He pressed the point further and I said that if the issue was as bad as he thought, then I would be ready to fly to America for talks with the President and the Federal Reserve Authorities.
>
> (Wilson, 1971, pp.128–9)

Not many of us can put a Prime Minister on the plane to Washington with as much speed as that.

ACTIVITY 13

Put together your own list of agenda setters on economic policy. Then think of a non-economic area of policy, like defence. Who sets the agenda there? How many of your economic agenda setters remain in play, and who are the new ones? For defence, do you need to add the military, arms manufacturers, NATO, the Pentagon ... the Russians?

4 What is also clear is that who sets the political agenda in one area of policy is not necessarily the same as who sets it in another. On *defence policy*, the agenda seems to be set by senior ministers, by foreign governments, by senior military figures, perhaps even by arms manufacturers, all as 'insiders'. The agenda can be influenced too, occasionally, by the conferences of the political parties from which ministers come, by peace movements and even by trade union lobbying — but all definitely as 'outsiders'. *Economic policy* has its insider groups too: political parties and ministers again, employers' organizations, the Bank of England, even the IMF, with trade unions sometimes as 'insiders', sometimes as 'outsiders'. The critical thing about the campaign for equal pay was that the women campaigning for it had to break into this cosy insider arrangement, to add the concerns of women to an agenda of economic policy which hitherto did not encompass them. The women's organizations

which made that breakthrough did not, in the process, consolidate themselves as 'insiders'. All they managed was a brief period in which they won the support of key insider groups — the unions and the Labour Party in this instance — and when that moment was over, their concerns were marginalized again.

─────────────────── ACTIVITY 14 ───────────────────

It is perhaps worth remembering how hard the trade unions had to struggle, before 1945, for insider status. My favourite story of this comes from the experience of the NUT who were rebuffed by the President of the Board of Education in the 1860s when they wanted him to alter the terms of teacher contracts (known then as 'The Code'). In sending them away, the minister said that 'teachers desiring to criticize the Code were as impertinent as chickens wishing to decide the kind of sauce in which they would be served'. Things have changed a little since then — for the teaching unions at least. Can you think of any other interest groups that have successfully moved from 'outsider' to 'insider' status? The only ones that spring to mind for me as even a possibility are green/environmental ones. Are any of these still being afforded 'insider status' by government departments as you read this? Is the political agenda still partly 'green', or was that just a passing fashion?

───

The picture with which we are left is of a fairly stable world of insider groups surrounding the government — with different insider groups in different areas of policy, but all regularly consulted on the direction and content of policy. Then around them are the excluded, the outsiders, who literally have to break into the charmed circle to be heard at all, and who normally can only stand outside — demonstrating, lobbying MPs, agitating inside political parties, writing to newspapers, going on strike — trying to create a climate of opinion which will help to open the closed circles of government to their concerns. Indeed it is possible to think of political parties, demonstrations and backbench MPs as key channels through which outsiders try to gain access to the corridors of power; see Figure 11.

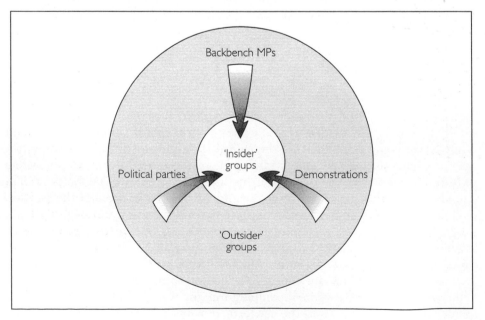

Figure 11

SUMMARY

- The political agenda is normally fixed by politicians and insider groups.
- Occasionally outsider groups break in — at least temporarily — to widen the range of issues being discussed.
- The 'visibility' of political agitation normally indicates outsider status. The powerful ones here are the quiet ones! The trick is to be heard but not seen.

WHAT FIXES THE AGENDA?

We have talked now about who fixes the political agenda, but that is only half the story. The insider/outsider picture is a fairly unchanging one. A new issue can occasionally be forced on to the political agenda by the pressure of outsiders — as we saw in our second case study — but normally the political agenda is fixed by those inside the charmed circle. Yet, though the groups inside the circle don't alter over time, the agenda they discuss does. So we still need to know from where the change derives.

We can get to that quite easily as soon as we remember that groups lobby government for particular reasons. They represent particular interests. If those interests don't alter much over time, nor will the issues they wish to raise. The pay of women has been less than that of men for a very long time: so what changed in our second case study was not the problem, just the ability of the women's movement to break through a wall of political indifference to have it discussed at all. And they were able to do that, in part at least, because of *wider social changes* that were altering the position of women in society, and altering general attitudes to the rights and roles of women. These changes (shortages of labour that made employers more willing to employ married women, new methods of birth control that gave women greater control over the size and timing of families, the spread of merchandized domestic appliances and so on) all created an environment within which women's groups were able to break through the wall of political indifference. Broad social changes helped to alter the political agenda by making it easier for women's groups to break into politics.

Yet in our first case study all the groups involved were already there. It was not a case of new groups having to break in, altering the political agenda as they did so. On the contrary, the unions, the bankers, the industrialists and the politicians had all been discussing economic policy with each other steadily since the war. So if — in the first case study — the political agenda around the economy changed, it couldn't be because some new group had broken in to join their discussion — as was the case with equal opportunities. It could only be because something had altered the interests and concerns of groups already there; and that indeed was the case. In the 1970s and 1980s the unions, the financiers, the manufacturers and the politicians all suddenly found themselves discussing unemployment, inflation and intensifying international competition. Those had not been their prime concerns in the decades before, but now the political agenda was dominated by little else. How are we to understand that change?

We can understand it by recognizing that none of these individuals and groups was in complete control of the main processes which shape the economy over which they presided. Of course it is true that each section of the economic power structure — civil servants, private businessmen, union leaders, international bankers — had a particular and often very complex view of the way prices and jobs, profits and growth, related to each other. Each enjoyed a limited degree of autonomy and leeway in the handling of their affairs — such that how they reacted to developments both in the world economy and in its British sector helped to determine the route which those developments would then take. There was a space for agency here — for human action to shape history: a right-wing trade union leader against a left, a monetarist-minded businessman against a Keynesian, and so on.

But the freedom of action of those key actors was itself constrained, and the nature of those constraints has also to be grasped. Simply because the reaction of significantly placed interest groups to their common experience of inflation and economic decline conditioned the development of these overriding features of economic life in the 1970s and 1980s, it should not be thought that any one interest group, or any group of interest groups, was actually responsible for the deliberate and conscious initiation of these problems. They did not put them on the political agenda. No group, and certainly no individual, no matter how well placed they were, controlled the entire economy. No group invented inflation, nor was responsible, as a conscious act of policy, for the rapid increase in prices after 1970. Not even the OPEC oil ministers had that power, though the media at the time often described them in such terms. No one group or individual could fix the rate of economic growth. No particular institution determined the relationship between levels of unemployment, levels of capital accumulation, and the rate of increase in the price of consumer goods. So it would be quite wrong to create the impression that the dominant economic agenda faced by governments in the first case study was given to them by key interest groups or chosen by them as politicians. Rather it was *imposed* upon them by wider economic processes and *inherited* by them from the UK's own economic past.

OPEC summit meeting in Stockholm, July 1977

I use the terms 'imposed' and 'inherited'. So what was imposed, and what was inherited?

What was *imposed* was the nature of the world economy that politicians met on entering office — what journalists and commentators often call 'the facts of economic life'. These are not timeless facts. They are merely current crystallizations of the state of development of the world economy. Politicians in Britain in the 1970s and 1980s faced a world divided into a capitalist and a state-socialist bloc, with the UK firmly fixed in the capitalist half of that divide. In 1974, as our first case study began, twenty-five years of unbroken economic growth in the capitalist part of the world economy were ending, being replaced by more sluggish and erratic patterns of growth. Inflation and unemployment were rising together across the entire capitalist bloc, as Keynesian policies of demand management stopped working for reasons which no one then fully grasped and which (as we saw in Block III) are still much in dispute between professional economists. What was not in dispute was that a new international division of labour was emerging, with competitor industrial economies coming on stream, particularly in the Far East. What was also beyond dispute were the commercial pressures on multinational companies, having to find new markets in progressively more difficult trading conditions, conditions eroded by the collapse of the fixed exchange rate system in 1971 and by the growth of protective barriers to trade in the 1970s and 1980s.

What all this *imposed* on the political agenda in London was the necessity to become more economically competitive if unemployment, falling living standards and impaired welfare services were to be avoided. There was literally no choice. Or, more precisely, the choice was being imposed from without, and what had to be settled locally was only the response to it. In the crucial sphere of economic activity, by the 1970s, *local* freedom of action was being drowned by *global* developments. That is what I mean by an agenda being imposed.

But it was also *inherited*. What was inherited was the particular weakness of the industrial sector of UK capitalism within that developing world system. Politicians of both parties inherited an economy with a traditionally low level of investment in manufacturing plant and equipment, an economy whose banking network had a tradition of international activity, and an economy whose labour force had a tradition of defensive trade unionism. To go back to our earlier metaphor of football pitches, if the start of the season was *imposed* from outside, what was *inherited* was an economy poised for relegation from the first to the second division. Local politicians had a number of options to avoid relegation — that is what the local struggle was about — but they could not begin at the top of the league any more, nor escape their participation in an internationally competitive system in which some would win and others would lose. The government here was like a football manager: desperate for team success in order to avoid personal dismissal, and able to avoid such a personal humiliation only by ensuring that football managers elsewhere went to the wall.

SUMMARY

- The agenda setters tend not to change over time. It is the issues they discuss which change.
- Agenda setters gather their interests from their position in particular social and economic orders: women's groups from the position of women in a male-dominated society; unions, firms and financial institutions from their positions in the UK part of a complex international economy.
- The economic agenda faced by governments alters as that economy generates new problems to which politicians need to respond; with the severity of the problems in the UK fixed by the particular place of the UK economy in the wider international economic order.

4.3   LEVEL 3: UNDERLYING PROCESSES

The image of the football manager struggling to survive in a *structure* which requires that teams lose as well as win is a useful one when examining the interplay of structure and agency in the sphere of the state. Here, as in football, agents struggle with each other for success, but do so in a framework which is already set. At least in the case of football, the framework of rules is not supposed to give advantage to some, and disadvantage to others. The match is literally played on level ground. But that is not the case in the area of state politics. The terrain on which political battles are fought makes some political objectives easier to attain than others.

—————————————————— ACTIVITY 15 ——————————————————

Take these political ambitions, some of which were mentioned in the case studies, others of which were not. List them in the order of the ease with which they could be achieved at the present time:

1   Equal access for men and women to senior positions in industry.

2   The abolition of all nuclear weapons.

3   The nationalization of the top 500 companies.

4   Full employment.

5   Reductions in trade union power.

6   Bigger state pensions.

7   More private schools.

I think the political ambitions are listed here in reverse order of attainability. The first is more difficult to achieve than the last, the sixth easier than the second, and so on. And that is so because the ones with higher numbers in the list do not involve anything like the same degree of challenge as do the low number ones to prevailing distributions of power, and to existing sets of institutional arrangements. The first requires a major dismantling of existing gender divisions. The last involves little more than local changes in tax laws and education regulations. The second involves the dismantling of entire power blocs in place since 1945, the sixth probably only a marginal redistribution of income between those in paid employment and those not. This is not to say, of course, that any are easy to attain, or that any are impossible. Agents can defeat structures. Even power blocs can disintegrate (as events in Eastern Europe show only too well). People make their own history, but not in conditions of their own choosing. They make it instead in conditions directly inherited from the past: and the achievement of radical goals is more difficult than more modest ones because radicals must mobilize vast social forces in the present before they can hope to shift the accumulated legacy of past practice and past privilege.

But what are these legacies which set the *gradient* on which the visible public debate takes place and which stack the deck against successful radicalism? No doubt they are many, but some of them at least surface elsewhere in this course, and can be signalled here.

Economically, the gradient is set by the organization of production and consumption — by the way, as we saw in Block III, that work and the home have been divided in this society, with work in the home organized around unpaid work overwhelmingly done by women, and with work outside the home organized in a capitalist fashion. Politicians inherit both. The entrenched world of gender divisions is so stable as to go literally unnoticed unless and until women raise questions of gender privilege. Economic activity within capitalism, on the other hand, is so perpetually in flux by comparison that its presence is everywhere. Politicians formulate and implement policy in a world dominated by the private ownership of the major means of production, the competitive struggle to accumulate capital, the reliance of the majority on wage labour, and the tensions between workers and owners which that reliance generates. Governments are forced to manage their economies in a world system, the capitalist bit of which (as we saw in Block I, and will see again in Block VI) has developed down the centuries in a combined but uneven way. Some economies are behind, some ahead: and like the football league, promotion for some can mean relegation for others.

Socially, that way of organizing work creates a world of immense inequality, as we saw in Blocks I and II. On the world scale, whole societies operate at different levels of affluence and poverty, the life-chances of their people being fixed by their position in a system of interlocking inequalities that are profoundly difficult to shift. Within each society, including this one, entrenched inequalities of opportunity are inherited: between men and women, between whole classes, and between majority and minority ethnic groups. Around these inequalities powerful structures of interest have consolidated themselves, so that movement in favour of one group can only be at the cost of the antagonization of others. Politicians may want to have it otherwise, but they must operate on a social terrain scarred by the social divisions of earlier generations.

Culturally, those inequalities have long been understood, and rationalized, by a series of dominant bodies of ideas — ideologies whose character and social consequences we shall examine later in this block. You only need the list — conservatism, liberalism, socialism, nationalism — to see that politicians inherit a cultural gradient: where the distribution of those ideas in the society as a whole makes some political projects easier to sell than others, and where shifting the balance of ideas thereby becomes crucial to the winning of popular support. We shall come to this dimension of politics in the UK in the two units which follow this one.

Politically, as we have already seen in this block, politicians inherit a system of nation-states with its own history, internal rivalries, and international bodies. They cannot wish that system away and bring in world government overnight. Nor can they easily disregard the sets of political practices already established as legitimate within their own nation-state. Three centuries ago, monarchs could rule across Western Europe because monarchs always had. Monarchs cannot rule here today. Politicians in Britain face a society which grants them power as *democratic* politicians, not as agents of autocratic rulers. They are expected to govern in a representative relationship with their society organized as an electorate; and they are expected as a result to rule through laws, and under law.

The electoral constraint on democratic politicians is the one we have not examined yet; and we have left it to the last not because of its lack of importance but because of its centrality. The representative relationship of politician and electorate is so vital that it will require a whole unit for its consideration. That will be the task of Unit 16.

5 CONCLUSION: TOWARDS A THEORY OF POWER

We have now seen how complicated it is to define and measure power. We have seen that power is a many-layered phenomenon. It can be isolated *one-dimensionally* (by looking at the actors battling with each other over a particular issue). It can be isolated *two-dimensionally*, by locating in addition the battle going on to get issues on or keep issues off the decision-making agenda. And it can be understood *three-dimensionally*, by seeing the wider social processes which make it so much easier for some actors to realize their goals than others.

We have also seen something of the complexity of the actual working out of power relationships between the UK government and the private individuals, groups and institutions over which it formally presides. On the surface of political life (when thinking of power only in a one-dimensional way), each case study still threw up a myriad of clashing politicians, insider and outsider groups, international pressures, economic crises and so on; and our own analysis of those case studies suggested an equal level of complexity beneath the surface, in the areas of agenda setting and underlying processes.

How can we make sense of, and place some order upon, all that complexity?

The placing of order on complexity is the job of *theory*; and we have now arrived at the point in this block when we need to introduce the question of theoretical choice. For here, as elsewhere in the course, different traditions of thought generate different theories of what is going on. They generate different theories of the state. There are liberal theories of the state, conservative ones, social reformist ones and marxist ones; and we shall survey them all in Unit 18. But for the moment I just want to introduce the two broad theoretical positions that recently have dominated academic discussion on the nature of power in contemporary industrial societies. One derives from a social reformist tradition of thought, and is normally referred to as a *pluralist* theory of the state. The other is a *marxist* one.

Your only task at the moment is to grasp the general character of each of these two theories, and to ask yourself what light, if any, they throw on all the detail that has gone before. Then in Unit 18 we will return to them and explore their strengths and weaknesses in a more systematic way. But for the moment just note these points about each of the two theories.

A *pluralist* theory of the state tends to argue:

(a) The modern state governs a society of immense complexity. It is one in which individuals play many roles and have many interests, some complementary, some conflicting. It is one in which there are many social, economic and cultural divisions.

(b) That complex society generates a multiplicity of groups to lobby government. If the society is democratically organized, it also establishes an electoral relationship between the government and each individual as citizen.

(c) No issue is entirely excluded from political debate, though insider groups find it easier to shape the agenda than outsider ones. Political parties play a crucial role as agenda setters, listening and responding to popular opinion, but also shaping that opinion by their own initiatives.

(d) The modern democratic state responds both to electoral pressures and to group lobbying. Policy shifts reflect the intensity of group lobbying and alterations in popular opinion. Political parties also act on their own initiative in making policy, but face the ultimate constraint of the electorate.

A *marxist* theory of the state puts those four points differently:

(e) The modern state faces a capitalist economy, which generates basic clashes of interest between classes, incessant competition between capitalists, and periodic economic crises. The capitalist nature of the economy dominates all other aspects of social life.

(f) That capitalist economy generates powerful interests which then lobby government. The inequalities of economic power reproduce themselves as differences in political leverage. If the society is a democracy, individuals enjoy formal equality with each other as voters; but that formal equality is robbed of most of its political significance by the existence of economic inequality.

(g) There is no formal barrier to the range of issues available for political debate; but in practice public opinion is moulded by a predominantly capitalist media, and any serious revolutionary agitation is invariably suppressed, if need be by state violence.

(h) The modern democratic state responds to group lobbying and to electoral pressure; but governments can meet electoral requirements only so long as these do not threaten major capitalist interests. Governments have an autonomy in the making of policy, but only within constraints set by the health of the capitalist economy over which they preside.

These two theories give very different readings of power relationships in the contemporary UK at each of the three levels of power with which we have been concerned. Indeed, each gives greater priority to one of these levels over the others.

A *pluralist theory* has lots to say about decision making at level 1 (points (b) and (d) are all about complexities at that level). Pluralist theory tends to discount the second level of power (point (c) is about that): though more refined pluralist thinkers are aware that not all groups can have their concerns discussed. Pluralists tend to the view that the most important thing about the third dimension of power is the *complexity* of social life (point (a)). For pluralists, politics goes on in a complex world, with democratic politicians trying to respond as sensitively as they can to the plurality of pressures upon them.

Marxists tend to be less enthralled by the sensitivity of democratic politicians. They characteristically start their analysis at the third level of power, and emphasize, not the complexity of social life there, but rather its capitalist nature (points (e) and (f)). That makes them sceptical about the range of issues actually available for political debate (point (g)). It also leads them to emphasize the constraints on democratic politics (point (h)) that derive from the social inequalities and economic competitiveness of an international capitalist system.

We can tabulate these differences between theories in the following way:

The three dimensions of power	pluralist view	marxist view
Dimension 1: Actors and issues	(b), (d)	(h)
Dimension 2: Agenda setting	(c)	(g)
Dimension 3: Underlying processes	(a)	(e), (f)

──────────────── ACTIVITY 16 ────────────────

As a final activity, look back through each case study again and see which of these two theories, if either, helps to make sense of what is going on there. Is the first case study better explained in pluralist/marxist terms? What about the second case study?

We will come back to these questions again in Unit 18.

===== READER =====

To complete your reading of the social reformism section of Chapter 22 of the Reader now read pp.274–85 of Section 2.3.

REFERENCES

Barnes, B. (1988) *The Nature of Power*, Cambridge, Polity Press.

Coakley, J. and Harris, L. (1983) *The City of Capital*, Oxford, Basil Blackwell.

Lukes, S. (ed.) (1986) *Power,* Oxford, Basil Blackwell.

Wilson, H. (1971) *The Labour Government: A Personal Record,* London, Weidenfeld and Nicolson.

ACKNOWLEDGEMENTS

Grateful acknowledgement is made to the following sources for permission to reproduce material in this unit:

p.53: Hulton Deutsch Collection; *p.57*: Chris Davies/Report; *p.58*: 'Chronology of the struggle', *The Independent*, 2 March 1990; *p.61*: Press Association; *p.63*: courtesy Barclays De Zoete Wedd; *p.64*: IMF Photo; *p.62*: Hulton Deutsch Collection; *p.70*: Hulton Deutsch Collection.

UNIT 16   POWER AND THE PEOPLE

Prepared for the Course Team by Peter Bradshaw

CONTENTS

1 EXPLORING THE CONCEPT OF DEMOCRACY

1.1 THE CONCEPT OF DEMOCRACY

This unit is concerned with the exercise of power by 'the people' and, like the other units in this block, the discussion centres on a particular concept — here 'democracy'.

Democracy is a familiar concept to us all. Consider, for example, how the term is used in an editorial from *The Sun*.

Who cares what YOU vote for?

A POLITICIAN is a man who knows nothing but thinks he knows everything.

That has never been more true than today.

Three issues make ordinary people angry because MPs are raising two fingers to public opinion: Hanging, gay sex and Europe.

Those we elect to make our laws in Parliament are totally out of touch with the kind of laws we want.

Contempt

Over 400 voted No to capital punishment, even though every opinion poll shows the majority of people want to bring it back.

Astonishingly, nearly 300 voted to make gay sex legal at 16, again flouting the polls. Fortunately, common sense prevailed and 18 is to be the age of consent.

Within hours, though, we saw the contempt in which the public is held.

Edwina Currie gleefully declared that it didn't matter what Parliament had decided because the European Court would change it.

What's the point in having a Parliament if Europe is to dictate our laws?

Most MPs fiercely defend what they perceive to be their right to vote according to their conscience or in line with what the party Whips order.

What's the point in electing them to Parliament if they're not going to reflect the views of the voters who put them there?

With breath-taking arrogance, MPs say if the voters don't like it we can dump them at Election time.

It's time to call their bluff.

Write to your MP today and ask which way he or she voted on hanging murderers or cutting the legal age for gay sex to 16.

Ask which way they voted over the Maastricht treaty. Find out how much they feel about handing so much of our way of life to the Brussels bureaucrats.

We know you'll be surprised at the replies you get from many of them. The people's voice must be heard. After all, this is supposed to be a democracy.

Politics is too important to be left to the politicians.

(The Sun, 23 February 1994)

Working perhaps from your reactions to the editorial we can begin to explore the concept of democracy more systematically. Take two or three minutes now to write down what the concept of democracy means to you.

——————————— ACTIVITY 1 ———————————

To me democracy is …

Most people's responses to this question focus, reasonably, on democracy as something like 'rule by the people'. But as we saw in Unit 9, although we often have understandings of concepts which may be quite widely shared in a particular society at a particular time, exploring these concepts more fully involves taking on some more challenging questions. What, for example, do we mean by 'rule'? Do we expect as members of 'the people' to be consulted on a daily, weekly, or only a five yearly basis about what the state does on our behalf? When we are consulted, over what issues do we expect to 'rule': What sixteen-year-old males (but not females) do in private? What the maximum fat levels in sausages should be? The distribution of wealth in society? Or are we simply prepared to accept the state's authority as long as we feel the government is accountable to us at elections? Did you notice that while *The Sun* questioned whether our representatives were responding sufficiently directly to 'ordinary people', it still assumed the use of representatives? The use of representatives to rule on the people's behalf is, however, only one form of democratic rule. Democracy has sometimes been, and sometimes still is, more direct: perhaps through the use of referenda, or even perhaps through handling more issues locally and then relying on mass meetings to take key decisions.

Citizens of a Swiss canton meet to take decisions directly

Some more questions surround which of the people are to rule? Who, for example, should decide the future of Northern Ireland: The people who live in the island of Ireland? The people who live in the present province of Northern Ireland? The people who live in the UK? The people who live in the European Union?

Although for simplicity we will concentrate for most of this unit on democracy in the contemporary UK, more key questions about the concept are raised by other societies. For example, how far are democratic processes to be found in one-party states? Such states usually have arrangements for assessing and responding to mass views within a certain framework, but does the concept of democracy reasonably encompass situations where the 'people's army' in a 'people's democracy' defines certain demands for change as undermining the very basis of the state? How many such forcible repressions of some people's views are needed before we cease to accept a state's claim to be democratic?

A supporter of the 'democracy movement' confronts members of a 'peoples army': Tiananmen Square

This unit tries to explore some of these issues and others surrounding the general nature of democracy and the particular forms it takes in the contemporary UK. The sequence it follows is, firstly, to focus within the rest of this introduction on three important but general questions about democracy:

• What should be the scope of democratic rule?

• Which 'people' should 'rule' and what should be the nature of that rule?

• How much should the mass of the people participate in politics?

These issues are returned to periodically in the unit when we move away from normative questions of what we think ought to happen, and concentrate more upon what has happened in the modern UK. The particular form of democracy which dominates the UK is usually referred to as 'representative democracy' and we examine this form more fully in Section 2. However, even though this form is the most dominant, the precise ways in which this system works changes through time, and we explore some of these changes in Sections 3 and 4. We will see that some of these changes are linked to different views of democracy in the different traditions recognized by the course; as changes occurred in the influence of particular traditions on how people viewed society, so changes occurred in the form of democracy the UK experienced. Finally, in Section 5, we review some of the main concerns of the unit and raise some general questions about the relationship between democratic forms and some of the social and economic patterns you have studied in earlier parts of the course.

1.2 WHAT SHOULD BE THE SCOPE OF DEMOCRATIC RULE?

Frequently in politics disagreements occur over how far problems should be handled publicly through the exercise of the state's authority and how far their resolution should be a matter for private individuals. Can you think of any examples of this?

You may have thought of issues such as: Who decides what is to be seen on television or whether women should have the 'right to choose' to terminate pregnancy, and, if so up until what point? Another example which occurs to me concerns the causes of crime and the best ways to deal with it. At the risk of oversimplifying, those who see crime largely in terms of wickedness or weakness in some individuals may advocate a relatively limited role for the state in this area: one largely confined to catching and punishing offenders. In contrast, others argue for a more extensive role for the state in attempting to deal with what they see as the social origins of crime by, for example, attempting to reduce unemployment and increasing the funding of social welfare and education. Arguments such as these form part of the history of democracy and illustrate the differing views of how far democratic rule should extend. At a broad level the liberal tradition has been associated with a view of democracy in which it is accepted that individuals should have certain rights, including the right to vote for someone to represent their interests. But this tradition is also associated with the view that democratically chosen representatives should be constrained from interfering too much with individual liberties in general and the right to hold private wealth in particular. Particularly among the rich, there was for a long time nervousness about giving the masses the potential opportunity to use a democratic state to redistribute wealth in their own favour.

In marked contrast to the liberal viewpoint is that of the social reformist and marxist traditions where the state is seen as needing to involve itself directly in the management of the economy if the mass of the people are to enjoy their right to the good life. In this view, a genuine democracy would involve much more than just allowing people legal rights and the right to vote. The state, acting on behalf of the people, ought to intervene extensively and powerfully to counter the inequalities inherent in capitalist economic systems: inequalities which mean that people not only have marked differences in their quality of life but also differing potential abilities to exercise power over others.

Of course while much of marxist and social reformist writing on these issues has concentrated on class it is worth remembering that, as we saw in Block II, inequalities also arise from gender and ethnic divisions. You might like to ask yourself at this point: How effective are democracies, which rely on relatively limited public interventions and guarantees of formal rights, likely to be in dealing with these types of inequality?

In considering this question you may like to recall the argument in Units 7 and 8 in which it was suggested that society is structured in a way which systematically favours the interests of whites and males. In this view, many of those in positions of public power often fail to see inequalities based on gender or ethnicity as matters to be dealt with by public policy seeing them instead as largely private matters. Of course, as you saw in the case studies in Unit 15, the women's movement has itself demonstrated the possibility of achieving change by working to get issues on the political agenda (remember Lukes' second dimension of power), and to win arguments about the shape of legislation and public policy (Lukes' first dimension).

We might also question common assumptions about the appropriate scope for democratic politics by mentioning briefly the potential for democracy in contexts other than the types of government activity emphasized in most of this unit. These include relationships in the workplace which often involve actions, for example threats of closure, informal consultation and strikes, which are not always recognized as 'political' but which, as we saw in Unit 15, clearly involve the use of power. They are not, however, usually resolved in ways which we would normally call 'democratic.' Although marxist writers have been the most critical of how this exclusion of democratic processes from workplace politics restricts the potential power of the working class, support for what is sometimes called 'industrial democracy' has been more widespread. Consider, for example, these comments from the Commission of the European Union:

> Employees not only derive their income from enterprises which employ them, but they devote a large proportion of their daily lives to the enterprise. Decisions taken by or in the enterprise can have a substantial effect on their economic circumstances, both immediately and in the longer term; the satisfaction which they derive from work; their health and physical condition; the time and energy which they can devote to their families and to activities other than work; and even their sense of dignity and autonomy as human beings. Accordingly, continuing consideration is being given to the problem of how and to what extent employees should be able to influence the decisions of enterprises which employ them.
>
> (European Commission, 1975)

"*Go on then, Entwhistle, participate.*"

'The problem of how and to what extent employees should be able to influence the decisions of enterprises which employ them.'

In 1994 the Commission's eventual proposals were accepted by all governments in the European Union (except the UK) but even these proposals offered relatively little power to 'influence decisions', recommending only the establishment of workers' councils with a consultative role. Moreover it is also worth remembering that for many people (for example the unemployed, retired people) there is no comparable opportunity in the workplace even to be consulted. Returning to the football analogy in Unit 15, not only is politics often played out on an uneven pitch, some groups cannot even get into the ground to play in certain games.

1.3   WHICH 'PEOPLE' SHOULD RULE?

Some other crucial general issues for democracy centre upon which people should rule and what should be the nature of that rule. To explore these apparently abstract concerns we can begin by looking at three sets of problems which in part derive from the UK having a system of government which, compared to most other industrialized societies, concentrates responsibility for policy making within one major centre and allows for relatively little authority being devolved either to the mass of the people themselves or to representatives elected to run local or regional governments. In consequence, groups out of sympathy with the policies of central government and concentrated in particular regions may find it more difficult to exercise political influence over their elected representatives than they would in some other industrialized democracies. How do you react to the following three examples of this general problem?

1   In the early 1980s the local government elections in many large cities brought to power with large majorities representatives who wished to pursue policies which cut across some of the preferences of the central government. In the disputes which followed the largest authority, the Greater London Council, was abolished, and other authorities saw their opportunities to run local affairs substantially reduced. The party which controlled central government claimed that it was representing the wishes or interests of the whole population and that attempts to represent the interests or wishes of particular groups in local areas was of less importance.

This example raises the key question: Precisely in which areas is it better to have a society-wide approach to problems rather than policies which try to be more sensitive to local needs? Taking this a stage further How far are there advantages in adopting standardized approaches to the problems of all the states in a grouping such as the European Union? When is this standardization likely to be more important than responding to the 'local' needs of individual countries or the even more local needs of regions within each country?

2   A different problem arises for voters, and potentially for certain governments, in cases where there are clearly identifiable regions in which the central government enjoys little electoral support. Consider for example, those voters in the 72 parliamentary constituencies in Scotland who in 1987 elected only ten MPs from the Conservative party and in 1992 increased this figure to eleven. In one sense their situation was similar to that of the approximately two-thirds of the electorate as a whole who also did not choose to be represented by members of the Conservative party. However, this particular group of non-Conservative voters were geographically concentrated in an area where ideas about the area's separateness from, or at least distinctiveness within, the rest of the UK were widespread.

The resulting levels of discontent have not in this case led to the kinds of developments seen in Eastern Europe in the late 1980s and the 1990s, but it is clear that the ideas people hold about their distinctiveness from others can change; as can their willingness to accept rule by those who may come to be perceived as outsiders — even if this form of rule incorporates democratic procedures.

Can you see how these issues surrounding where political decisions should be taken also link with what you read in Unit 14 and saw in TV07? Challenges to state sovereignty are arising through such processes as the increasing globalization of the economy, the tendency of environmental and health problems to cross national boundaries and the constraints on states placed by membership of organizations such as the European Union. If we wish to control such challenges through democratic processes might we need to consider how far demo-

Teenage girls working in a single sex school and wearing what is, within their religious tradition, appropriate clothing. How far should the state accept, facilitate or encourage such diversity?

cratic control can be exercised in contexts other than nation-states, for example through the European Parliament, perhaps through a reformed United Nations, or perhaps also through giving local (rather than national) communities more control over more aspects of their lives?

3   A final set of issues is raised by the complaints of Unionist politicians in Northern Ireland about the abandonment of the Stormont assembly in which they used to command sizeable majorities. The deterioration in community relations in the 1970s led the British government to revoke the special arrangements that had allowed a degree of regional autonomy in Northern Ireland, and to replace these by direct rule from London. In effect central government had been faced with a problem which is as old as democracy itself: 'In systems which emphasize majority rule, what is to be done to prevent the majority imposing conditions on the minority which the minority find unacceptable?' While most people's understanding of democracy involves the idea of majority rule, how far can we also expect the majority group to respect the wishes and rights of minorities?

You may have noticed that in the examples we have examined so far the 'minority' groups have been concentrated in particular geographical areas (large cities, Northern Ireland, Scotland). But we can also quickly see that this general problem of how far minority wishes can be accommodated within systems committed to majority rule need not necessarily have a geographical dimension. Can you think of any other current examples where the need to accommodate minority views has become controversial?

Two general areas you might think about are: firstly issues of free speech, blasphemy, pornography; and secondly, questions surrounding how far society is prepared to accept cultural and religious differences.

Insofar as most of us emphasize the 'majority rule' aspect of democracy it is worth introducing briefly at this point the major justifications for balancing this with a sensitivity to minority views. The first of these is the practical argument that governments find it easier to rule if they have the consent of most of the population — including all those who at various times form a 'minority'.

A second set of arguments emphasizes that the more important principle in a democracy is not so much *majority* rule as rule *by the people*. As David Beetham puts it

> ...it can be argued that democracy means, literally, rule by the people, and this signifies the people as a whole, not the rule of one part of it, however large, over another. Such a conception requires procedures of debate which ensure that all significant points of view are heard, and decisional procedures, such as those of amendment, which allow an initial majority position to be modified to take account of other viewpoints.... So while democratic institutions may require a majoritarian voting procedure to ensure that decisions cannot be determined or blocked by a minority, democratic principle requires that such a procedure should always be used as a last, and not a first, resort.
>
> (Beetham, 1993, pp.361–2)

1.4   HOW MUCH SHOULD THE PEOPLE PARTICIPATE IN DEMOCRATIC POLITICS?

Finally, in this introductory section we can briefly consider issues of political participation. While a political system may offer the people some opportunities for democratic rule, how far the system can really be said to operate democratically may be partly dependent upon how far people take up those opportunities. In this context you may find it interesting to reflect upon your own participation in the various processes often seen as central to modern democratic politics. Try comparing your own behaviour with that of a sample of 1,570 adults representative of the major groupings in the contemporary UK.

─────────────────── ACTIVITY 2 ───────────────────

When you have looked through the figures in Table 1, think for a moment about whether it would be better for society if the figures for voting and for other forms of political participation were higher. Then in the space below write down one or two of the general advantages, as you see them, of having high levels of political participation.

Table 1 Percentage rates of past and potential participation in politics.

	Have done at least once in past five years	Would 'certainly' or 'probably' consider action in future	'Might consider'	Would 'never' consider
Contacting				
Local councillor	20.7	33.3	40.4	26.3
Town hall	17.4	28.4	41.1	30.5
MP	9.7	24.2	39.5	36.3
Civil servant	7.3	18.8	38.6	42.6
Media	3.8	11.0	30.7	58.3
Group activity				
Informal group	13.8	16.4	34.9	48.7
Organized group	11.2	14.4	31.3	54.3
Campaigning				
Fund-raising	5.2	6.2	14.8	79.0
Canvassed	3.5	5.0	13.1	81.9
Clerical work	3.5	4.0	14.3	81.7
Attended rally	8.6	8.8	23.9	67.3
Protesting				
Attended protest meeting	14.6	23.8	39.8	36.4
Circulated petition	8.0	14.0	36.4	49.6
Blocked traffic	1.1	2.4	9.2	88.4
Protest march	5.2	7.3	20.3	72.4
Political strike	6.5	8.0	15.8	76.2
Political boycott	4.3	9.5	25.8	64.7

Note: Among this sample the percentages who had voted 'at least once' in local, general and European elections were: local 68.8; general 82.5; and European 47.3.

Source: Parry, G., Moyser, G. and Day, N. (1992) *Political Participation and Democracy in Britain*, Cambridge, Cambridge University Press, p. 423.

Very broadly it seems to me that the claimed advantages lie in two main areas. You might like to comment in the margin on how significant you see each of these.

1 Participation in the public affairs of a society potentially contributes to a society's sense of being a cohesive entity in which all are involved. When a government exercises its power to make binding decisions over a society, it can, if it so wishes, ultimately rely on force. But although all governments have this option, and occasionally use it, they prefer situations where the mass of the population accept that it is right and proper for the government to exercise its power. The people accept what is often termed the state's 'legitimacy' to make binding decisions over them. The concept of legitimacy is closely linked to another, and probably more familiar, concept — that of authority. A basic argument for advocates of greater participation in democratic processes is that if people feel that their views are being taken into account, the state is better able to use that form of power which we can call *authority* more than that form of power known as *force*.

2 Advocates of democracy also sometimes suggest that if people are offered genuine opportunities for participation, not only are the probabilities increased that they take their responsibilities seriously, but they also become better informed about the issues with which they are dealing. Well informed

participation ought in turn to offer increased chances of developing policies which are both responsive to people's needs and likely to be successful.

You must form your own judgements as to how far these arguments would support changes to forms of democracy which allowed more frequent and more powerful mass participation, perhaps for example through the introduction of regular referenda on key issues. Your judgements may, of course, partly depend on your responses to our earlier questions about the appropriate 'scope' for democracy, the most appropriate 'levels' for handling political problems, and the extent to which democracies should be 'minority sensitive'. Whatever your views are they should provide a useful base for the analysis, in the next sections, of the existing formal political system in the UK: a system usually described as representative, but sometimes as parliamentary or liberal, democracy.

SUMMARY

- Democracy is a concept which usually centres upon some notion of opportunities for the mass of the people to exercise collective control over important parts of their lives.

- A key question in any system of democracy concerns the range of issues which should be subject to democratic control.

- Also of crucial significance to any democracy is the question of balancing majority and minority preferences.

- Within democratic systems there are variations in the frequency with which the people are able to exercise influence and the procedures available for this to occur.

---

2 REPRESENTATIVE DEMOCRACY

What strikes you about the version of democracy which seems to underlie the response of a former British prime minister, Edward Heath, to the suggestion that the electorate should express directly through a referendum their views on the government's acceptance of the Treaty of Maastricht?

> Britain's political system is founded upon the principle of parliamentary democracy. This means that the British people have the right to elect representatives, who then represent their interests and those of the country in all debates and votes in the House of Commons. MPs must vote according to what they judge to be the best interests of their constituents. Every time we hold a referendum in this country we are effectively undermining an age-long tradition of parliamentary democracy...

> The public, understandably, show little interest in the fine print of complex, often highly technical legislation. I believe that any referendum on the Maastricht Treaty would not produce a reasoned and rational debate on the subject. In the main the public would vote according to their general perceptions about the subject, these in turn being largely shaped by the media's handling of the issue.

> (Edward Heath, 1993)

Heath's version of democracy — based on **representatives** chosen periodically through voting and then operating through multi-party competition in the House of Commons — is the one most familiar to most of us and the one on which we will therefore concentrate in this unit. (The terms 'representative', 'parliamentary' and 'liberal' democracy are sufficiently close for our purposes to be used almost interchangeably.)

Before we examine the key elements in representative democracy it is worth commenting that what is understood by this broad concept of representative/ parliamentary/liberal democracy does change through time. For example, despite Heath's reference to 'an age-long tradition of parliamentary democracy' even the right to vote is of relatively recent origin and was arrived at not so much through 'tradition' as through protracted struggles principally by the working class and by feminists. As late as 1914 only 30 per cent of the adult population enjoyed this right, and it was only within the lifetime of some of the people reading this sentence (1928) that the franchise in the UK was finally extended to most women. It is worth remembering that through most of history discussions about the concept of democracy have been discussions principally about the rights and responsibilities of men.

In the rest of this section we can now concentrate on what is usually seen as being at the core of most people's participation in representative democracy — the relationship between voters and their representatives. We will examine each side of this relationship in turn, starting with the voters.

2.1 THE VOTER'S CONTRIBUTION TO REPRESENTATIVE DEMOCRACY

Basic to the concept of representative democracy is an assumption that each voter knows what s/he wants and will express a preference for the candidate who appears most likely to influence public affairs in the directions favoured by the voter. (A slight variation on this is that some voters vote for whoever has the greatest chance of defeating the candidate who goes most *against* what the voter wants.) How far voters do behave in this way is the subject of an extensive and complicated body of research, and as a way of raising some of the issues involved you might first reflect upon your own voting.

———————————— ACTIVITY 3 ————————————

Consider the following list of potential influences on your voting. Try to rank them according to their potential influence on your own behaviour in the past.

Potential influences	Ranking
The party preferences of your parents	
Your 'social' class	
How your friends/spouse/colleagues vote	
Your age	
Your gender	
Your ethnic group	
Whether you work for the state	
Your reliance on state services, for example housing, NHS, public transport	
Party policies on:	
— the welfare state	

Potential influences	Ranking
— power of trade unions	
— defence	
— managing the economy	
— other issues	
Your opinion of potential Prime Ministers	
How parties present themselves during the election campaign	

When you have considered what influences your own voting, think about the influences on other voters for a moment. Do you think that most other voters are influenced in similar ways to yourself? You might explore this issue further by comparing notes in a tutorial or discussing it with non-OU acquaintances with whom you still have time to spend.

Whenever I have asked similar questions of OU students in the past they almost invariably suggest that the greatest influences on them are found in the bottom half of the list. The impression one gets is of individual voters carefully weighing up all the alternatives afresh before each election. This general view is in fact broadly shared by some researchers in this field. One frequently quoted work, for example, compared voters to shoppers, developing what it termed 'a consumer model of vote choice, to emphasize that the same principles hold as those which guide the individual in purchasing goods for consumption' (Himmelweit *et al.*, 1985, p. 10).

This view clearly has its attractions. Many of us have complex sets of ideas which might appear contradictory and ill-informed to others (especially those who do not agree with us). But when we listen carefully to others we can normally see how their views reflect different value positions, different exposure to others' views, different interpretations of what is heard and seen, and perhaps different interests. However, at the same time we also know that if we take an overview of voting we can find some patterns which seem to be related to aspects of social structure. Some interesting questions about the nature of representative democracy arise from how far these patterns have changed and are changing.

Through much of the 1950s and 1960s, for example, research suggested that most voters in the United Kingdom regularly voted for the party most associated with their social class. Table 2 provides a typical illustration of this relationship (and its apparent partial decline in the 1970s and 1980s).

Table 2 Social class and the vote

	Average 1945–1970		1979 election		1983 election		1987 election		1992 election	
	Non-manual	Manual	Non-manual	Manual	Non-manual	Manual	Non-manual	Manual	Non-manual	Manual
Conservative	65	30	55	36	51	35	49	37	49	35
Liberal/other	10	8	19	17	31	28	31	23	25	20
Labour	24	62	26	46	18	37	20	40	26	45

Source: Crewe, I. (1993) 'Values: the crusade that failed' in Dunleavy, P. *et al.*, (eds) *Developments in British Politics*, Basingstoke, Macmillan, p. 99.

Attempts to *explain* these correlations at the time emphasized principally the influence of family background and adult contacts. Voters were seen as developing their basic attitudes largely under the influence of their family (class background). Then, within a society with relatively little social mobility, most voters would as adults mix with others from similar (class) backgrounds — in marriage, socially, and at work. For large groups of voters their political preferences would be learned and reinforced within one class. Leaders, policies and campaigns would be relatively unimportant, as what any government or party did or said would be interpreted within a particular view which ignored or forgave the favoured party's mistakes and applauded its successes.

It is worth pointing out here that researchers differed in the extent to which they saw the link of voting and class as understandable or even rational. To the extent that people's life experiences were affected by their class position, and to the extent that the main political parties could be seen as favouring the interests of particular classes, then class-based voting need not be seen as unthinking or irrational.

It also needs to be noted that even when the general alignment of class and party support was at its strongest other factors also affected some voters. Religion, for example, was, and is, strongly associated with voting patterns in Northern Ireland. Also significant across all classes were: age (increasing tendency to vote Tory with age); gender (greater Tory support among women); and region (Labour support higher in Scotland, Wales, and Northern England).

While the picture of voting in the 1950s and 1960s was dominated by a few straightforward divisions — admittedly some of them cross-cutting one another — the tendency since the 1970s and 1980s for greater numbers of voters to switch their support in successive elections has led to some rather more complex explanations of voting with more dividing lines needing to be found. My explanation of these developments is set out below as a list of several, sometimes interrelated, elements. As you read through them you might like to make some notes in the margins about how far each of these developments has continued in recent years.

1 It appears that the traditional allegiances of many voters were loosened, particularly in the 1970s, by what voters perceived as the failures of governments from *both* major parties to cope with the economic problems of the time. Notice here an illustration of the *local and the global* course theme operating within the connections between stresses in the UK's domestic politics and changes taking place in the global economy.

2 Those same changes in the global economy led to changes in the working lives and class positions of many voters. (You may recall how in Unit 10, and more specifically in Chapter 7 of the Course Reader, recent major changes in the numbers of people doing various kinds of work were described.) The significance of this for voting can be illustrated, for example, by pointing to the implications for Labour party support of: on the one hand the run down of large workplaces, with unionized workforces, and traditions of working class solidarity; and, on the other hand, the increase in numbers of smaller workplaces, with different forms of work, and sometimes with 'no-union' agreements.

3 In the 1980s the Thatcher governments not only provided a sympathetic context for these globally-led changes, but also, with policies encouraging wider ownership of shares and houses, set out to change how voters experienced and perceived their position in society, for example, as an important part of a 'share-owning, property-owning democracy' rather than as 'one of us' (the working class) set against 'all of them' (bosses, government, and so on).

4 Traditional allegiances on class lines were for some voters further undermined by the increasing significance of potential conflicts surrounding the

welfare state. The 1970s began to see a divergence in the major parties' attitudes to the welfare state. Consequently how voters were themselves positioned *vis-à-vis* the welfare state became increasingly significant.

Many voters from *all* occupational classes are, for example, employed by the state and may be potentially hostile to public spending cuts. Similarly people's attitudes, whatever their occupational class, may be affected by the degree to which it is the public or private sector which provides the important goods and services they consume, for example in housing, education, medical care and transport. Finally, party differences towards the state are likely to be noted by many among those groups, for example the unemployed and many pensioners, whose major source of income is from some form of state benefit. Overall the numbers in such groups have grown since the 1970s. Of course, on the other side of this coin are the potential views of other groups, whose interests in the welfare state take a different form. Among many of those who are employed, especially those employed in the private sector and especially those who rely on private provision of some, or all, major services they consume, attitudes to the welfare state may focus less on its benefits than on what they may see as the 'burden of taxation' it imposes.

5   There have been a series of changes over the past twenty-five years in the ways in which voters learn about and handle information about party politics, and these too may have affected traditional allegiances. Thus, for example, the increase in the average time spent in formal education may have negatively affected the strength of commitment to single parties. (As someone involved in higher education you may be particularly interested to learn of evidence linking further or higher education and willingness to switch voting support.)

Similarly, some researchers have argued that increases in the amounts of time spent watching television's attempts at 'unbiased' and extensive coverage of party politics may have, as it's most probable effect, a reduction in people's stereotyping of party positions. At the same time, of course, newspapers feel less responsibility for impartiality, and the growth in recent decades, of what many would see as substantial 'anti-Labour' bias in much of the popular press may have weakened traditional Labour support. Moving further along the 'bias' spectrum, we might finally mention the public relations efforts of the major parties. Increasingly sophisticated work in this area has probably loosened the traditional allegiances of some voters, even if the switches concerned may largely cancel one another out in any single election.

To recap for a moment, this long list has covered a series of changes to the socio-economic positions voters have found themselves in, and to the ways in which they have learned about and experienced party politics. Very broadly they suggest that: firstly, the 'long-term' influences on voters are both complex and subject to change; and, secondly, that there has been an increasing likelihood of more voters being more receptive to such shorter-term influences as persuasive campaigns or the personalities of party leaders. However, you should be aware that researchers in this area often differ about the degree to which voters as individuals, or groups, or classes clearly identify their interests and vote for candidates most likely to represent those interests. My own view is that while the allegiances of many voters may have been relatively constant and they may not always have been based on extensive investigation of contemporary controversies, this does not mean that they blindly follow tradition or are 'brainwashed' by the mass media or party propaganda.

We will return to this question of the influences on people's ideas later, particularly when we examine, in Sections 3.3 and 4.4, marxist interpretations of contemporary democracy. But, before moving on, it is worth illustrating again the main point of this treatment of voter behaviour: how one views voter behaviour is connected to what kind of democracy one advocates. You may recall Edward Heath's view of voters' views being 'largely shaped' by the media. Would you share this picture of the typical voter (including yourself)?

2.2   THE CONCEPT OF REPRESENTATION IN DEMOCRATIC POLITICS

So far we have been looking at what voters do, but now we turn to those who are chosen to be representatives and at what we understand by their provision of representation. Have another, and perhaps more critical, look now at the first paragraph of the Edward Heath quote at the beginning of the section, and then attempt the next activity.

———————————————— ACTIVITY 4 ————————————————

Write down as many things as you can think of to explain why your views on every issue may not be 'represented' fully by your representatives.

It may be that some of the problems you have listed related to the particular individuals concerned, but it may also be that they arise from some basic problems in what is meant by 'representation' in party politics. (Note here that we are using the word representation in a different way to how it is used in the context of the course theme of *representation and reality*.) Firstly, and quite commonly, the term representation is used in situations where your representative can use her/his contacts and expertise on your behalf to persuade some part of the state to deal with your problems more quickly and/or more sympathetically. Much of the work of representatives at all levels of government, from local to European, is involved with being something like a 'legal representative' on behalf of constituents, dealing largely with specific problems arising from how existing policies are being implemented.

However, when we look at those situations commonly seen as being at the heart of politics — situations where different groups disagree with one another about the development of public policies — the concept of representation becomes more problematic. What can representation mean when a representative does not share the views of some, or even most, of her/his constituents? Many representatives claim to see themselves as something like 'messengers' carrying the people's wishes into arenas which have formal responsibility for shaping public policy. The people's views are said to have been expressed in their reactions to party manifestos, and representatives then bring these messages to the policy-making process claiming to have a 'mandate' from 'the people'. Unfortunately such claims hardly stand up to serious scrutiny. We can quickly list three obvious problems which arise through the way in which representatives are usually chosen:

1   Although most candidates express their views on a range of issues or
    attach themselves to the stated views of a particular party, the voter has

only one vote with which to express her/his preferences for a package of policies.

2   The voter's preference is expressed infrequently — despite the rapidly changing circumstances to which public policy often has to respond.

3   In political systems like that of the UK, the method of choosing those candidates who simply have more votes than their nearest rivals means that manifestos are often not endorsed by majority views either in a constituency or nationally. On a national scale, 'first past the post' voting allows those parties whose supporters are concentrated in particular constituencies to win seats at the expense of those with widely scattered support and candidates who may do well but still lose. Figure 1 illustrates this by showing the percentages of the electorate voting for the two main parties in the period 1950 to 1992 and the number of seats they won.

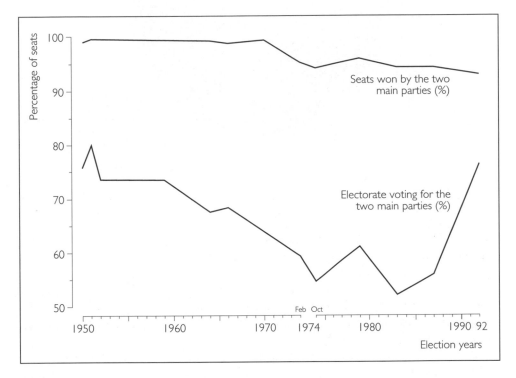

Figure 1

Source: B. Coxall and L. Robins *Contemporary British Politics: An Introduction*, p.266, Macmillan Ltd, 1989 (up-dated)

These features of the voting system complicate the question of how far successful candidates are likely to be representative of their constituents, but in addition, of course, once these representatives enter the relevant assembly — be it local government, a national assembly or even the European Parliament — they operate in a context which may be notable not so much for its responsiveness to electors' detailed preferences as for the ability of political parties to control the behaviour of their members. The willingness of a United Kingdom MP, for example, to represent any specific needs in her/his constituency often become secondary to what is perceived to be the greater needs of the party. The essence of representative democracy almost seems reduced to whether party leaders operate in ways which satisfy the general demands for competence and responsiveness among enough voters to deliver continuing majorities of Parliamentary seats. And all this is within an electoral system which translates votes into representatives in a very distinctive way.

Edmund Burke, one of the leading figures of the conservative tradition

These features of the political system potentially allow representatives not to feel closely bound by what many of their constituents want. However, we should also note that some party leaders and other representatives may not always even see it as desirable to respond to mass preferences, at least in the short term. You may have noticed earlier that Edward Heath argued that 'MPs must vote according to what *they judge* to be the best interests of their constituents' (my italics). Heath often seemed to me to adopt ideas from liberal and social reformist positions, but here he seems to be reflecting a view which is often associated with one of the leading figures of the conservative tradition, Edmund Burke. This is the view that representatives may be a better judge than their own constituents of what is in the interests of those constituents or of what is in the so-called 'national interest'. (Although, given what you already know of the divisions which exist in most societies, you may wonder about how often it is possible to recognize a clear national interest on most issues.) In these cases we seem to see representatives failing to follow mass preferences because of their own strongly held convictions. But, in passing, we should also note that, as we saw in Section 1.3, the reluctance to follow majority preferences may also sometimes reflect an attempt to remain sensitive to minority views.

2.3   DIVERSITY AND CHANGE IN SYSTEMS OF REPRESENTATIVE DEMOCRACY

Although this exploration of representative democracy may have emphasized some of its problems, I certainly would not wish to write off either the UK system in particular or representative democracy in general. However, it is also worth re-emphasizing that attempts to provide popular control via a voting system can take many forms. Many other states also have multiparty systems, but the particular mechanisms they use are very different to those in the UK. They may allow more authority to be exercised locally, or provide more opportunities for voting in referenda, or less flexibility in fixing the timing of elections, and so on. The particular forms taken by these institutions affect the degree to which the people could be said to 'control' the state or, more modestly, the way in which their views and interests are 'represented'.

What should also be emphasized at this point is that although the relationships between voters and their representatives may be central to the concept of democracy they are only part of a wider range of relationships. We began this unit with a simple notion of democracy as 'rule by the people', but we can now move on to a more complex view. Read carefully through the following passage which suggests that in modern times the concept of representative democracy has come to imply:

> A cluster of rules and obligations permitting the broadest participation of the majority of citizens in the selection of representatives who alone can make political decisions (that is decisions affecting the whole community).
>
> This cluster includes elected government; free and fair elections in which every citizen's vote has an equal weight; a suffrage which embraces all citizens irrespective of distinctions of race, religion, class, sex, and so on; freedom of conscience, information and expression of all public matters broadly defined; the right of all adults to oppose their government and stand for office; and associational autonomy — the right to form independent associations including social movements, interest groups and political parties.
>
> (Held, 1992, p.17)

Notice here that while voting may be at the heart of the 'cluster', the people also have other rights and responsibilities, for example, the right to exert influence through membership of 'independent associations' such as pressure groups or trade unions. The relative importance of these different elements in democracy can be shown to change through time, and in the next two sections we will examine some of these changes in the UK's relatively recent past. For the sake of simplicity and convenience, we will explore some contrasts in how some of the UK's democratic institutions were made to work in the periods broadly on either side of the Conservative victory in the general election of 1979.

SUMMARY

- The most visible opportunities for the people to exercise influence in the United Kingdom are found in a set of institutions and processes based on representative democracy.

- One basic concern in representative democracy is that voters choose candidates who seem most likely to provide, within the decision-making process, a continuing expression of voter preferences. Research shows that the socio-economic positions of the voters concerned have a major influence on the way they vote and that furthermore these positions have become increasingly complex in recent years.

- Features of the voting system inevitably make it difficult for representatives to represent the preferences of all their constituents on all issues at all times.

- In addition, differences of view exist about the extent to which representatives should try to follow directly mass preferences if the representatives themselves conflict with what they see as being in the public interest.

3   DEMOCRACY AND CORPORATISM: THE UK IN THE 1960s AND 1970s

In this section we will concentrate on the nature of democracy within a style of policy making already referred to in earlier units. In Unit 12, for example, you saw how, for thirty years after the war, governments pursued sets of economic policies aimed at producing high levels of employment, sustained improvements in standards of living, stability of prices and a favourable balance of payments. They were also generally committed to the continuing development of the welfare state. Unit 15 developed this picture further but also associated it with a particular style of making policy. Look back briefly now at the analysis in Unit 15 of how decisions were made about economic policy. The treatment of this in Section 3.1 and Section 4 is quite lengthy. So it might be best to skim through these sections quite quickly.

In this unit we are particularly interested in the involvement of 'the people' in this particular style of policy making. To do this we need to examine two things. The first concerns what the package of public policies developed in this period tells us about the general relationship between the state and the rest of society — for example which aspects of society were seen as appropriate areas for public policy and those which were seen as being the responsibility of private individuals. Our second set of concerns is with how far, and in what way, various sections of 'the people' influenced policy making.

3.1   THE POLICIES

The package of policies making up what is known in the UK context as the 'post-war settlement' is seen by many as having its origins in the coalition government of the wartime years. And, following the Labour victory in 1945, the government intervened extensively and directly in many areas of economic and social life. Policies such as the establishment of the National Health Service or the nationalization of certain industries, attempted to transfer important areas of social life or economic relations from the private control of doctors or large firms to public control by a state which sought to act on behalf of all its citizens. State intervention was seen as being more likely to deliver economic growth and greater equality in living conditions than the free markets of earlier years.

Admittedly by the 1950s, government interventions, in the economy at least, began to be less directive, and settled into a broadly Keynesian emphasis on attempts to influence overall levels of demand in ways that brought full employment and economic growth within a mixed economy. (Have another look at Unit 12, Section 2 if you want to remind yourself of the key elements in this package.) However, there was less retrenchment in other areas of public policy, and the idea of an extensive welfare state was gradually consolidated. Through central government, local government, and a variety of semi-official agencies the state became involved not only in the provision of public housing, public health services, public transport and so on, but also in attempts to regulate many areas of private activity in ways which were seen as benefiting the public good. Some indication of this growth in the public sector can be seen from the figures in Table 3.

Underlying this considerable growth in state activity were some differing views about the questions raised in Section 1.2 about the scope of public policy in a democracy, and more specifically about how far the state had a responsibility to reduce the worst effects of inequality in society. For some writers and

Table 3   Number of state employees (000s)

	1923	1931	1951	1961	1971	1975
Central Government	160	110	1,136	1,302	1,561	1,910
Local government	227	292	1,415	1,782	2,651	2,993
Nationalized industries	—	—	2,789	2,196	2,001	2,003
Armed Forces	250	189	827	474	368	336
Total	637	591	6,167	5,754	6,581	7,242

Source: Coates, D. (1984) *The Context of British Politics*, London, Hutchinson, p.220

professional politicians, state action in this area was seen principally as a necessary concession to secure a continuing 'consent to be governed' among the mass of the population. Others, however, argued that an important aspect of any democracy needed to be the delivery of a variety of rights to all citizens. These were seen as encompassing not only civil rights (such as the right to a fair trial) and political rights (to be delivered by free elections and so forth), but also a series of welfare rights aimed at removing what Beveridge, one of the architects of the Welfare State, referred to as the 'five giant social evils of unemployment, want, disease, ignorance and squalor'.

3.2   THE POLICY-MAKING STYLE

At the risk of oversimplifying we can also identify in this period a broad style of handling political problems which for our purposes is best referred to as 'corporatism'. Before we examine this style of policy making it is worth noting that its main justification has been developed largely by a group of writers many of whose ideas derive from what this course terms 'the social reformist tradition'. In particular this style is often defended by those who adopt broadly 'pluralist' ideas of how the modern state works within capitalist societies.

——————————————— ACTIVITY 5 ———————————————

You came across these ideas when they were contrasted in Unit 15, Section 5 with views of the state developed within the marxist tradition. Take five minutes to remind yourself of the key arguments in that section now.

The discussion in Unit 15, Section 5 is conducted in very general terms, but earlier in the course we have come across several references to the corporatist style of policy making defended by many pluralists. For example, we have seen how much of economic policy in the post-war period was formed through the cooperation between Treasury officials, senior Cabinet ministers and officials of both the TUC and CBI. Think for a moment about how far this style could be described as essentially 'democratic'?

Defenders of corporatism claimed as its major advantage its incorporation into the centre of government policy making those with expertise and with the potential power to promise that policy would ultimately be accepted. However, it offered relatively limited opportunities for control or scrutiny by voters. At best 'the people' enter into this process in three main ways:

1   Their voting for parties with a broadly similar approach could potentially be seen as providing very broad support for the set of policies being pursued — achieving full employment and steady growth through Keynesian techniques of demand management, through the maintenance of the mixed economy, and through the development of an extensive welfare state.

2   It could be argued that many people had their interests represented by leaders of groups or organizations which were operating at the heart of policy-making even if this was outside the formal parliamentary process. For pluralists democracy in modern societies has to involve a plurality of ways for the people to influence public policy.

3   All voters are regularly given the opportunity to choose a different set of representatives in Parliament, and these representatives act as a kind of referee managing the inevitable conflicts between groups in society. The fact that groups have differing resources and potential power is seen as less important than the existence of democratic processes which make each member of 'the people' formally equal and which formally give them ultimate control over the political system.

To illustrate the essential features of this style in the running of democracy we have, so far, used the example of policy making in the overall management of the economy, but there is evidence that similar processes and institutions also operated in many other areas of policy. Figure 2 attempts to illustrate this in a simplified way. The diagram shows policy making in central government as a series of concentric circles with the greatest potential to exercise power being found near the centre. This distribution of power was to be found in each of the sectors which went to make up the system as a whole. Within each policy sector the most important relationships were those between the civil servants in central government and the representatives of key 'insider' interest groups. These groups were invited to become involved in policy making partly because they were seen as having the technical expertise to deal with the often complex technical issues with which the state was faced, and partly because their cooperation might ultimately be needed when policy was implemented. Perhaps unsurprisingly, as the state took on a wider range of functions it became clear that it could not itself implement all the policies fully. To this extent it needed the cooperation, or at least the acceptance, of those who would actually put into practice government policies on health, pollution, policing, and so on.

In addition to insider interest groups, also closely involved in policy making were large numbers of organizations which were often referred to as QUAN-GOs (Quasi-autonomous nongovernmental organizations). Organizations as diverse as the Office of Fair Trading or the United Kingdom Atomic Energy Authority shared common characteristics of having considerable autonomy in developing and implementing policy, but being expected to pursue policies which reflected what were seen as national interests rather than the sectional interests of individual firms or groups.

In passing we should note here that the willingness to incorporate these groups into policy making and policy implementation had some important, but perhaps unsurprising, consequences for the type of policy changes which usually occurred. Frequently policy changes emerged gradually, tended to be relatively minor, and were usually confined to those issues on the political agenda which the groups involved defined as being important. If you bring into the heart of policy making those with a major stake in the status quo, they are unlikely to want that status quo disturbed very much.

Finally, on the 'outside' of each sector were interest groups who attempted to influence policy but who were less likely to be directly involved in raising issues, in discussing them or in implementing policy.

Take a few minutes now to follow these points through for yourself by examining one segment of Figure 2. You might also notice that the diagram potentially depicts the way in which those involved in individual sectors might find themselves 'competing' with other sectors. Certainly Cabinet ministers and their civil service departments often developed an interest in their own sector and its problems to the point where cooperation between departments was hindered and particularly when there were perceived to be competing priorities for a limited overall total of government expenditure.

So what kind of democracy is being offered here? We have a style of democratic politics which emphasizes:

1   Ultimate overall control of policy making is formally held by 'representatives' who are elected largely for their general effectiveness in managing the status quo, and bringing about some change in society.

2   Such changes that do occur are largely incremental and are often worked out and put into practice through compromises between, on the one hand, civil servants pursuing some version of what they see as the public interest and, on the other hand, interest groups in their widest sense. As the term suggests such groups concentrate principally on advancing their own interests —

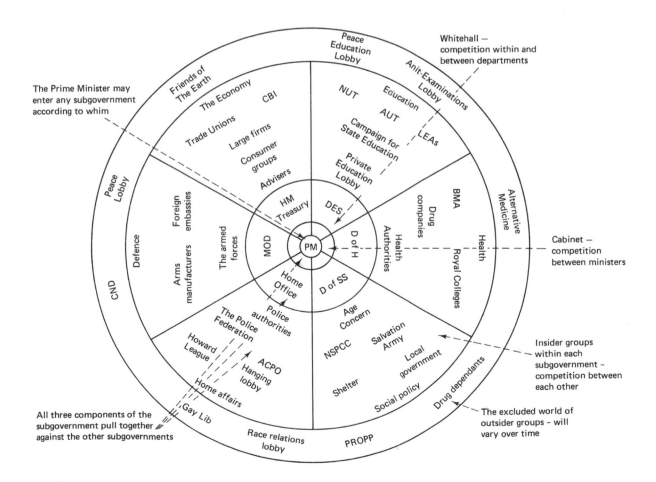

Figure 2

Source: Kingdom, P. (1991) *Government and Politics in the UK*, Cambridge, Polity Press, p. 421.

although they may well wish to identify their own interest with those of the population as a whole. (Groups in these situations tend to adopt their own version of the memorable aphorism 'what's good for General Motors is good for America'.)

3   There is in some cases an extra potential opportunity for the public to influence policy through membership of any interest groups which can establish themselves with ministers and civil servants as being, at least in their eyes, worth consulting. In practice, of course, many of these groups are not 'open' to the mass of the public. Furthermore, in some cases even where groups are more 'open', questions may still exist about the degree to which they are representative of their members. In the 1960s and 1970s, for example, it often appeared that many workers were less accommodating to the demands of employers and government than their 'representatives' among the leadership of the TUC.

Thinking back to the general questions raised in Section 1.4 about how much mass participation is envisaged within the political system it is clear that, within this style of policy making, the mass of the public have a very limited direct role. In addition, they also implicitly forego using their vote to bring about radical change: for example there is technically nothing to stop them from voting for redistributing wealth substantially in their direction. So why do the mass of the population find this form of democracy acceptable? The defence of this style — normally advanced by followers of the pluralist theory introduced in Unit 15, Section 5 — usually involves four main elements.

Firstly, it is suggested that most of those who are directly involved in policy making do share with most of the public a broadly similar set of ideas about how society operates, how it should operate, and how it might be improved and reformed — a priority on economic growth, an extensive welfare state, little radical change, and so on. In this sense you might like to note that of the major traditions identified in the course, social reformism has the strongest connections with this particular style of democracy. Notice, however, that although what we called in Section 1.2 the *scope* of democratic rule is extensive in this system, the degree of change likely to occur through government action is likely to be gradual and largely confined to items which are already on the conventional political agenda.

Secondly, pluralists suggested that for their part, the mass of the people could in a sense be characterized as being prepared to accept relatively little control over government — either directly or via their MPs — in return for promises of technically well-informed policies framed within the broad consensus of ideas supposedly shared by most of society.

Thirdly, the existence of a plurality of actors (in interest groups, local governments etc.) able to exercise power on behalf of particular sections of the people acted as a counterbalance to any central government tempted to interpret its majority of seats in Parliament as giving it a mandate to introduce extreme policies.

Finally, while most of the people are aware that certain groups, for example those in business, may have a privileged position in the running of many parts of society and particularly the economy, these privileges were seen by pluralists as being ultimately subject to a political system and a legal system which, at the very least, promised equal rights for all citizens, legal impartiality, and the opportunity to remove through voting the crucially important elected parts of the state.

SUMMARY

- A corporatist emphasis in policy making was associated with an extensive role for the state and with incremental changes to a set of policies supported by both major parties.
- Within this system the people were said to 'rule' by providing general approval of the set of policies pursued, by choosing members of political parties to oversee the development and implementation of these policies, and by involvement in interest groups.
- Limits on the extent of democratic rule were sometimes explained in terms of the scope and technical complexity of the problems faced by government.

3.3 A MARXIST CRITIQUE

Pluralist writers clearly thought that within the corporatist period western democracies had developed new democratic forms which retained a limited degree of popular control, made possible economic growth and provided opportunities for all to benefit from the good life. However, many others were not so convinced. Feminist writers, for example, have observed that the relatively extensive scope of government action during this period still left largely unchallenged many aspects of gender based inequality. A political structure in which men dominated government and insider interest groups was not conducive to getting onto the political agenda legislation for enhancing the opportunities of women. You should be familiar with this argument from the case study in Unit 15. Also in Unit 15 (Section 5) you came across the criticisms made of pluralist views by writers from the marxist tradition, and it is this critique that we will examine further now.

To many writers in the marxist tradition the corporatist form of democracy was seen as one more way of dealing with the inevitable problems of capitalist societies. For them capitalism is inevitably associated with class conflict, and yet giving the majority working class the vote potentially allows it to triumph in this conflict and to end the conditions of its own exploitation. The very compatibility of capitalism with democracy is therefore something which needs to be explained.

It can certainly be argued that even the corporatist form of democracy did relatively little to remove those fundamental inequalities and conflicts of society which, as we saw in Block II, have continued to exist despite the existence of an extensive welfare state. Nevertheless, the state does seem able to reduce the potential for class conflict both by increasing the chances of economic growth and by offering certain concessions to the population as a whole. These included for example, access to the welfare state, formal equality before the law and the opportunity to express political views through voting and interest group activity. But at the same time government policy seems from a marxist position inevitably oriented to the preservation of a capitalist economic order. Making this possible, there is at the heart of political relations what one writer in the marxist tradition usefully expresses as an understandable 'accord' or compromise. He suggests:

> It is easy to see why and how the existence of this accord has
> contributed to the compatibility of capitalism and democracy ... each

class has to take the other class into consideration: the workers must acknowledge the importance of profitability, because only a sufficient level of profits and investment will secure future employment and income increases; and the capitalists must accept the need for wages and welfare state expenditures, because these will secure effective demand and a healthy, well trained, well housed and happy working class.

(Offe, 1984, pp.193-4)

We can see that this analysis does not need anything like a conspiracy of big business and government to hold down the working class. Indeed capitalist firms often have an interest in making some concessions to the working class. Similarly governments wish not only to be re-elected in the short term, but also, in the long term, to avoid challenges to the state's overall authority. However, marxist writers would still point out that the requirements of capital are so strong that they effectively constrain the state's actions. Not surprisingly governments believe that their electoral success, and what they see as the general well being of society, depend on their successful operation of a capitalist order. Here is one example of how these constraints can work:

> In his valuable and revealing *Diaries of a Cabinet Minister* R.H.S. Crossman gives an account of how the Labour Cabinet of which he was a member had to decide whether to allow an oil company to build a refinery on Canvey Island in Essex. Not surprisingly, the proposal was strongly opposed by many residents of the area, and Crossman, as Minister of Housing, had some sympathy with them. But when the issue came before the Cabinet it decided in favour of the oil company.
>
> 'The Foreign Office, the Commonwealth Office, the Ministry of Power, the DEA (Department of Economic Affairs) and the Treasury all insisted that we couldn't afford to upset a foreign oil company. The risks involved in displeasing the company were deemed to be too great ... Against that local opposition counted for very little' (Crossman, 1975)
>
> Here is an example of a political decision being taken at the highest level by an elected government which nevertheless felt itself to be more or less powerless in relation to a large transnational company. It is clear that the power of the company is political as well as economic. But unlike the local community, which would have had to organize, collect signatures for a petition, demonstrate and lobby in order to make its views heard and get them noticed, the company needed to do very little. Certainly it had no need to solicit public support. Provided that the Cabinet was aware of the company's power, which of course it was, the company had little need to campaign or lobby for its case. Its mere possession of power was enough to overawe the Cabinet into acceding to its 'request'.
>
> (Arblaster, 1987, p.101–2)

In many cases this exercise of power is not seen by state officials (or many of the public) as unreasonable. There may be a routine and unquestioning acceptance of the ideas, firstly, that economic growth is crucial and, secondly, that it is best secured through the operations of large companies. For their part most marxist accounts would also accept that the state does have some flexibility or autonomy in deciding what is the best way to make capitalism work. You will be aware, for example, that there are often differences of view about interest rates between businesses who want to borrow money and banks who want to lend it. In such cases governments have to make choices between competing capitalist interests. But these are choices made from within a particular set of ideas, or ideology, about how societies do work and should work.

The acceptance of the prevailing order is explained in marxist accounts largely by referring to the prevalence in society of sets of ideas, or ideologies, which have the effect of making the status quo seem normal or natural. The next unit examines this role of ideology in more detail, but to illustrate the point at its most basic we might suggest, for example, that our attachment to ideas such as 'a fair day's work for a fair day's pay' and 'we're all in the same boat' potentially incline us to see our place in the economic system in ways which do not challenge the existing order of things. Of course, you may wonder why suggestions like these are referred to as *ideas* and not simple *facts*. There may be some truth in saying 'we are all in the same boat', but we should also recognize that this is not a simple factual statement. We could also ask, for example, if we are all in the same boat whether we are all on the same deck. Can you also see that the ways in which democracy itself is often represented as popular control — for example in expressions like 'Government of the people, for the people and by the people' — only partially reflects the reality of representative democracy?

The key point from the marxist tradition is that some ideas, which happen to support a particular set of political, social and economic arrangements come to be accepted as true and, to the extent that this occurs, questions about those arrangements are rarely asked. You may recall that this suggestion was raised by Lukes in Chapter 12 of the Reader where he discusses his third 'dimension' of power: that dimension characterized by structures and processes which perpetuate power relations and which largely depend upon the widespread acceptance of sets of ideas about society. Lukes asks:

> ...is it not the supreme and most insidious exercise of power to prevent people, to whatever degree, from having grievances by shaping their perceptions, cognitions and preferences in such a way that they can see or imagine no alternative to it, or because they see it as natural and unchangeable, or because they value it as directly ordained and beneficial?
>
> (Lukes, 1974, p.24)

In these terms it might not be surprising that, in the sphere of politics, people might accept, however grudgingly, a form of democracy which by relying on representatives, infrequent elections, a powerful civil service etc. distances the people from opportunities to bring about fundamental change. Moreover, as both of the major political parties in the UK of the 1950s and 1960s endorsed broadly similar sets of policies, marxist commentators would not be surprised that the dominant ideas among the mass of the population followed similar lines. Electoral contests came to be carried out within a particular framework. As Coates puts it:

> The broad mass of the British electorate expected governments to oversee prosperity and guarantee full employment. They expected good health care and proper education, but otherwise there was no political mileage in major social reform, or in any further erosion of the powers/ rights of private property.
>
> (Coates, 1991, p.162)

Finally we can note that writers from the marxist tradition are more likely to remind us of the state's willingness to use violence when necessary. Writers from all traditions recognize that most governments are able to exercise their power partly because the mass of the people accept what they do as being more or less appropriate. Some of the people accept the state's authority as being totally right, proper and legitimate. Others may be indifferent or even afraid to resist. However, in all states these varying forms of acceptance of the state's authority are supplemented by the state being willing and able to use force to enforce its particular set of rules. From this starting point writers from a marxist tradition would then want to emphasize the way in which those rules frequently favour a particular class, and may be used to suppress demands for radical change to a structure in which the interests of capital are paramount. In the post-war United Kingdom instances in which the state had to resort to force to maintain the existing order within its own territory were relatively rare. But when they did occur how should they be interpreted? If we take an example such as the miners' strikes of 1974 and 1984, do we see an image of those responsible for upholding order protecting the right of some citizens to work in the face of violent intimidation? Or do we see agents of the capitalist state using force in an attempt to break the power of the working class?

The maintenance of order or another skirmish in the class war? Miners' strike 1984

SUMMARY

- Marxist writers suggest that within a corporatist style of government and administration the incorporation of representatives of capital into policy making and implementation inevitably produces outcomes favourable to capital in general, even though different interests within capital still compete with one another.

- They also suggest that in capitalist societies the widespread acceptance of ideologies, or sets of ideas (including ideas about the nature of democracy), contributes to making existing power relations seem normal and legitimate.

- The state can, and will, ultimately rely on force to sustain the existing social, economic and political order. Economic growth through much of the post-war period and the success of ideologies which legitimated the existing order meant that only rarely was it necessary to use force.

4   SOME VIEWS OF POLITICS AND DEMOCRACY IN THE 1980s AND 1990s

4.1   THE SETTING

What I have termed the 'corporatist' style of politics provided some of the major features of UK politics in the period between 1945 and the mid- to late-1970s. (Indeed elements of the corporatist form of policy making continued to be found in many aspects of state activity through the 1980s and into the 1990s). However, in the 1970s, the package of policies associated with the post-war settlement and the corporatist style of policy making began to face major criticisms. In Section 3.3 we examined some of the critiques from writers within the marxist tradition, but another major challenge came from a set of ideas which developed largely from what this course terms the 'liberal' and, to some extent the 'conservative', traditions. In the UK these ideas particularly came to prominence with the election in 1979 of the government led by Margaret Thatcher. Admittedly there was evidence that by the mid-1970s the Labour government of the time was also beginning to question whether the corporatist style and package of policies was adequate to deal with the range of problems facing government. Ultimately more significant, however, was the fact that in 1979 enough voters were sufficiently disenchanted with the government's performance to vote in a general election for a party some of whose leaders shared many of the ideas of what is often referred to as the 'New Right'. The set of ideas, or ideology, associated with the New Right sees the role of the state, and the nature of democracy, in different ways to what had become common in the corporatist era.

4.2   NEW RIGHT VIEWS

Although the ideas of the New Right on the nature of the state and the nature of contemporary democracy have their own complex history a good way to introduce them here is essentially as a critique of the corporatist style. To illustrate this we can look critically at the activities of each of the three main types of actors identified earlier as being at the heart of policy making under corporatism: civil servants, interest groups, and elected representatives.

The first element in the New Right's critique of *civil servants* is their tendency to behave in ways which reflect not so much their expertise or their willingness to pursue the public good, but more their desire to build up their own 'empires'. According to the liberal tradition, individuals are likely to behave most rationally when they have a direct interest in the resources they spend. As this is largely absent for civil servants, they are said to look for rewards in other ways — such as the number of people they employ and the areas over which their department is responsible.¡

(*Cartoon reproduced from* 'Little Boxes' — *a collection of Bryan McAllister's work from* The Guardian)

One view of the bureaucracy in the National Health Service

Civil servants could also be accused of a tendency to slow down much needed changes through what were seen by many as cumbersome bureaucratic procedures. Some of these difficulties may admittedly arise from the difficulty of producing coordinated action from a complex bureaucracy of many departments. But, to the New Right, the size and complexity of a bureaucracy is more likely to form part of an indictment of an over large and unwieldy structure rather than an acceptance of the difficulties of developing a coordinated approach to complex problems.

Linked to this, the New Right criticized an overall culture within the bureaucracy which emphasized consensus and compromise rather than decisive action. Part of the defence of this by civil servants themselves has been that, in the long run, good government may be better served by searching for compromise positions which are sensitive to the views of significant minority groups, especially when the electoral system delivers central governments who do not receive the majority support of most electors. In response New Right critics would question whether the backgrounds of many senior civil servants were appropriate for dealing with the problems of rapidly turning around an economy and a society in crisis. The elected government could also claim that the overall support of 40 per cent of those who voted gave them more legitimacy to shape policy than totally unelected civil servants.

Turning to the participation of *interest groups* in the making and implementing of public policy, the New Right's critique is based on grounds of economic efficiency and its view of the nature of democracy. In most cases these groups pursue relatively narrow sets of interests, and questions therefore arise about how far such interests are compatible with any supposed general interest of society as a whole. As you know, a major assumption of the liberal tradition is that individuals in society are best able to decide what is in their own interests, for example whether they wish to join a union or not, or whether to buy products made in the UK. In this light, therefore, it may be reasonable to ask why governments should, for example, give the TUC a particular influence on the law relating to unions, or provide a sympathetic ear to requests for state assistance to declining industries.

Such interventions can be characterized from the New Right view as not only stifling the development of a genuinely competitive economy, but also allowing powerful minorities to thwart the wishes of the majority as expressed in general elections. (Can you see how, in terms of the issues raised in Section 1.3 the New Right may take a distinctive view on how 'minority sensitive' a democratic government should be?)

Finally, some in the New Right questioned the general ability of *elected representatives* to represent in detail what individual voters really want. As you saw in Unit 11, Section 2 the liberal tradition is associated with an attachment to market mechanisms as a means of allowing individuals to indicate what they want in the light of their available resources. In this view our buying provides signals to the rest of society about what we value. As Enoch Powell put it:

> The free enterprise economy is the true counterpart of democracy: it is the only system which gives everyone a say. Everyone who goes into a shop and chooses one article rather than another is casting a vote in the economic ballot box: with thousands or millions of others that choice is signalled to production and investment and helps to mould the world just a tiny fraction nearer to people's desire. In this great and continuous general election of the free economy nobody, not even the poorest, is disenfranchised; we are all voting all the time.
>
> (Powell, 1969, p.33)

This provides an interesting approach to one of the major questions introduced in Section 1.4 about the extent of mass participation in politics. The New Right's position is that the number of issues handled by conventional political processes should be greatly reduced, thus allowing individuals more opportunities to decide for themselves what they want — subject of course to the resources at their disposal.

In contrast to private individuals, elected representatives, acting in the public sphere, are not constrained by the discipline of spending their own money. In their attempts to win votes they are seen as often using state expenditure to get individual voters 'off the hook' of making difficult choices. In this they are aided by the complicity of many voters who can be seen as being unable or unwilling to connect what they want with the taxes they ultimately pay. As one commentator, describing these types of ideas put it, the voter

> ...is like a skinflint dining in an expensive restaurant with a party of friends who have agreed to share the bill equally between them. However tight-fisted he may be, it is not rational for him to order the cheapest items on the menu. If he does, he will probably end up by subsidising his fellow diners. It makes more sense for him to opt for the caviar and champagne.
>
> (Marquand, 1988, p.76)

Similarly, using another memorable food-based metaphor, New Right views essentially suggest that 'democracy is to adults what chocolate is to children: endlessly tempting; harmless in small doses; sickening in excess' (Marquand, 1988, p.78).

If we now pull together these critical comments on how civil servants, interest groups and politicians worked together under corporatism we can see how the New Right views them as having produced policies which were damaging for the economy, for social relationships and for the political system as a whole.

We can take these three areas in turn.

1 In the case of the economy, a large and relatively inefficient state is seen as giving in to inevitably selfish interest groups and voters, and providing a wide range of services which require high taxation levels, which then undermine the levels of initiative of those in work. At the same time the unemployed are seen as preferring handouts from the state to either working or moving to places where work is available. Employers are, in turn, seen as having to provide relatively high wages to attract labour into employment. We thus have an overall picture where high labour costs, low levels of initiative, an inflexible work force and high levels of taxation all combine to impose burdens on business — the mainspring of economic well-being. In this context it may not be surprising that many thinkers on the political right also began to doubt whether the corporatist style of democracy was compatible with a capitalist economy increasingly experiencing the effects of globalization. (You may recall that Unit 12, Section 6 identified several significant trends in this 'globalization of the local economy', for example 'the emergence of multinational corporations, the establishment in the UK of foreign-owned firms, the internationalization of banks and financial institutions, the emergence of a new international division of labour, and shifts in the nature of the world trade'.)

2 However, while the liberal critique of 'excessive' democracy may concentrate on the problems it is said to cause for the economy, it also has a pessimistic view of the implications of this type of democracy for *social relationships*. Here what is seen as the tendency for the state to encourage dependence on itself supposedly comes at the expense of traditional forms of social organiz-

ation in the family and in the local community. Extensive state benefits, employing social workers, providing large amounts of residential care for the elderly and so on are seen as potentially undermining those supposedly traditional values which emphasize individual responsibility, mutual support in families, care in the community and so on. Prime Minister Thatcher expressed the basis of this position clearly in what became a much quoted view.

> Too many people have been given to understand that if they have a problem it's the government's job to cope with it. They're casting their problems on society. And, you know, there's no such thing as society. There are individual men and women, and there are families. And no government can do anything except through people, and people must look to themselves first. It's our duty to look after ourselves, and then, also, to look after our neighbours.
>
> (*Woman's Own*, 1987)

3 Finally we can identify some criticisms more explicitly concerned with issues normally labelled as 'political'. The first draws upon a central value in liberal positions: personal liberty. You may recall from Unit 11 that liberals see markets not only as the optimum means for resolving economic and social problems but also as crucial for the exercise of personal liberty. In their eyes those forms of democracy which allow for control by the masses of a state with a wide range of functions may be represented less as 'the people controlling their affairs for the common good' and more as the 'tyranny of the majority imposing their wishes on individual liberties'. As the leading liberal theorist, Hayek, put it, 'if democracy is taken to mean government by the unrestricted will of the majority, I am not a democrat' (Hayek 1982, p.39). Note that comments such as this do not imply that governments should be more sensitive to the wishes of minorities: they are part of the argument that even democratically elected governments should, as far as possible, leave individuals to make their own choices.

A second 'political' element within some liberal critiques is their suggestion that governments in representative democracies can easily become 'overloaded'. The suggestion here is that governments, attempting to increase their popularity by acceding to public demands for state intervention or help, may take on increasing responsibilities. Unfortunately, however, the relevant problems may not in fact be remediable by any form of government action, and certainly not by governments which by repeatedly trying to please have become large and unwieldy. Ultimately the danger may arise of a public, disillusioned by continual promises and continual failures, beginning to question the authority of government in general.

Together these criticisms led many liberals to advocate what they termed a 'rolling back' of many state activities: abolishing some of the state's functions (for example in running nationalized industries) and reducing levels of involvement in some of those activities which remain. Using the course theme of *public and private*, we can see that while the role of the state in administering the *public* sphere of society would contract, individual firms and citizens are seen as needing to take on more responsibility for handling what now become *private* concerns. Individual citizens have some of their requirements met by the state, but increasingly they come to rely on doing things for themselves or entering into markets which are seen as being much more sensitive to people's demands. At the same time, however, the state is still seen as needing to retain a number of functions (protecting the rights of individual citizens, maintaining law and order, defence, and a 'safety net' welfare state). In addition ultimate control over this more limited range of activities still resides in a government chosen by the people in periodic elections within a system of representative democracy.

4.3   THE LIBERAL AND CONSERVATIVE INHERITANCE

So far I have suggested that this broad set of ideas derives mainly from a liberal tradition, and that in the UK context they had a considerable influence on the Thatcher governments of the 1980s. However, it is important to note that these particular governments drew some of their other ideas not from the liberal but from the conservative tradition. Thus, while they drew from liberalism an emphasis on the importance of markets and a 'free' economy, they also supported the idea of a strong state preserving a social order based on supposedly traditional sets of values. From your own experience you might remember, for example, the emphasis on the importance of the family, the firm positions on law and order issues, the sympathy for a return to traditional methods and so-called 'standards' in education, and the taking up of what were claimed to be traditional positions on issues of public and personal morality — often even setting themselves against what were seen to be the 'trendy permissive society' positions of many elements in a variety of quarters from the modern Church of England to academic social science.

Interestingly the pursuit of these types of ideas, in a sense springing from the conservative tradition, sometimes gave rise to attempts to provide 'firm' central government, and this formed an interesting contrast with the more liberal emphasis on personal liberties, rolling back the state, and so on. The general point you should take from this is that, although for the sake of simplicity we are here identifying broad styles in the handling of national politics, few individual politicians draw all their ideas from one intellectual tradition. Moreover the complexities of party politics and changing events mean that most political parties or governments rarely move as a unified body in one single direction at all times.

SUMMARY

- New Right critiques saw the extent and the style of public policy under corporatism as contributing to economic malaise, social problems and restrictions on individual liberty.

- Solutions to these problems are said to lie partly in 'rolling back the state' and a change in the balance between public and private responsibilities.

- In practice the liberal emphases in New Right positions were combined with some views traditionally associated with conservatism.

4.4   A VIEW FROM THE MARXIST TRADITION

Following the pattern used with the account of corporatism, we can now examine how the New Right's version of representative democracy appears to writers in a different tradition — marxism. As a starting point, however, I need to make two general points.

Firstly, the marxist tradition is not the only source of critical views of the New Right. Feminist writers, for example, have explored among other things the implications of New Right policies for the real opportunities available to women in areas such as family life and the emphasis on 'care in the community'.

Secondly the account given here is inevitably highly selective. The application of New Right ideas was neither uniform across areas nor consistent through time. Moreover different schools within the marxist tradition have different interpretations of the period. The most we can do here is to illustrate how writers from a different theoretical position interpret at least some of the key developments during this period.

One useful starting point is to examine the way in which New Right ideas came to be in a position to influence policy in the first place. The account you read earlier linked the arrival of these ideas with the electoral success of a particular individual, Margaret Thatcher, who, through the operation of the British electoral system, came to be elected as Prime Minister in 1979. We could account for these developments by concentrating on Mrs Thatcher's personal history, her rise in the Conservative party, the events of the general election and so on. However, a marxist account would also want to place all this in a wider context, perhaps stressing that the levels of dissatisfaction with corporatist policies which were the most obvious influence on the election result were part of a wider phenomenon which was substantially linked to changes in the international economy.

In several countries, as scattered as the USA, France and Sweden, it became particularly apparent during the late 1960s and early 1970s that problems were arising as high state expenditures and high levels of taxation contributed to rising costs and thus to declining competitiveness in an increasingly globalized economy. The global order in which states had to operate was one in which firms could easily transfer significant parts of their operations to low cost locations. In this context, 'local' attempts by individual states to combine economic growth with high welfare expenditures appeared to many to be increasingly problematic. At the level of individual voters, rising levels of unemployment coupled with inflation led to higher levels of dissatisfaction with parties associated with corporatist policies and approaches — even if there was little evidence of any clear endorsement of the policies which New Right governments were about to put into effect.

In the UK during the 1980s, the application of New Right thinking meant firstly that the state retreated from involvement in some areas of policy such as attempts to secure full employment particularly through management of overall levels of demand. We have already mentioned the end of corporatist consultation in the formulation of economic policy. In other areas there were moves to deregulation, for example, in the abolition of wages councils which, by fixing minimum wages, were seen as interfering in the ability of market forces to set a market price for labour. The switch from public means of shaping society to private means was also evident in the privatization of large areas of the economy previously run by the state or its agencies. Moreover in those areas of state activity which remained there was a greater use of market principles in setting and implementing policy. (You may remember TV06's treatment of the markets operating in health care.)

The success of these efforts to roll back the state should not, however, be overstated. For example, when British Telecom and British Gas were privatized anxieties about their abilities as potential private monopolies to dominate relevant markets led to the government establishing new regulatory bodies such as OFTEL and OFGAS. But, the government's aspirations at least remained those of reducing state activities in some areas and altering the balance between public interventions and the operation of markets. As we saw earlier, New Right thinking claims that, in a sense, markets deliver to individuals and organizations greater potential freedoms to choose what they wish to consume. Marxist writers are critical of this view of freedom, pointing out that even the freedom to buy certain goods, for example a higher probability of rapid medical care, or the education of one's children in smaller classes, depends on having the necessary resources in the first place.

Moreover, in the absence of state intervention to reduce inequality, major differences in access to resources will persist indefinitely. In the case of the UK there is considerable evidence that inequalities in a number of areas increased significantly in the 1980s. For example, if we examine the share of national income taken by the 50 per cent of households with higher earnings and the share taken by the 50 per cent with lower earnings, we find that in 1979 the higher earners took approximately two-thirds of the total and lower earners took the remaining third. By 1993, however, the differential had widened to approximately three-quarters versus one-quarter. Successive governments contributed to these widening differentials by their acceptance or encouragement of the restructuring of the economy, by their attempts to constrain rises in their own expenditure, and by their own taxation policies. To illustrate the latter point, in 1993 while the 10 per cent of the population with the highest incomes paid back approximately 32 per cent of their income in various forms of tax, the 10 per cent with the lowest incomes paid back 43 per cent of their already smaller amounts (*The Guardian*, 10 July 1993).

Another notable aspect of how Britain's political institutions worked during this period was a general strengthening of central government, particularly at the expense of other state agencies and local government. One particular target for the New Right was the tier of non-elected authorities known in the United Kingdom as QUANGOs. In the early 1980s many of these were abolished and many of their former areas of interest became more subject to regulation by markets. However, where abolition was perceived to be unnecessary or impossible there was evidence that the former practice of choosing representatives on the governing bodies of these organizations from a range of political views and interests became less common. Senior positions were increasingly filled by individuals with similar political views to those of central government, thus making it less likely that a plurality of interests would be represented in these important bodies (see for example Colenutt and Ellis, 1993; and Cohen, 1994).

In the context of local government, the application of a New Right approach provided some interesting changes in the style of democracy enjoyed in the UK particularly with regard to the issue, first raised in Section 1.3, of where political decisions ought to be taken. Although local governments had been chosen and controlled through a system of representative democracy, they were often perceived by central government as wishing to undermine policies which the centre claimed had national — rather than local — support. In some cases local authorities were abolished and those that remained were subjected to more direct central control. The bypassing of local government in the area of education was particularly interesting. In general the powers of local education authorities were reduced as central government provided major incentives for schools themselves to be funded by central government but also to be subject to market principles in the hiring of staff, the purchase of books, and so on. At the same time, however, the state began to intervene actively, through the National Curriculum, in what was to be taught in most schools. In addition, that curriculum was justified most frequently in terms of the need to provide a workforce more able to contribute to a competitive economy.

This example of attempts to change the content of the school curriculum leads us to what the marxist position would see as another crucial aspect of government during this period, the state's attempts to shape the way people saw themselves and their relationships with one another. We saw earlier that marxist accounts of the state emphasize the way in which sets of ideas or ideologies come to justify a particular way of doing things. We are, of course, familiar with part of this argument through our awareness of the way in which the ideas voters hold about issues and political parties can to some extent be 'influenced' by the ways in which political issues are represented to them by the mass media and by political leaders. Using the terminology of one of the course themes, aspects of *reality* can be *represented* in ways which voters may gradually come to share. While voters are clearly not infinitely pliable or likely to be 'brainwashed', some of them may be led to concentrate on certain aspects of reality and to downplay or disregard others, for example to focus on welfare 'scroungers' rather than on those eligible for benefit but sometimes too proud to claim it. Those aspects of reality which *are* focused upon can also be represented in ways which get people used to seeing the same set of facts differently by using a particular set of ideas. A strike among NHS employees might be represented as 'workers defending eroded living standards and protesting against deteriorating conditions in our health service' or as 'militant unions holding the country to ransom by picking on helpless sick and aged people'.

To the extent that such processes are seen as 'helping voters to understand' they may be part of a healthy democracy, but they also raise the possibility of what might justifiably be termed 'manipulation'. In this sense the exercise of power might be seen as depending partly on the ability to shape people's ideas. (Remember what Steven Lukes in Chapter 12 of the Reader had to say about the third dimension of power.) Writers from within the marxist perspective have a particular interest in how far ideas shift and how far they are shaped. Although disagreeing about how far the process has gone in the UK in recent years they generally share a broadly common approach on why it was necessary. In their view changing conditions in the international economy made it increasingly difficult for western states to remain competitive while still maintaining high expenditures on social welfare and still securing high levels of employment. In these conditions democratically elected governments were seen as having to find ways of persuading their electorates to accept reduced government expenditure on social welfare, higher levels of unemployment, shifts in the relative power of employers and employees, and even, as we have seen, changes in the style of democratic rule. Certainly at various times Mrs Thatcher and her ministers proclaimed themselves as seeking changes in the basic ideas people held about society: how they saw their responsibilities to their families, their communities, their employers; and, in the more 'political' sphere, how they viewed the role of the state and their own rights and responsibilities. For example, the then Chancellor of the Exchequer, Norman Lamont claimed in a major speech to Parliament in 1991:

> The eighties were years of remarkable progress in our economy, but even more striking was the change of attitude. The crucial importance of the market is now widely accepted both in this country and even in this House. It is that change of ideas and attitude that will be the lasting legacy of Mrs Thatcher.
>
> (Quoted in Coates, 1991, p.164)

The governments of the time certainly had some advantages in potentially bringing about ideological change. Apart from their normal opportunities to make persuasive public statements, they enjoyed wide support in the editorial columns of a majority of newspapers. They also pursued a number of policies, for instance, in restricting the power of the unions, selling off council houses and nationalized industries, encouraging private pension schemes, and so on, which ultimately were intended to have the effect of encouraging individualist rather than collectivist approaches to people's problems. In these circumstances, it appeared possible that a new and distinctive set of ideas about society, the economy and politics could become increasingly dominant over alternatives.

Political interaction in the context of the 'community charge'

--------------------------------- ACTIVITY 6 ---------------------------------

Try writing two contrasting captions for the above image of a mass protest/riot.

How far such change actually occurred is still unclear. Surveys of mass atti-tudes generally seemed to show little evidence of mass moves to New Right positions (see for example Rentoul, 1990; Crewe, 1989). As one example Table 4 shows some of the results of a series of careful surveys of mass attitudes during the 1980s. It gives the percentages choosing different responses to a question about appropriate levels of taxation and public spending.

Table 4   (Figures shown are percentages of responses given.)

	1983	1986	1990
If the government had to choose it should:			
— reduce taxes and spend less	9	5	3
— keep taxes at the same level as now	54	44	37
— increase taxes and spend more	32	46	54

Source: Taylor-Gooby, P. (1991) 'Attachment to the Welfare State' in Jowell, R. *et al.* (eds), *British Social Attitudes: the Eighth Report,* p.25

However, at the same time many writers, not only from the marxist tradition, have argued that within the area of party politics there was evidence that the ideas of competing parties were gradually shifting. Parties with a stronger tradition of support for the welfare state were seen as gradually placing more emphasis on 'caring for the needy' and the need for 'value for money' rather than the *right* of all to benefit from the welfare state or 'the need to seek economic equality'. In this context the appearance of continuing competition between parties might be less significant than the fact that they were all moving in the same general direction. In this way one might see gradual long-term shifts in the general terms of reference (what is sometimes termed the 'dominant ideology') within which the major parties competed and through which most people saw themselves and their society.

SUMMARY

- For most writers within the marxist tradition attempts by the New Right to 'roll back the state' can be understood in terms of reducing those regulations and levels of taxation which constrain profitability at a time of increased international competition.

- This perspective would also emphasize that in many parts of the public sector not subject to direct central control, mechanisms have been established which are overwhelmingly sympathetic to the interests of private capital.

- Continuing electoral support for governments expressing New Right views can be explained less by success in changing mass attitudes and more by policies which deliver greater wealth to certain groups in society while preserving the electorally popular core elements of the welfare state.

- Central government has strengthened its position over other levels of government by arguing that its policies have been accepted by the electorate as a whole and cannot be undermined by sub-national groups with different preferences.

  Despite shifts in the public statements of the major parties, most of the available evidence seems to show only limited influence of New Right ideas on mass attitudes to the role of the state and the role of individuals within it.

---

5 HOW FAR CAN CAPITALISM AND DEMOCRACY WORK TOGETHER?

This final section involves you in working on Chapter 14 of the Course Reader. You should find that this activity consolidates and develops further many of the major concerns of this unit, and raises some interesting questions about the relationships of politics and the economic system.

However, Chapter 14 was originally written as a reflective conclusion to a carefully argued and lengthy textbook, and you need to approach it in ways appropriate to your own requirements. As a first step in this you may find it useful to remind yourself of *The Good Study Guide's* introduction to the skills involved in reading new material and making notes. Take a few minutes now to glance through Chapter 2, Sections 5 and 6 of *The Good Study Guide*, but ignore the activities on the Gardner article.

———————————————— ACTIVITY 7 ————————————————

Before you start work on Chapter 14 of the Reader I would like to make three suggestions:

1 Skim through the piece for 5-10 minutes getting a feel for its general content, approach, and sequencing. This should help you in deciding on the style and possible extent of any notes you make later.

2 Work through the piece again in a more systematic way making notes as you go. The form of these notes is up to you. You might, for example, make your own summary of the main points on a separate sheet. Alternatively, you might work principally on the printed page by highlighting/underlining the important generalizations, writing a few extra comments in the margin, etc. Doing this should in itself help you to engage actively with the ideas explored in the chapter. In addition, however, you should remember that, in the future, you will need a system which helps you retrieve the key points in the chapter without having to read systematically through several pages of text.

3 Try not to get too 'bogged down' by apparently new but unexplained concepts. If this occurs, try to work out the meaning of the term from its context. You might also get some help from the *Glossary Index*. In addition, if you are using the system of compiling 'concept cards' suggested in *The Good Study Guide*, jot down a few words on a new card or possibly on a card for what appears to be a related concept. Your grasp of central concepts will develop gradually as you come across them being used in slightly different ways in different contexts. To take one example, you have already seen in the course several references to 'ideology' and you are probably becoming familiar with this term as meaning something like a 'cluster of ideas'. As the course progresses you will also see how an ideology is a cluster of ideas which helps one group exercise power over others. In Chapter 14 of the Reader you will come across the term 'dominant ideology' which, as you will probably grasp, implies that a particular set of ideas comes to dominate most people's thinking. Similarly you will come across a reference to the 'ideology of liberal democracy'. If you reflect on what you have already read, you should see that this suggests there is a common cluster of ideas about how democracy works which, because it springs from the liberal tradition, emphasizes the supposed power of individual voters in running the country.

My advice is now in danger of becoming longer than the reading itself. So have a go now at skimming through the chapter and making some notes on it.

═══════════════════════ READER ═══════════════════════
Now read and make notes on Chapter 14 in the Course Reader.

Welcome back. My guess is that you probably found this extract quite demanding. However, your note taking should have helped you with your grasp of its main points. Additionally to give you some further help with both the extract and the development of your note-taking skills, I have set out below, as an example of someone else's notes, the ones I made in my preparatory reading for writing this unit. To make the text legible I have used less abbreviations than normal. If you glance through these notes you might notice some useful tips, for example the use of abbreviations, the use of a very brief summary at the beginning, the inclusion at some point of precise information about the source of the original article. You should also see that for me notes do not always attempt to provide a complete summary of the piece in question. I only took

---

Dearlove and Saunders : NOTES

- Compatibility of democracy + capitalism?
- Competing perspectives
- Economic + social change → feasibility of democratic styles.

1 Roles of government vs. markets. Balance between govt. (public power) and markets. (arena of private power). Note New Right's emphasis on individuals exercising private power in markets rather than attempting to shape society via use of (public) state power.

2 Importance of politics/economics relationship in different traditions. Traditions here:
- 'Left' – links with Marxist tradition.
- 'Mainstream' – links with liberalism

3 Traditions differ in views on overall compatibility of democratic policies and capitalist economy. But these views also change over time.

4 Traditions also use concepts differently.
- democracy – 'procedural' emphasis in mainstream views (votes, formal procedures, etc).
  – 'substantive' emphasis in Left tradition. (Sensitivity to need to deal with continuing existence of economic power. Need for a more participatory democracy.)
- capitalism – disagreement about real extent of 'freedom' and 'opportunity'.

5 Paragraph 8 very good on New Right. 'Overload'. Implications of big government for economy. Need for 'limits' to democracy – or at least the democracy of competing for votes and seeking compromises between major interests.

6 Conditions for compatibility of democracy and capitalism.

GENERAL	IN 90s?
i) Deference – in politics – at work	Much reduced?
ii) Representative democracy; limited role for elected elements (strong civil service); links between capital and state.	Little change in view
iii) Buoyant economy to create tax revenue for meeting popular demands	Problem of reconciling low taxes, demands for welfare, high profits as difficult as ever – especially given international economic competition
iv) Supportive dominant ideology	How far has ideology of New Right permeated elites and/or mass of population?

7 Capitalism finds easiest fit with liberal democracy. But democracy has 'impulses' to move to participatory style. Really?? Wishful thinking?

8 Socialism + democracy have different sets of tensions. East Europe in 90s?

(J. Dearlove and P. Saunders, _Introduction to British Politics_, 1984 Cambridge Polity Press, pp. 436–444)

Figure 3

notes on those parts of the reading most relevant to this particular unit. Nor do I always feel able to provide answers to all the questions which occur to me as I am trying to get to grips quickly with a large amount of new literature. You may see parallels with your own situation here!

I hope you can now see how this reading builds upon some of the key issues raised earlier in the unit. To close let me mention just three of these.

Firstly, there is the importance of recognizing that major concepts, such as democracy, are represented in very different ways within different academic traditions and within political practice. Have another look, for example, at the different representations of democracy and capitalism referred to in the fifth paragraph. At various points in the unit you may have also seen that the basic questions with which we began — about the appropriate scope for democratic rule, the problem of which people are to rule, and what are appropriate forms of participation — are also answered differently by writers from different traditions and by political leaders who draw many of their ideas from those traditions. You will return to the question of how the traditions see democracy and the general links between state and society in the closing unit of this block and in Block 7.

A second important issue for you to reflect upon is the position taken in the unit and the reading on the extent to which the institutions of *representative* democracy make possible the exercise of power by the mass of the population. You will have noticed the comments in the reading, for example, on the dangers of 'procedures which fall far short of participatory democracy and which represent a mere shadow of a substantive democracy in which all citizens have relatively equal chances to influence and control the making of decisions which affect them be they in politics or the market.' Similarly this unit, for example in Section 2.2, raised some of the problems which face systems of representative democracy. Of course you may still find this form of democracy preferable to alternatives. But the more general point to make is that there are potentially lots of different ways of organizing mass inputs to the taking of public decisions, and how we organize these matters affects to a large extent the type of society we experience every day (and study in this course).

A final set of issues raised in both the reading and the unit involves both the extent of and the causes of changes in how democracy operates within a society. While the common view in the UK is predominantly one of gradual and inexorable development of democratic forms, Dearlove and Saunders point, for example, to relatively recent and intense debates about the desirability of universal voting rights. They also argue that the form of democracy adopted in a society is closely related to changes in economic conditions and in mass attitudes. While the unit made similar points through its brief account of post-war history, the reading concentrates on the general relationships between its 'four conditions.' A fitting activity with which you could wind up your work on this unit would be for you to go through each of these four conditions, reflect upon what is happening in each at present, and consider what this might mean for the type of democracy you experience in the near future.

=========== AUDIO CASSETTE ===========

Now listen to Audio-cassette 4, Side A, where David Held traces some of the key developments in thinking about the concepts of democracy, and the contributions to this made by the four traditions. He also discusses the contemporary challenges to the democratic governance of sovereign states areising from globalization.

══════════════ GOOD STUDY GUIDE ══════════════

This would be an appropriate point for you to continue developing your essay writing skills. By the end of this week you should have completed Section 5 of Chapter 6 of *The Good Study Guide*.

REFERENCES

Arblaster, A. (1987) *Democracy*, Buckingham, Open University Press.

Beetham, D. (1993) 'Political theory and British politics' in Dunleavy, P. *et al.* (eds) pp. 353–70.

Coates, D. (1984) *The Context of British Politics*, London, Hutchinson.

Coates, D. (1991) *Running the Country,* Sevenoaks, Hodder and Stoughton (in association with the Open University).

Cohen, N. (1994) 'One party Britain', *The Independent on Sunday*, 3 April, p.17.

Colenutt, B. and Ellis, G. (1993) 'The next quangos in London', *New Statesman and Society*, 26 March, pp.20-1.

Commission of the European Community (1975) *Employees' Participation and Company Structure*, 5th Directive Green Paper, Supplement 8/75, Brussels.

Coxall, B. and Robbins, L. (1989) *Contemporary British Politics: An Introduction*, Basingstoke, Macmillan.

Crewe, I. (1989) 'Values: the crusade that failed' in Kavanagh, D. and Selsdon, A. (eds) *The Thatcher Effect*, Oxford, Clarendon Press, pp 239-50.

Crewe, I. (1993) 'Voting and the electorate' in Dunleavy, P. *et al.* (eds) *Developments in British Politics 4*, pp.92–122.

Crossman, R.H.S. (1975) *Diaries of a Cabinet Minister*, London, Hamish Hamilton and Jonathan Cape.

Dearlove, J. and Saunders, P. (1984) *Introduction to British Politics*, Cambridge, Polity Press.

Dunleavy, P., Gamble, A., Holliday, I., and Peele, G. (eds) (1993) *Developments in British Politics 4,* Basingstoke, Macmillan.

Hayek, F.A. (1982) *Law, Legislation and Liberty, Vol.3*, London, Routledge and Kegan Paul.

Heath, E. (1993) 'A referendum would be a squalid deal', London, *The Observer*, 14 March.

Held, D. (1992) 'Democracy: From City-states to a Cosmopolitan Order' *Political Studies,* Volume XI, pp. 10-39.

Himmelweit, H., Hilde, T., Humphreys, P. and Jaeger, M. (1985) *How Voters Decide*, Buckingham, Open University Press.

Hodgson, G. (1984) *The Democratic Economy,* Harmondsworth, Penguin Books.

Jowell, R., Witherspoon, S. and Booth, L. (eds) *British Social Attitudes: the seventh report,* Aldershot, Gower.

Jowell, R., Brode, L. and Taylor, B. (eds) (1991) *British Social Attitudes: the eighth report,* Aldershot, Dartmouth.

Kingdom, P. (1991) *Government and Politics in the UK*, Cambridge, Polity Press.

Lukes, S. (1974) *Power: A Radical View*, Basingstoke, Macmillan.

Marquand, D. (1989) *The Unprinicipled Society*, London, Jonathan Cape.

Offe, C. (1984) *Contradictions of the Welfare State,* London, Hutchinson.

Parry, G., Moyser, G. and Day, N. (1992) *Political Participation and Democracy in Britain,* Cambridge, Cambridge University Press.

Powell, E. (1969) *Freedom and Reality*, London, Batsford.

Rentoul, J. (1990) 'Individualism' in Jowell, R. *et al.* (eds), pp. 167–82.

Taylor-Gooby, P. (1991) 'Attachment to the Welfare State' in Jowell, R. (ed), pp. 23–42.

Thatcher, M. (1987) interview in *Woman's Own*, 31 October.

ACKNOWLEDGEMENTS

Grateful acknowledgement is made to the following sources for permission to reproduce material in this unit:

Text

'Who cares what you vote for?' *The Sun*, 23rd February 1994, Rex Features Ltd; Heath E. (1993), 'A referendum would be a squalid deal', *The Observer*, 14 March 1993.

Figure

Figure 1: Coxall B. and Robins L. (1989), *Contemporary British Politics: An Introduction*, Macmillan Ltd; Figure 2: Kingdom, P. (1991) *Government and Politics in the UK*, Basil Blackwell Ltd.

Tables

Table 1: Parry G., Moyser G. and Day N. (1992), *Political Participation and Democracy in Britain*, Cambridge University Press; Table 2: Crewe I. (1993), 'Voting and the electorate', in Dunleavy P. *et al* (eds), *Developments in British Politics 4*, by permission of Macmillan Press Ltd; Table 3: Coates D. (1984), *The Context of British Politics*, Hutchinson; Table 4: Taylor-Gooby P. (1991), 'Attachment to the welfare state', in Jowell R. *et al* (ed), *British Social Attitudes: The Seventh Report*, Dartmouth Publishing Co Ltd.

Photographs

p 79: Swiss National Tourist Office; p 80: Stuart Franklin/Magnum; p 84: Joan Russell/Guzelian; p 94: Mansell Collection; p 104: John Sturrock/Network; p 113: Justin Leighton/Network;

Cartoons

p 82: Punch; p 106: Cartoon reproduced from *Little Boxes*, a collection of Bryan McAllister's work from *The Guardian*; p 115: Steve Bell 1987.

UNIT 17 THE POWER OF IDEOLOGY

Prepared for the Course Team by Gregor McLennan

CONTENTS

1   THE CONCEPT OF IDEOLOGY

1.1   INTRODUCTION

The topic of this unit is the concept of ideology. This concept is among the most weighty and hotly debated in the whole of the social sciences. It is also quite a slippery notion to grasp hold of at first. This is partly because it is a term which crops up in a number of very different contexts. Right back in the D103 Preparatory Pack, for instance, you were asked to examine the images of society that are conveyed in the popular press, and Stephen Wagg stated in Reading 7 that his main task was to ascertain the 'ideological essence' of such tabloid journalism. In Unit 16, Section 4.4 the question of whether the mass media 'shape' or merely 'reflect' ideas about electoral democracy was raised. These references indicate how useful social scientists find the concept of ideology in analysing the nature of power in society, and that the concept can be applied to a wide range of social phenomena. Now, the authors of previous units clearly felt that 'ideology' was valuable in expanding on the subject of their units, but they did not have the concept of ideology itself as their main focus. In this unit, however, that is precisely our focus. We want to know: what does ideology mean and how and why does it manage to crop up in so many different areas?

In spite of its exciting capacity to 'unlock' insights into very concrete and 'live' issues, there is no getting away from the fact that ideology and its exploration involves a degree of relatively *abstract* thinking. And since it is not always clear what people mean when they use the term 'ideology', the first thing we need to do in this unit is to lay out some theoretical definitions of the concept. That is our agenda for Section 1 of the unit. As you work through this section, you should try all the time to track back and forth in your own mind between the 'abstract' theorizing and 'concrete' examples of ideologies in action, especially ones that *you* regard as politically significant.

In Section 2, I go on to relate the discussion of ideology to our understanding of the traditions of social science thinking that are featured throughout D103. We shall see not only how each tradition analyses ideology, but also how the traditions themselves can be seen as ideologies in action within society. Then, in Section 3, the guidelines of the first two sections will be reinforced in depth by discussing the ideological aspects of a major political phenomenon of modern times, namely nationalism.

By the end of the unit you should be able to:
* understand the meaning of ideology;
* discuss its possible social roles;
* indicate how ideologies work and how they get transmitted;
* explain how ideology is handled in the *traditions* of social science thinking;
* apply these insights to examples of ideologies in action, especially with respect to *nationalism*;
* begin to form a view on the overall significance of ideology in the maintenance of a social order.

1.2   THE MEANING OF 'IDEOLOGY'

What, then, do we mean by the term 'ideology'? When first coined by French thinkers in the late eighteenth century, 'ideology' was intended to refer to the scientific study—the 'ology' —of ideas, in much the same way as 'psychology' was to be the scientific study of the 'human mind', and 'sociology' was to be the scientific study of society generally. Gradually, however, it has become more usual to see 'ideology' as referring not so much to the *study* of beliefs and ideas in society, as to the beliefs and ideas being studied. Thus, ideology came to be regarded not as a scientific discipline in itself, but rather as a specific type of belief system within society, to be examined as such by the social scientist.

You should note here that already we have gone beyond the possibility that ideology simply refers to any and every kind of 'idea' or 'belief'. After all, people have beliefs about lots of things which may or may not be about society and which they may or may not share with others. However, to regard ideas and beliefs as specifically 'ideological' requires a minimum of three conditions:

1   that those ideas are indeed *shared* by a significant *number* of people;

2   that they form some kind of coherently related *system*; and

3   that they connect in some way to the nature of *power* within society.

To start with, then, we can say that ideologies are systems of collective, widely-held ideas and beliefs concerning the nature of society and its dominant power structures.

The case of religion is instructive in clarifying this distinction between ideas and ideologies. On the one hand, religions involve ideas and beliefs about gods, spirituality and salvation. Religious doctrines in this sense are not necessarily about society and could perhaps be regarded purely as a matter of theological truth and individual faith. Put that way, it would appear that religious ideas should not be thought of as ideological. On the other hand, most religions also involve definite notions of rightful authority, moral conduct, of the good society, of heaven on earth, and so on. Religions often carry implications about whether a particular type of hierarchy of *social* power is legitimate or not. Put that way, religion *can* be regarded as ideological in some respects.

Take Catholicism as an example. In medieval times, it could be argued, Catholicism served to reflect and support the typical threefold social hierarchy of feudal lord, priest and peasant in that everything on earth was believed to have a fixed and unalterable place in a divinely ordained order. Given that doctrine, the idea of rebelling against the worldly order of the day was treated as a sin as well as a crime. Today, by contrast, Catholicism in some South American countries is labelled 'liberation theology' because it holds that there is absolutely *no* theological justification for social and political inequality. Quite the opposite. So the priest is in this case united with the peasant *against* the landlords rather than being in league with them as in medieval times. In both these cases, religion plays a distinct ideological role, though the ideological contents of the two Catholic outlooks point in radically different directions, the one serving to sustain the social order of its time, the other attempting to challenge it.

Looking at religion from the point of view of ideology is interesting partly because its ostensible subject matter is usually spiritual rather than socio-political in any direct sense. Many other belief systems, though, do have a very direct link with issues of social structure and political power. In particular, ideas concerning equality or inequality, social justice, freedom and progress are classic grounds for ideological contestation. Such ideas are either about whether the *present* state of society—the social order—is right and good; or they are about how some *future* social order would greatly improve the human condition.

Ideologies, in other words, serve either to sustain or to undermine the *legitimacy*, the rightfulness, of a socio-political order. Ideas which are both widely held and tend to support the prevailing social order are sometimes referred to as *dominant ideologies*. Ideas that strive to undermine the dominant order, or which propose alternatives to existing society (which may sometimes be 'utopian' alternatives) can be designated as *counter-ideologies*. In this unit, I shall concentrate, for convenience, on the nature of dominant ideologies, though from time to time I shall bring in how counter-ideologies differ from these in important respects.

The idea of a socio-political order as used to describe the context of ideology is itself quite broad. It certainly includes the various short-term 'regimes' of particular political parties, monarchs or leaders. But equally importantly, it also refers to the longer-term, deeper-lying economic, social and moral bases upon which politics in the narrow sense operate. Whether a society is basically capitalist or socialist, whether it is liberal or not, whether it is democratic or authoritarian, whether it is culturally 'western', or white, or male-dominated: all these sorts of issues can validly be included in the notion of a social order. When a political regime or social order is legitimate, this means that it is generally accepted and endorsed as fair, appropriate or right in the minds of its people. When it is considered illegitimate, it has little moral support of a popular kind.

SUMMARY

- Ideologies are collective beliefs which help to legitimize or de-legitimize a social order.

- Ideologies encourage us to view the social world in a particular light, and by adopting an ideological framework certain consequences follow about how we *live*.

- Ideologies are in a sense always about *power*, even where their belief-content is ostensibly to do with something else (such as God, or masculinity, or the national character).

1.3   WHAT IDEOLOGIES DO

In developing a proper definition of ideology in this way, to say what ideologies *are* involves beginning to ascertain what they *do* in society. So, for example, to say that ideologies are collective beliefs about society is useful, but only up to a point. A better analytical purchase is gained when we add that what these ideological beliefs do is to sustain or challenge prevailing social orders. Our definition of ideology, in other words, will tend to be closely bound up with what we think the *point* of ideology is; that is, with its potential social *role* or function.

It is worth elaborating on this by considering some of the ways in which dominant ideologies sustain a social order. To see the social world through the lens or frame of an ideology is to put things in a certain perspective, to perceive social life according to relatively stable values, assumptions and images. At this point, I want to emphasize that the components of ideologies are not only 'ideas' as such. Often they take the form of fairly vague background assumptions, prejudices and inclinations. But these ideological assumptions are in practice no less potent or coherent for being imprecise. So one role of ideologies is simply that they give shape to people's perceptions and values: they help them make sense of society.

A second and related role of ideologies is that they perhaps fulfil a general human need to feel psychologically 'at home' in an awesome, infinite universe. Ideologies in that sense provide some local answers to the metaphysical puzzle of 'the meaning of life'. They deliver a definite sense of social order and sometimes cosmic order. Ideologies thus serve to link theory and practice closely together: through *identifying* as individuals with their values and perspectives, we can come to see ourselves as having a definite place and purpose within the larger scheme of things.

A third general role of (dominant) ideologies is that they can help to secure social integration, so enabling societies to 'hang together' over time in a viable way. Virtually all known societies have contained serious differences of wealth and power, talent and education amongst their members. How, then, have they managed to avoid continually breaking apart? One answer is that ideologies provide a potent reservoir of beliefs and values out of which a kind of social glue or cement can be made and used to mend the cracks of internal social division and conflict, thus preventing social disintegration.

A fourth possible way in which ideologies sustain a prevailing social order is that they serve the particular interests of dominant groups or ruling classes (thus the term 'dominant' ideology). For example, it has often been asserted that liberal ideas of the free market and competitive 'winner-takes-all' attitudes are simply ideologies which further the specific interests of the capitalist class. Similarly, the 'vanguard' role of the proletariat as highlighted in Soviet Communist doctrine prior to the 1980s was arguably little more than an ideological cover for the self-interest of Party bosses in state socialist societies. So the ultimate purpose of ideology from this point of view is to gain widespread social acceptance of beliefs which in the end serve the interests not of the masses at all, but rather of particular élites.

SUMMARY

We have identified four possible roles or functions of dominant ideologies. Ideologies:

1 help us make sense of society from within a particular framework of meaning;
2 provide metaphysical security and a sense of social identity;
3 act as a 'social cement' in circumstances of social division;
4 serve the material interests of ruling groups.

Counter-ideologies also fulfil these roles to an extent, but clearly they are less concerned about cementing the *existing* order than presenting an alternative order. Also, counter-ideologies attempt to serve the interests of subordinate groups, not ruling groups.

There are some important things to note at this stage about these social roles that are played by ideology. First of all, although each role has its own distinctive emphasis, these roles are often compatible with one another. You could accept some or all of them to some extent. You could accept, for example, that ideology acts as a social cement, then go on to argue that it does so by serving privileged social interests. (This combines roles 3 and 4.) Or you could hold that the larger part of making sense of society (role 1) is really about feeling personally 'at home' in the world (role 2).

The second thing about the list of roles is that it is by no means complete. You could add to it. You might, perhaps, want to say that ideologies are the means by which powerful *individuals* get the *masses* in society to endorse their dicta-torial tendencies. Or, if you were a psychoanalyst, you might want to argue that ideological attachments are social reflections of deep-seated, psycho-sex-ual conflicts within individuals.

A third point to emphasize is that we are talking of *possible* social roles for ideology, not proven roles. Indeed, it is seldom the case that any particular role is wholly fulfilled. Take the view that ideology furthers the interests of domi-nant groups. Such a role is unlikely to be totally realized within any given society, and moreover there will probably be quite significant variation in its embodiment in different societies. What we are getting at here is that whilst it is tempting to think in terms of the single, definitive function of ideology, it might be better to think of its potential *roles* in the plural. Although there is a tendency to speak of *ideology*, in general and in the singular, it is sometimes more appropriate to think about ideolo*gies,* in the plural. It is not wholly improper to talk of ideology in general and its main social roles; the point is simply that we must be careful not to overgeneralize.

––––––––––––––––––––––– ACTIVITY 1 –––––––––––––––––––––––

Consider at this point whether you have any initial views on the main role of ideologies. You may, for instance, be inclined to see the 'meaning of life' ques-tion as tedious and unreal; or again, perhaps you regard psychoanalytic theory as just so much mumbo jumbo. It's all simply about élite power, you might say. Maybe that's right. But if that is your current view, I would encourage you at this stage to 'bracket off' some of these definite opinions in order to review the range of other possible social functions that ideologies fulfil.

If, on the other hand, you find all the proposed roles for ideology *equally* attractive, and so don't have any fixed view of your own, that's fine. But try now to indulge your prejudices a little more: what main purpose, in the end and in your view, does ideology serve? Try to make a provisional choice between the four roles outlined in the Summary above.

1.4   INTERPRETING THE 'BASELINE' CONCEPTION OF IDEOLOGY

From the points made so far, we can now put forward a 'baseline' conception of ideology:

Ideologies are sets of ideas, assumptions and images by which people make sense of society, which give a clear social identity, and which serve in some way to legitimize relations of power in society.

Whatever else you take from this unit you should try to understand, and reflect upon, this formula. However, the formula remains a 'baseline' conception only. It is possible to go on to *interpret* it in slightly different ways. In particular, you could be relatively 'restrictive' or relatively 'relaxed' about just what *sort* of ideas or practices ideology is supposed to include. For example, if we were inclined to see ideology as referring only to those bodies of ideas that are theoretically systematic and politically explicit (such as Hitler's *Mein Kampf,* Marx and Engels's *Communist Manifesto*, or J. S. Mill's *On Liberty*), then we would be interpreting our baseline conception in quite a restrictive way. If, on the other hand, we wanted to include as ideology just about any common-sense assumptions, images or rituals, then we would be adopting a very 'relaxed' interpretation of the baseline conception with regard to what sort of thing ideology is.

It is also possible to take a relatively restricted or relatively relaxed view about how *directly* the ideas are connected to power. If you look again at the 'baseline' conception you will see that it leaves this question fairly open. A restricted view of the ideas–power connection would want to go on to say that ideologies are actually fairly *directly* and *deliberately* linked to the interests of particular social groups, especially dominant élites (e.g. party bosses, rich capitalists, white people, men, etc.). A more relaxed interpretation of this point would by contrast say that ideologies connect to power relations in all sorts of *indirect* and *accidental* ways, and that we should be careful not to exaggerate the element of conspiracy and deliberate brainwashing in the dissemination of dominant ideas.

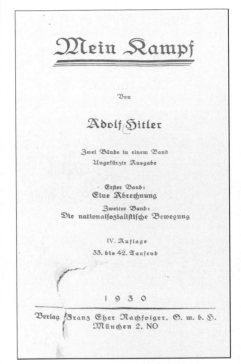

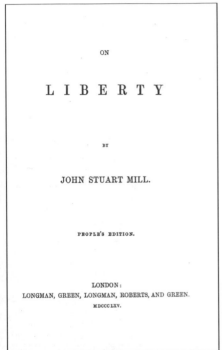

What does ideology include?: a 'restricted' view—specific political doctrines

What does ideology include?: a 'relaxed' view—everyday images, rituals, cultural norms

A third area of interpretation concerns exactly *how* ideologies support dominant interests. A restricted position here would be that ideologies achieve this by spinning webs of *illusion* and *distortion* in people's minds. Ideologies, in this sense, are doctrines which merely *pose* as 'the whole truth' about their subject matter (e.g. racial superiority). But in fact such ideological dogmas are precisely the opposite of the whole truth—they are at best very partial distortions and at worst outright lies and propaganda. So says a restrictive view on this third issue. A more relaxed interpretation of the relationship between ideology and truth would, however, not be happy with this. Instead, it would emphasize that we are *all* creatures of ideology in its broadest sense. We all have values and make assumptions which probably 'fit' the dominant social order in some way. It is therefore somewhat unrealistic (indeed a bit of an *illusion*, ironically) to assume that some of us can magically step outside of all ideology to pronounce on how 'distorted' everyone else's ideology is. All 'truth', in a relaxed interpretation, is relative to existing cultures and ideologies, and restricted interpreters should not presume to claim for themselves the special status of being 'above' the ideological influences within which everyone lives and breathes.

SUMMARY

- The baseline conception of ideology leaves three areas open for further interpretation:

what ideology is supposed to include;

how directly it serves dominant interests;

whether ideologies legitimate power by promoting illusions and distortions or not.

- On each of these issues it is possible to favour a more 'restricted' interpretation or a more 'relaxed' interpretation.
- These terms ('relaxed' and 'restricted') refer not so much to an outright *opposition*, as to a spectrum of different *emphases*.

———————————————— ACTIVITY 2 ————————————————

Bearing the spectrum of interpretations of ideology in mind, consider whether you previously thought of yourself as having 'ideological' views. Perhaps you have never thought of yourself as holding ideological beliefs, and thought only of *others* as being ideologically motivated. If so, can you now see that this involves a 'restricted' interpretation of ideology which can be summarized in the slogan 'you have (false) ideology, I have (true) insight'?

Alternatively, perhaps you *did* previously think of yourself as having an ideology. *Everyone* does, you might say, regardless of whether or not they realize it. If this is your view of ideology, can you see that it is a relatively 'relaxed' one?

Some of the pros and cons of the different interpretations of ideology are worth noting. One novel feature of a relaxed view of the *content* of ideology is how far it extends the concept of ideology away from an equation with *thinking* as such. Not only ideas but all sorts of 'representations'—everyday conversations, the arts, marriage ceremonies, tribal dances, openings of parliament—form part of the symbolic world of ideology. By contrast, a very restricted view of ideological content narrows the field tremendously. Indeed, in some restricted versions, ideology is not merely confined to the realm of ideas, but is virtually equated with the kind of dangerously irrational or false ideas that only supposed 'extremists' or 'fanatics' would hold.

The problem here is that when we equate ideology with irrational and extreme beliefs, it always turns out to be *someone else* who is the 'fanatic', the slave of irrational ideologies, whereas we (of course!) are the exclusive guardians of truth and enlightenment. There are serious moral and scientific pitfalls in taking this kind of omniscient posture. It discourages self-criticism and turns the concept of ideology into a crude weapon of polemic rather than considered analysis. A more relaxed view at least encourages a certain humility and openness to other cultural values, since we are all equally the children of ideologies.

On the other hand, a very relaxed view of the content of ideology perhaps goes too far in the other direction, since ideology appears to become so vague as to lose its distinctive critical edge. After all, the term 'ideology' implies a strong element of condemnation or *critique*, which restricted views to their credit certainly preserve. If, for example, I call your belief in the monarchy 'ideological', it usually indicates that I am being critical of your attitudes, that I think they justify what cannot wholly be justified, and that in some way they give a very *partial* view of social reality. So if you happen to like the Queen's dresses simply as a matter of personal taste in clothing, the concept of ideology probably does not arise. But if, on the other hand, that sartorial appreciation forms part of a more general opinion that the Queen is not only a smart dresser but also a lovely person, an exemplar of family values, and a bulwark against disorder in a turbulent world, *then*, if I were a republican, I would be inclined to say your views were verging on the ideological. This is precisely because they form a set of approving images and assumptions which upholds what from a republican standpoint is an absurdly antiquated institution and an indefensibly aristocratic power structure.

By drawing into the symbolic sphere of ideology all manner of beliefs, practices and attitudes, a relaxed view of the content of ideology risks equating ideology with culture generally. Now it may well be that most cultural phenomena do have an ideological *aspect,* but 'culture' as such is a much broader and more descriptive term than 'ideology', covering just about everything to do with human beliefs, habits and artifacts. So if ideology becomes so broad as to cover the whole symbolic realm, and begins to lose that important implication of critique, then we might well ask: Why bother with 'ideology' at all? Why not just stick to 'culture' or 'common sense'?

On the question of whether ideology is the opposite of 'truth', a relaxed view tends to suggest that we are all *equally* creatures of ideology. Certainly, this helps dispel the inflated idea that mere humans can aspire to an omniscient 'God's eye' view of truth beyond all taint of ideology. And it is now widely accepted amongst scientists and philosophers that all truths are formulated from within *some* perspective or other. To that extent, it is important not to take the restricted view of ideology as being equivalent to sheer *distortion* too far. Nevertheless, a very relaxed view would have it that because all views, without exception, are ideological, then no theory or assertion can be more valid or truthful, less ideological, than any other. This stance, you may remember from Unit 9, is known as a *relativist* position, and if pushed far enough it can lead to intellectual complacency or despair. Moreover, if the claim 'all is relative' is itself valid, it appears to be valid in a distinctly *non-relative* sense. In other words, when pushed to the limit, relativism appears to *contradict* itself, and this to some extent supports a more restricted interpretation of ideology because the latter is very firmly non-relativist in spirit.

Finally, throughout these debates between 'restrictive' and 'relaxed' interpretations of what ideology is and how ideologies sustain the social order, we need to remember that they still share an overall 'baseline' conception: that all ideologies are a way of making sense of the world, offer social identities, and connect directly or indirectly to prevailing power structures.

1.5   HOW IDEOLOGIES WORK

We noted earlier that ideologies do not necessarily succeed in fulfilling their supposed roles/functions, such as securing social integration or sustaining the interests of dominant groups. But let us assume for a moment that they do always succeed; that ideologies work; that they are effective. A question then arises which we have not yet fully addressed: How do they manage this? How do (dominant) ideologies work? There are probably five main features which can be identified when they are working effectively.

1   Firstly, ideologies present their ideas as being both *rational* and *natural*. In spite of the fact that ideologies are very much social products, having only a limited currency in time and place, they encourage their adherents to believe that the states of affairs they endorse are perfectly natural. How many times, for instance, have you heard the opinion that it is only 'natural' that women are more caring and less competitive than men? Or that 'boys will be boys'? Or that tribal societies are 'primitive', or that black people are unwelcome because it is only 'human nature' for people to stick with their 'own kind' against outsiders? In each of these examples, part of the force of the ideology is to assume that its norms are the only rational or natural ones to adopt, so that other views are correspondingly unnatural, deviant or irrational. A closely related feature of ideologies is that they do not present themselves as valid just for a particular time and place, for the here and now; rather they are usually projected as stretching way back in time to the very roots of what is culturally important for a society.

2   The second feature is that ideologies work to cover over or resolve the sources of *conflict* in a society. Dominant ideologies usually attempt to conceal social contradictions; counter-ideologies for their part usually propose that a wholly different form of society is the only way to remove the very sources of such contradictions. Unit 16, for example, considered the suggestion that the liberal belief in equal opportunities in democratic capitalist societies plays down the fact that the wealth and power structures of such societies make effective equal participation by the mass of the people highly *un*likely. Or again, the widespread official use of the term 'people's democracies' to describe various Communist states prior to the mid-1980s was one way in which the general *lack* of popular control in these societies could be rationalized. In striving to secure conformity and cohesion, dominant ideologies tend to play down or counteract endemic conflicts.

3   Thirdly, ideologies present what are in practice rather partial or sectional ideas as being *universal*. Ideologies are partial in that they never give a complete picture of the phenomena they deal with. But the implication is usually that they are doing just that: presenting the true essence of the matter. Ideologies are also partial, in the sense of being *sectional*; that is, they often emerge from or speak for the values and interests of particular groups. Yet they come across as being appropriate for everyone without exception, and thus claim a universal validity.

4   The fourth feature of ideologies is that they tend to come in *packages* or *chains* of meanings. Rather than putting forward single ideas which are to be judged strictly by their logical force or empirical validity, ideologies tend to generate a whole series of connected terms and emotive mental associations. These associations combine to create very distinctive 'discourses': distinct ways of seeing, thinking and talking. The favoured ideological meanings of the preferred discourse are then invested with a very *positive* approving 'charge' whilst contrary ideological messages are charged *negatively*. This feature thus highlights the centrality of *language* to ideology and the remarkable way in which the use of language in a particular style can trigger off a whole chain of ideological images and reasoning.

Perhaps the best source of illustrations of this crucial feature of ideological language is to be found in the mass media. In China, in June 1989, for example, there was a major political upheaval which resulted in at least 1,000 students and other 'pro-democracy' forces being killed by troops in Beijing's Tianenmen Square. The Chinese authorities, through the mass media, made every effort to convey the view that the initial protest was in no way a legitimate political movement or genuine contribution to democracy in China. Rather, it was presented as an instigation of social 'turmoil' fomented deliberately by alien 'bourgeois' agents and 'criminals'; it was these 'counter-revolutionary' elements and not the 'people's army' who were violently destroying the possibility of civilized, ordered change in China's evolving democratic system. In this case, a momentous ideological struggle was being waged around the chains of association of such words as 'democracy'—'freedom'—'the people'—'social order'. For the students and their allies the events in Beijing's Tianenmen Square represented a popular democratic protest against corruption and authoritarianism in the Chinese leadership, and against stagnation and repression in the Chinese Communist system. For the Chinese Communist Party leadership, Communism had no need of the kind of 'capitalist-style' democracy that the dissidents were advocating—it already had its 'higher' brand of people's democracy. Above all, they wanted order to be firmly re-established, no matter what the temporary cost. Neither the rights and wrongs of this episode, nor the evidence in favour of either standpoint are our concern at the moment. It is the sheer power of language and the way it distributes positive and negative charges along the chains of ideological meanings that are most significant for our purposes.

———————————————————— ACTIVITY 3 ————————————————————

Examine the following press cuttings. They concern the 1985 Tottenham 'riot' in Britain. What 'chains of association' can you identify in these reports of events?

81 hurt in Tottenham rampage

RIOTERS KILL POLICEMAN

Six are shot as black mobs hurl firebombs

By BRIAN SILK, GRAHAM JONES and JOHN WEEKS

A policeman was slashed to death with a machete last night in a huge riot by hundreds of black youths in Tottenham — the first officer to die in the 1980s clashes. Another is critically ill after concrete was dropped on his head, and three colleagues, a TV technician and two reporters were hit by shotgun blasts.

A total of 81 people needed hospital treatment — 58 of them police. One of the shot officers was seriously ill with a stomach wound. The slashed constable died in North Middlesex hospital, Enfield, while being treated for a wound in the neck. Police reinforcements brought in from all over London included marksmen from the crack D11 firearms unit, and teams with teargas equipment.

The riot followed the death of Mrs Cynthia Jarrett, a 20-stone West Indian divorcée who collapsed — apparently from heart failure — as police searched her house in Tottenham on Saturday.

They had earlier arrested and charged one of her sons.

As one unconscious policeman was carried away by colleagues, one shouted: "The bastards are using shotguns."

There were cheers from police shortly before midnight when a Metropolitan Police helicopter swooped over the flats in the Broadwater Farm council estate, the rioters' stronghold, illuminating them with a searchlight in an attempt to pinpoint any gunmen.

At 12.30 a.m. Chief Supt Michael Jeffers reported "a large number of men lying in ambush" on the estate. Police were prepared to wait for the situation to cool.

"We'll wait" he said. "Time is on our side."

Scores of police relaxed, many of them collapsing exhausted, on the pavements, lying down on their shields, or sitting with their backs against garden walls.

"We're obviously in for a long night," said one.

A chilling echo of Ulster

Sir Kenneth Newman, Metropolitan Police Commissioner, visited the scene of the rioting early today and then went straight to visit injured police officers in hospital.

The escalation of rioters using weapons, and the sheer viciousness of young thugs using a tight complex of flats to battle police, brought a chilling parallel with Belfast to London.

And unlike all other race riots in Britain since 1980, this was confined to a residential area, with few shops and targets for looters.

The all-too-familiar mob armoury of petrol bombs, bricks, bottles and chunks of paving stones showered down on squads in riot gear.

Smoke from blazing cars swirled over the estate.

Police claimed to have spotted a gunman on a first-floor balcony in Griffin Road with what was described as "a long black-barrelled weapon."

Violence had exploded at nightfall after a weekend of growing tension following the death of 49-year-old Mrs Jarrett, who suffered from high blood pressure.

A demonstration outside Tottenham police station yesterday afternoon was dispersed, but nightfall gave the black mobs the protection they needed.

Youths began stoning police after community leaders addressed a meeting in the estate about a mile from the Spurs football stadium on the other side of Tottenham High Road.

Soon scores of youths, many of them masked, were involved. Then hundreds.

Police advanced, batons pounding Zulu-style on their riot shields. The petrol bombs began arcing through the night with their comet-tails of fire.

"Police made a charge, but they were devastated," said a resident. "They just had not been expecting it."

Just in front of the police line in Adams Road, flames shot into the air from burning cars, occasionally releasing deafening explosions.

Daily Telegraph, 7 October 1985

RED BUTCHERS

By BRIAN HITCHEN

They have made three children fatherless

The brave widow of murdered policeman Keith Blakelock spoke last night of her grief.

Mrs. Elizabeth Blakelock said she had no hatred for the rioters who killed her husband.

"I feel pity for them. I don't think they can know what they have done," she said.

"They left me a widow and made three children fatherless. Do they know that?"

She talked as police revealed there was evidence that Trotskyist and Communist agitators were behind the violence sweeping Britain's cities.

Pc Blakelock, 40, was hacked to death by a gang armed with knives and machetes during the Tottenham riots.

Suffered

A witness said: "They went for him like a pack of hyenas."

Police suffered 223 other casualties in the violence, 60 of whom needed hospital treatment.

There were just 20 civilians injured and only 16 arrests made.

A .38 calibre bullet was removed from the stomach of one officer last night. Pc Stuart Patt, 25, was said to be "comfortable" in Whittington Hospital.

The bullet, fired from a hand-gun confirms police fears that heavy-gauge weapons were used against them on Sunday.

Pc Patt, a married man, lives in Barking.

Metropolitan Police Chief Sir Kenneth Newman spoke publicly last night for the first time of the part played by the hard Left in racial clashes sweeping Britain.

"Activists are engaged in stirring up this kind of trouble," he said.

Left-wing infiltrators aim to spread race hatred and set black against white. Their object is to wreck and destroy.

While buildings blaze and shops are looted, the agitators melt into the night before the police can arrest them.

"Then they wait for the next excuse in another town to rip apart the very fabric of British life," a security specialist said.

Many senior police officers believe that the hard-Left are succeeding in the campaign of terror among inner-city communities because of the law enforcement officers' fears of upsetting a delicate racial balance.

Daily Star, 8 October 1985

My own reading of these excerpts was as follows (though I do stress that this is my personal understanding, since in discussing the ideological associations of language use there is always room for differences of nuance and interpretation).

Perhaps the first thing I noticed was that, although presented as 'reports' or factual descriptions of events, the excerpts seem to set off what are actually highly controversial trains of thought. In the very title of the *Telegraph* piece, I get the impression not only that very serious violence has occurred, but that it has been perpetrated, perhaps deliberately, by blacks against the police, the officers of the state. The headline 'Rioters kill policeman' could in that sense be taken to imply that the violence against the police was not only a major *outcome* of the disturbance, but may also have been one of its *aims*. Throughout the report, the impression is given (through remarks about the 'ambush', the 'rioters' stronghold', 'masked youths', etc.) that the violence was well-disciplined on the night,and perhaps even organized in advance. Notice how important the use of the little ordinary words are in suggesting things. For example, we are not told that 'hundreds of black youths' were *involved* in the 'huge riot', but that the latter was '*by*' the youths. Again, the key difference this linguistic nuance makes — to me at least — is to suggest organization rather than chaotic spontaneity.

Beyond this overall picture of the character of the riotous disturbance, there seems to me to be two main emotive chains in play. One is to a greater or lesser extent racist. The popular racist phrase 'black bastards' is intimated, through the mouth of the unconscious policeman's colleague. The reference to 'black mobs' excludes by definition the possible involvement of white people, and moreover conjures up time-worn white prejudices to the effect that black people are inherently dangerous and uncivilized. Indeed, even though the phrase 'pounding Zulu-style' is used ironically to describe the actions of the *police*, the very phrase triggers the thought that, in spite of the irony, the police are not only the 'thin blue line' in times of trouble, but also the thin *white* line, using like tactics against like, just as in the glorious days of British colonial pacification of tribes in 'darkest Africa'.

Similarly, in paragraphs 7–10, a brief dramatic narrative is presented, where the police are portrayed in a seige-like situation and we are drawn into their words and feelings 'on the ground'. Such a technique of reportage invites our identification with the 'collapsed' and 'exhausted' officers as they face an arguably unreasonable degree of 'viciousness' directed against them. The report does not include a similarly dramatic story line from the other participants' standpoint, yet later there were numerous accusations of *police* violence and police racism, made by residents of the Broadwater Farm estate. The point, then, is not that the reporters are failing to report what they see. Rather, what they see, the information they receive, and deeply-buried assumptions about the norms of our society, all inevitably make a brief snapshot of events somewhat *partial*, and always governed by ideological associations of one kind or another.

A second ideological chain around the idea of *terrorism* is then blended in. In itself, of course, 'terrorism' is another of those terms which provokes familiar stereotypes and strong responses. And yet, on closer inspection, its exact meaning is hard to pin down and it is often difficult to decide just *which* people and *what* causes are to be condemned in its name. Notoriously, one person's 'terrorist' is someone else's 'freedom fighter'. Although the word 'terrorist' is not used, in the *Telegraph's* set of stereotypes (whether consciously intended or not), black youths on a North London high-rise estate become associated with images of political terrorism through use of the language of 'petrol bombs', 'comet-tails of fire', 'masked youths', 'gunmen', 'a chilling parallel with Belfast', and so on.

There is another, apparently minor, ideological thread in this report, namely the description of the civilian who died. Cynthia Jarrett is described as a '20-stone West Indian divorcee'. However, this short reference actually reveals a great deal about the *sexist* ideology of news reportage and our culture generally. The marital status and weight of Ms Jarrett have very little to do with what happened to her, and yet those few words contrive to present an unsympathetic and disapproving character portrait which seeks out a similar response in the reader. Again, as with the other 'threads' of meaning I have discussed, it is unlikely that such sexist ideological associations were deliberately *intended* by the journalists concerned. But then again, ideological connotations are very powerful precisely *because* they are often partly subconscious.

Turning to the other report, the *Daily Star* introduces a new set of 'negative' images, namely those associated with 'reds'. Here, the ultimate goals and alleged 'planning' of the riots are associated not with black youth but with 'Trotskyist and Communist agitators'. There is, however, a very similar *logic* at work which asks us to identify positively with some things and to recoil in anger from others. Indeed, in spite of their other political differences, there are interesting similarities between the Chinese Communist authorities and the British capitalist press. Both prey on and encourage popular fears of disorder.

The Chinese Communist Party spoke of the damaging spread of the turmoil, the British press talked generally of the 'breakdown of order' and occasionally of an 'orgy of rioting'. In the Chinese case a political movement is being identified as essentially criminal, in the British case a social protest is being presented as politically subversive. In both instances, the feelings of the 'people' are assumed to be on the side of order, and the authorities claim to be more 'democratic' than the protesters, so that any disorder is assumed to be both threatening and undemocratic. It follows that 'turmoil' must therefore be the deliberate work of a band of subversives—bourgeois elements in the one case, red and black malcontents in the other.

5   The fifth and last feature of ideology that I want to discuss is the way in which such chains of ideological meaning, or ideological *discourses*, attempt to make a very personal appeal to you as an individual. The French Marxist philosopher, Louis Althusser coined the term 'interpellation' for this very feature (Althusser, 1972). This useful but unfamiliar piece of jargon means that ideologies address or 'hail' you as a person, in your heart of hearts, for the ideological cause or the discourse in question. It is vital here to repeat that ideologies are not just systems of logical ideas in the abstract, but that they operate through *language* and that they circulate compelling moral images.

Lord Kitchener's famous poster which sought recruits to fight in the First World War

That is why we speak of ideological 'discourses'. Within ideological discourses you personally are being inescapably addressed and appealed to. You are being asked to identify yourself with the values and perceptions of the ideology. You are being 'interpellated' as one of 'us' and not one of 'them'.

This assumption of *you* being one of *us* is very powerful. Other key terms which attract us to particular ideological standpoints include the reference to what is 'normal' as opposed to what is 'deviant'; what is 'healthy' as opposed to what is 'sick'; what is 'rational' as against what is 'irrational'; and so on. An interesting feature of ideologies, it follows, is that although their overall importance lies in their *mass* political character, they actually work at a surprisingly concrete, subjective level. 'Your country needs *you*' said Lord Kitchener's famous poster which sought recruits to fight in the First World War.

His authoritative finger almost bursts through the hoarding to single out you personally, even though of course the message applies to everyone, to every 'you' that happens to be out there. Now according to Althusser, this is how *all* ideologies work. We are all 'recruited' by the appeal of the language of the ideological discourse in question. We are both *invited* and yet *commanded* to display our allegiance to the authorities of that ideology. Such authorities might be particular authority figures (generals, presidents, queens, ruling classes, party leaders, etc.), or they might be sets of beliefs and values (patriarchy, capitalism, Islam, Communism, liberalism, etc.). This capacity of ideology to operate on our subjective sense of identity is crucial, and it reminds us that subscribing to an ideology is never just a matter of intellectual agreement. It is also a matter of emotional allegiance. (In Unit 20, this connection between ideology and social and personal identity will be developed further.)

SUMMARY

Ideologies 'work':

- by making their values appear natural and rational;
- by concealing or denying contradictions;
- by appearing truly universal;
- by weaving together linguistic chains of association;
- by addressing or 'interpellating' you as a subject.

1.6   HOW IDEOLOGIES ARE TRANSMITTED

The power of ideology lies in its capacity to activate a strong sense of what is right and proper as against what is deviant and wrong. But ideologies can activate us in this powerful way only if they become part of the general cultural currency. In other words, they need to be effectively and publicly *transmitted*. Ideological transmission can be thought of in two main ways, and these coincide with the relaxed and restricted interpretations of ideology discussed in Section 1.4.

On a relaxed interpretation, emphasis is placed on the general effects of the process of *socialization*. Inevitably, as we are socialized into language and reflective ability, we gradually 'pick up' the values and beliefs of the wider culture into which we are born. From our parents and immediate family in early life, we absorb general social and political norms as well as the unique personal 'ambience' of those people and their way of life. In school too, we are encouraged to grow intellectually to an extent, but within the limits set by the form and contents of the knowledge we are taught. This knowledge is normally organized quite strictly around the very specific traditions, requirements and perspectives of our society, a society in which we are eventually expected to play a responsible adult role.

Workplaces and neighbourhoods are further channels of communication in which political and cultural values are circulated. Of course, it may be that these ideological channels do not have a 'one-way' message to deliver. Factories and neighbourhoods, for instance, have sometimes served to sustain a strong working-class identity, one which is precisely *not* that of the 'middle' or 'ruling' class. Even so, factories and other workplaces are dominated by the fact that people have to *work*. And the logic of work involves routines and rewards which depend upon the smooth operation of the labour process and social system. A predominantly capitalist economy, where private firms compete in a 'free mar-ket' and where the overall aim is to produce optimal profits, produces one kind of economic rationality, whereas a centralized 'planned' economy with little private ownership produces a quite different set of norms and goals. In all cases, however, there is bound to be encouraged a sense that the best way of running any economy is the one currently prevalent.

Often in local communities a sense of collectivity undercuts possible differences of interest or political attitudes between people. To that extent, neighbour-hoods are no more one-way transmission belts of dominant ideology than workplaces. On the other hand, neighbourhoods are the places which, for the most part—even in economies which are moving towards 'flexitime' and home-work—people return to *after* work. There, they pick up the pieces of their domestic lives and leisure activities. They shop and socialize and raise famil-ies. They watch TV, play sport, and worry about their house or street. These 'private' pursuits, however, are themselves deeply reflective of 'public' social norms. In modern Britain, for example, sport is predominantly a matter of male competitiveness, and shopping, as Unit 3 made clear, involves the buying and selling of commodities, commodities which are given intense ideological definition through the medium of advertising.

The point, then, is that across the gamut of socialization, individuals' ideas are shaped by a number of settings and institutions. They develop their own sense of identity and 'belonging' within these settings. They absorb the predominant social codes of behaviour, interaction and expectation. In innumerable half-conscious ways, they take on and reproduce prevalent ideological meanings.

It is open to us at this point (as in Section 1.4) to adopt a more restricted interpretation of the process of ideological transmission than is perhaps allowed for in the general notion of socialization. This way of looking at trans-mission would involve thinking of ideas as being *deliberately* and *actively* disseminated through institutions by specific groups and agencies. Take the mass media, for example. On the restricted view of ideology, newspapers and television have owners and controllers, editors and programme makers, who are major opinion formers—hidden persuaders, as Unit 3 put it. Even if these agencies *do* try merely to 'reflect' public opinion, such opinion already has a limited ideological range owing to the influence of the other components of socialization. In addition, it is hard to believe that those in leading positions in the media do not seek to mould the public in their own image. This critical line of thought effectively suggests that the mass media is in the business of thought control by way of creating 'necessary illusions' (Chomsky, 1989). This debate around the ideological role of the media is extended in TV 09, which should be regarded as essential viewing for this unit. A number of cartoons indicating similarly sceptical views of the media in the East and the West are reproduced in Figure 1.

'We now present a press conference with neither questions nor answers'
Source: *Polityka*, 17 November 1982

'They keep on saying there's a crisis but they broadcast the same news'
Source: *Polityka*, 19 March 1983

Figure 1   Similar sceptical views of the ideological role of the media in the UK and Poland

Other key ideological institutions are the education and legal systems. For example, the validity of assumptions about what girls and boys ought to do in life, how they ought to behave, depends greatly upon whether those expectations are reinforced or challenged in schools and colleges. Legal ideologies, such as the idea that all citizens are equal before the law and that the law is 'above' politics, are also very powerful. Of course, as social scientists, we are interested not only in assessing the power of such ideological themes, but in checking them against the reality of power as it is exercised within institutions. We need to find out whether, for example, there is genuine equality before the law, or whether there is 'one law for the rich and another for the poor'.

In terms of agencies who transmit ideological discourses, there are several possibilities. Organized political parties are certainly important. Business concerns (newspaper proprietors, state enterprises, multinational companies) form influential and powerful interest groups, which have the resources to fundamentally affect the stability and character of the economy on which a society draws for its survival and well-being. Trade unions too can sometimes assert their influence. Professionals of one type or another (editors, teachers, judges) are also important in the process of ideological transmission.

Recalling our overall Block IV theme of *power*, it is worth emphasizing here that *the state* itself has a crucial interest in the content and transmission of dominant ideological themes. Many of the key ideological institutions—the public broadcasting networks, education, the law—are after all *state* institutions. We have seen how the 'forces of order'—whether in China or Britain—move swiftly to stigmatize political challenges to the state. This portrayal of deviancy and subversion existing amongst an evil 'minority' is a powerful way of 'agenda setting' (to cite Unit 15). So the state is a key player in the ideological game, and it has the ultimate coercive power to reinforce the rules of the game. Moreover, some of the other agencies just mentioned—businesses, political parties, professions—can only further their own interests and ideologies by either securing the goodwill of the state, or even by seeking to control the state in various ways.

SUMMARY

The transmission of ideologies is achieved through a variety of institutions and informal channels. They are circulated and reinforced, more or less consciously or deliberately:

- in the general process of socialization (through families, peer groups, neighbourhoods and workplaces);
- in the institutions of the private and public sectors (the media, education, the law);
- by parties, business concerns, professions and other interest groups;
- by the state itself.

1.7 THE IMPACT OF IDEOLOGY

We have assumed so far that people *are* susceptible to the power of ideology; that ideologies *do* indeed work, in other words. But now we must ask: is this really the case? What if ideologies on the whole do *not* work? After all, the impression given when discussing ideology is that all our tiny minds are 'filled' with or moulded by systems of ideas that are not of our own making nor in our own interests. This is a very *deterministic* picture of the impact of ideology; that is, it makes it seem as though we as individuals have no free choice in the matter. Yet we clearly do have some choice, and the impact of ideology is unlikely to be total for a number of reasons.

For one thing, the key terms of ideologies can be contested from different perspectives. 'Freedom' and 'democracy' are classic examples of ideological principles which are claimed as exclusively theirs by political movements of both the Right and the Left. Yet there is something slightly ambiguous about such terms when they are extracted from their wider chain of ideological meanings. This ambiguity of ideological language reduces the possibility of a monopoly of ideological meaning being established.

A second, related point is that in seeking to establish one ideological 'chain' of meaning, alternative meanings are inevitably referred to, albeit in a very negative way. This opens up a space for debate, however small, in which *counter-ideologies* to the dominant ideologies can emerge. The popularization of the revamped Conservative Party in the late 1970s, for example, depended as much on its success in stigmatizing *socialist* and *social democratic* principles as on the affirmation of its *own* values. Much of the ideological repertoire of modern conservatism is designed to show that socialist policies are 'extreme', 'alien', 'un-British' and 'inefficient'; and that social reformist compromises are 'weak' and 'wet'. Yet in the very moment that such alternatives are castigated, their availability as some sort of alternative is actually confirmed.

Thirdly, ideological 'ideals' seldom square *totally* with people's lived experience. There is thus always some room for people to argue out ideological themes in relation to their own stock of values and practices. And frequently these experiences happen to contain elements which 'chime' better with *counter-ideologies* than with *dominant* ideologies, thus challenging to an extent the latter's 'reign' over the political culture. For instance, it is appropriate to think of the feminist challenge to male domination in this kind of way, in that many women, who might be reluctant to call themselves feminists as such, nevertheless often reel off a stream of negative experiences and feelings concerning the conduct of men which in effect support the contentions of feminist theory.

Another way of putting this point is to say that we often encounter ideological *dilemmas* or contradictions, rather than one-way messages. Even everyday expressions of sheer ideological bias can reveal ambivalence as well as prejudice. Take, for example, the statement of one respondent to a social science survey of racist attitudes: 'I have nothing against foreigners. But their attitude, their aggression is scaring. We are no longer free here. You have to be careful' (Billig *et. al.,* 1988). This declaration opens with an apparently tolerant attitude which takes the familiar form, 'I am not prejudiced, but ...'. The 'but' then indicates the main emphasis, which often turns out in fact to be an expression of prejudice! Yet, all is not totally clear-cut even in this case. The general attitude strikes me as being more *apprehensive* than simply bigoted, and the opening sentence does not have a completely hollow ring. Furthermore, the concern about freedom is a little too pat. It sounds like a repetition of *someone else's* beliefs (perhaps those of a popular newspaper or a National Front acquaintance). I want to ask: he or she says that, but what does the speaker *really* think? In other words, although the overall emphasis is undoubtedly of a racist character, there does seem to be some evidence of a contradictory ideological dilemma in play here.

A fourth reason why the impact of ideology is seldom total is that there are usually *several* ideological possibilities as to how our 'identities' are developed, and these sometimes crosscut and undermine one another. You might, for example, happen to be a mother with no 'official' paid job, and so you will be subject to all the pressures around you *to think of yourself* as being a mother at home—with all the various positive and negative images that this role carries. But you may also be white, middle-class, involved in a neighbourhood watch scheme, an expert on yoga, a hillwalker, a member of the SNP, and an Open University student. Whilst it is easy to construct ideological stereotypes or 'packages' out of such attributes, it could also be the case that some of the interests and images clash with others. In our male-centred culture, for example, the image of the studious mother at home does not readily square with that of being a political activist. So whilst our subjective ideological profiles contain an important element of external imposition, there is usually enough 'space' within the ideological 'field' for us to negotiate our self-images and to contest dominant expectations and values. This aspect of social identity is extensively explored in Unit 20.

Fifthly, ideologies are not static entities: they change and adapt over time and in accordance with circumstances. For example, in the eighteenth century, British 'patriotism' was considerably more radical or 'Leftist' in its implications than today, when it is normally regarded as a 'Rightist' or at least a conservative sentiment. The idea of the 'freeborn Englishman' often served as the banner under which labourers and artisans challenged—often in a distinctly 'riotous' manner—élite rule within the British state. Similarly, Mikhail Gorbachev's version of Communism was significantly more 'capitalistic' than that of preceding Soviet leaders. So ideologies change, sometimes quite dramatically, and the ambiguous nature of many key ideological terms (such as 'freedom', 'justice', 'efficiency', 'the individual') ensures that even apparently inflexible ideologies have the potential to be 'massaged' in different directions.

The view I've been developing is that the power of ideology in general is strong, but that no particular set of ideological associations is likely to rule completely unchallenged or is wholly free from ambiguities. Societies and individuals are perhaps better seen as ideological targets rather than ideological puppets. Within this approach, it is still possible to accept that there are dominant or at least *prevalent* ideologies which have a distinct advantage. And this is partly because they stem from the actions or interests of powerful groups in society who either control or have special access to the means of ideological transmission. So although I've tried to give a complex view of how we 'make sense' of society within the process of ideological subjectivity, I would still want to stress that a central function of ideology is maintaining the social power of dominant groups.

Other social scientists might disagree with this conclusion. They would ask: what if political and social power can readily be maintained *without* the assistance of ideology? They would argue that society 'holds together' not so much because ideology provides the 'glue', but because people are generally preoccupied with much more *pragmatic* concerns. The dramatic collapse of Communist Party power in the nations of Eastern Europe in 1989–90 would seem to suggest that many citizens of those countries 'went along' with Communist control for thirty or more years without truly internalizing the substantial degree of ideological pressure put on them during that period to see themselves as legitimately represented by the Party and the state. This shows that people can *comply* with a social order, without necessarily *endorsing* it. They may go along with the dominant power structure, not because they believe in the dominant ideology, but because they need to get on with the business of working for a living, and keeping themselves and their households simply ticking over.

Apart from active opposition, many people just feel completely *alienated* from all available political ideologies, and are *apathetic* as a result. Much research data supports this interpretation for liberal democratic societies as well as state socialist ones. Reviewing research on working-class attitudes to the British social order, one group of authors note that 'the common conclusion' is that working-class people mostly reveal an attitude of 'pragmatism, rather than either acceptance of or opposition to the dominant values' (Marshall *et al*., 1989). Some writers have further concluded that if there are any dominant ideologies at all, then they serve not so much to persuade the *masses*, but rather to provide a comforting world-view for the social *élites* themselves. The masses remain pragmatic or apathetic.

This argument is effectively that ideology is *not* in the end terribly important for the maintenance of social order. And the argument gains in strength once we remember the role of sheer *force* in holding society together. As Unit 15 indicated, there are enforceable laws and serious penal sanctions which control what can be legitimately tolerated in all known societies. And if you do happen to fall foul of these laws, you are liable very quickly to feel the physical power which lies behind the everyday social 'consensus'. This reality is often quite enough to persuade people to 'go along with' the prevailing order.

There is no easy resolution to this debate about whether the power of ideologies amongst the mass of the people in modern societies is strong, weak, or non-existent. It is something that always requires further research and discussion. And it is something that you must begin to make up your own mind about. My own personal view is that the power of ideologies *is* strong. I *do* think that we develop compelling images, ideals and expectations that contribute significantly to the maintenance (and occasional overthrow) of existing power relations. Certainly, there remains every indication that any vacuum left by the decline of one major ideological influence (such as Communism) will be quickly filled by the revival of other potent visions (such as ethnic and religious fundamentalism) or by the emergence of new ideological 'combinations'. But having said that, the impact of ideology is seldom so strong as to rule out many contrary considerations, such as the contradictions between and within ideologies, or the important elements of pragmatism and even cynicism which frequently dictate how we think and behave.

2 IDEOLOGY AND THE TRADITIONS OF SOCIAL THOUGHT

The discussion in this unit connects closely with some of the points made in the course about the four traditions of social thought.

===================== READER =====================

Before reading on, you should read Section 4 of Chapter 22 on 'Traditions of social thought' in the Course Reader. The section is entitled 'The presence of the traditions in the society to be studied'.

The main point of the section you have just read is that the traditions have a kind of double-sided existence in modern Western society. First of all, they exist as *intellectual traditions*, acting as veritable storehouses of ideas, categories and approaches which we can draw on for analytical purposes. So we would want to know how the concept of 'ideology' is used in each tradition. Secondly, the traditions themselves exist as *political ideologies*. Thus, David Coates relates how the traditions have developed as crucial resources for practical social movements in history. In the heat of this political battleground, it can be seen how easily abstract theories are converted into a variety of political programmes and values, moulded to suit the needs of the moment, and the needs of the movement.

Considering the traditions as *political ideologies*, we would want to think about how they strive to make sense of reality, what kind of social identity they appeal to, and whether they can be associated with the interests of particular social groups or relations of power. For example, liberalism as presented in the Traditions essay, understands society mainly in terms of self-regarding individuals. Moreover, liberalism 'constructs' this sense of identity by forging a chain of positive images around notions such as competition—reward by merit—the market—private property—personal freedom—equality of opportunity. By the same token, liberalism involves the attempt to *discredit* various alternative chains of association which favour 'collectivist' norms or values. Thus, liberalism casts a negative aura around ideas of solidarity, planning, the state, freedom from exploitation, and equality of condition.

A further point to be drawn out from the way liberalism functions as an ideology is that the liberal vision attempts to secure *social integration*, or acts as a 'social cement', insofar as it seeks to counteract tendencies towards social disintegration. For liberals, these tendencies are usually held to stem from the awareness of class or group conflict. At the same time, liberalism itself had a distinct class origin amongst the rising commercial and agrarian bourgeoisie of the eighteenth century. It was later associated with the industrial 'captains of industry' in the nineteenth century and to this day has its greatest appeal amongst the aspiring middle classes in the private sector of the economy.

In order to assess the *impact* of liberal ideology, the extent of various commonsense 'I'm all right, Jack' or 'I did it my way' attitudes would have to be examined. So too would the extent of the popular commitment to a sense of individual liberty in relation to the powers of the state. Also relevant is the electoral success during the 1980s of Margaret Thatcher's neo-liberal brand of Conservatism.

As to the *transmission* of liberalism, individualistic themes are amply conveyed through the mass media, whether in news reports of events in countries with different political cultures, or in TV dramas featuring successful but idiosyncratic heroes. As mentioned, neo-liberalism is advocated by (part of) the modern Conservative Party in a general way, but in a still more tightly focused manner by institutions such as the Adam Smith Institute and organizations such as Aims of Industry.

The preceding account of liberalism is really only a first step in approaching liberalism as an ideology. There are two reasons for this shorthand approach. One is that my main example of an ideology 'in action' is not liberalism but nationalism, which is the subject of the next section of this unit. Secondly, you will be pursuing the analysis of the traditions of social thought in detail in the D103 Summer School. So I only want to trigger off that process here. However, I do suggest that you make a start on that activity by thinking about each of the traditions as an ideology and considering:

- how it constructs distinctive chains of ideological association;
- how it constructs a sense of social identity (e.g. around individuals in the case of liberalism, around social class in marxism's case);
- how it is related to the rise or current interests of particular social movements and groups;
- its means of transmission and degree of impact.

———————————————— ACTIVITY 4 ————————————————

From your reading of Chapter 22, and following my analysis of liberalism, try to complete the following grid. To get you started, I have filled in the whole of the first column, and also the rows for liberalism and conservatism. Try to work out what the rows for marxism and social reformism would look like. And don't be afraid to add question marks after particular entries—as I have done under the 'Current group interests served' column. Often our entries depend some-what on *which* tradition we generally favour. To cite class interests rather than other group interests, for example, is generally an indication that a marxist analysis is being adopted. So some care is needed here—it is the *attempt* to complete the matrix which matters, not the end result.

Tradition	Social identity high-lighted	Related associ-ations	Group source	Current group in-terests served	Measure of impact	Means of trans-mission
Liberalism	Individuals	Private property Competition Personal freedom Merit	Eighteenth-cen-tury commerce Nineteenth-cen-tury industrial bourgeoisie	Private sector Middle class	TV heroes Thatcherism Common—sense individualism	(Part of) the Con-servative Party Aims of Industry Adam Smith Insti-tute
Marxism	Social classes					
Conservatism	Loyalty to estab-lished authority	Family values Authority of state Human nature	Eighteenth- and nineteenth-cen-tury patrician reac-tion to democratic revolution Landed interests	Upper class in coun-try and city?	Fears about law and order Support for monarchy Popularity of cen-sorship	(Part of) the Con-servative Party *Salisbury Review* 'Old school tie' networks Anti-permissive-ness movements
Social reformism	Common citizen-ship					

Let us now turn to the other important 'face' of the traditions: their existence as *intellectual traditions*; that is, sources of ideas and approaches to be drawn upon in social science analysis. Here, the traditions offer a number of ways of 'making sense' of ideology; and, as might be expected, these offerings compete with each other in certain respects. Marxists, for example, argue that ideol-ogies are essentially rationalizations of *class* identities and class advantages. And in the modern world, they maintain, the most powerful dominant ideol-other political phenomenon (socialism, fascism, etc.) matches nationalism's ogies are those which serve to rationalize the capitalist system of economic production. Liberalism would thus be regarded as a form of bourgeois ideology. Liberals, for their part, see ideologies as intolerant and often 'extreme' doc-trines which dangerously raise collective passions (the state, class, religion, etc.) above the interests of individual people. Doctrines such as marxism would fall into that category as far as liberals are concerned.

Conservatives are less inclined to see ideology as having a particular content. Rather they see ideology as a *type* of thought pattern, one which imposes artificial and abstract theoretical conceptions of what society *should* be like on *existing* social bonds (such as those generated by the family or the monarchy) which have proved of durable value in the past. From that angle, conservatives would see both the individuals of liberalism and the classes of marxism as ideological impositions, contrivances which undermine traditional loyalties, and which serve only the interests of intellectual élites.

The social reformist tradition is rather more difficult to place in the discussion. As the Traditions essay indicates, this is probably to do with the relative lack of clear theoretical lines in the reformist tradition. In relation to ideology, as in other theoretical areas, social reformism falls sometimes towards liberal propositions, sometimes towards marxist theses. Social reformists are inclined to share the liberal view that ideologies, usually being 'extreme' beliefs, are politically dangerous. On the other hand, reformists also draw on marxist categories, to the effect that ideologies stemming from class interests—including the liberal-individualist world-view itself—are socially divisive, impeding progress towards the reformist goal of a 'fair' society.

For all their differences in terms of *content*, the traditions do share certain analytical ideas. They all draw attention, for example, to the partial and selective nature of ideological thinking. They all highlight its powerful emotive force, as well as its explanatory ambitions. Furthermore, there are relatively 'restricted' and relatively 'relaxed' versions of all four traditions. In the strict versions, ideologies are commonly perceived as mystifications of reality, perpetrated in order to advance the interests of particular groups. Each tradition then, of course, singles out a different group, and indeed tends to present the *other* traditions as being typical ideological mystifications.

Relaxed advocates of all traditions are more sensitive to the possibility that *all* ideas are necessarily partial, and that *several* interests may be served through ideological means. Thus, whilst highlighting the concepts that are distinctive of each tradition, relaxed advocates of each are less inclined than their stricter colleagues to see ideology as straightforward, deliberate distortion.

3   IDEOLOGICAL ASPECTS OF NATIONALISM

3.1   THE 'IMAGINED COMMUNITY' OF NATIONALISM

As a way of consolidating your work in Sections 1 and 2, I now want us to consider the nature of *nationalism* as an ideological framework. One reason for this focus is that the spread of nationalism has been a major feature of modern times. Indeed, one scholar has argued that 'The history of Europe since the French Revolution has been the history of the rise and development of political nationalism' (Kamenka, 1976). That is no small claim, since it implies that no influence on the growth of modern society. Yet in another sense that claim is not big enough, since it is restricted to 'Europe'. This reveals a kind of 'First World' bias which omits to mention the centrality of nationalism to 'Third World' states, movements and ideologies.

Another reason for the focus on nationalism is that, as we go into the last decade of the twentieth century, both the strength and variety of nationalism seem to be growing very significantly. From the revival of Scottish nationalism in Britain to the escalation of ethnic and nationalist conflict in the USSR, Eastern Europe and Asia, there is little sign of nationalist ideology losing its special power to motivate and mobilize people.

Lastly, the peculiar intensity of nationalist feeling is difficult to account for fully. At times we might even feel that it simply defies explanation. Certainly, no explanation is likely to be uncontroversial. Yet as another writer has said, 'nation-ness is the most universally legitimate value in the political life of our times' (Anderson, 1983), so as social scientists we are under some obligation to try to understand it in analytical terms. And our earlier conceptual discussions of ideology in general do in fact go a long way towards this understanding.

Nationalism, you should note, is not simply a matter of ideology; it is a type of political *movement*. Nevertheless, nationalism has an important ideological aspect, and can readily be seen to conform to our three initial conditions for ideology and our baseline conception of ideology, as presented in Section 1. The central nationalist tenet is that the boundaries of the political state should coincide with those of a distinctive people and culture (i.e. a nation). In attempting to develop this thesis into a popular movement, nationalism certainly aspires to:

1   project a set of *shared ideas* amongst a particular social group;
2   form a relatively *coherent system* of political and social belief;
3   involve a distinctive picture of *power relations*.

In terms of the baseline conception, nationalism:

1   provides meaningful images, ideas and assumptions which help us *make sense* of society;
2   proposes a clear basis for our sense of *social identity*; and
3   legitimizes (or challenges) *power structures* from a particular standpoint.

Beyond this, again following the guidelines of Section 1, we need to look at the typical subjective appeal of nationalist ideological themes, as expressed

Figure 2   Map highlighting the Baltic States of Estonia, Latvia and Lithuania

through language and symbol. We need also to consider the possible social roles of nationalism, its transmission and its impact.

Something of the ideological power of all nationalist sentiments is captured in the following graphic passage describing Estonian nationalism. (Estonia, at the time of writing this unit, was a republic within the Soviet Union. However, being ruled ultimately from Moscow, it was not an independent state—see Figure 2.):

> From a week's television, I keep this image: a young Estonian woman in national costume, standing with others on a stage, with tears streaming down her cheeks. She was not sobbing. On the contrary, she was singing. But the streams of tears flowed on until they were running off her chin in tiny waterfalls.
>
> All this for old songs once forbidden; for a rectangle of cloth striped black, blue and white. Perhaps somebody had spoken of the dead thousands in Siberia who were denied the joy of these days in Tallinn, or of the hero Lembitu slain by the German 'Knights of the Sword' more than 700 years ago. Whatever the prompt, she was weeping for her nation.
>
> Once again, we were being shown the most powerful and enduring of all the spells which are used to bind human beings. Nationalism is the force which Tom Nairn compared to a Janus-head looking back to the reactionary past and simultaneously forward into the future. It is the religion of what Benedict Anderson called 'imagined communities', those passionate identifications with other people far away, never to be met, for whose very existence the patriot has no proof.
>
> (Ascherson, 1988)

Many other nationalisms also invoke the *historic* unity of a people, even though their political objectives are usually very immediate. Nationalist language is full of the phraseology of shared bonds and origins. For example, it frequently summons up images of the 'homeland', or 'motherland', or 'fatherland', in a way which suggests that within a national community people are bonded so closely together as to be almost 'flesh and blood'. Regardless of whether or not you 'get on' with your parents, family bonding is irrevocable. In a similar way, one's national belonging generates strong memories and loyalties, which sometimes seem beyond rational assessment. Thus, most people today, even those who are not nationalist in any organized, party-political sense, find it hard to resist the 'call' of nationalistic discourses. Even hardened Scottish marxists, for example, who would normally seek to foster a spirit of *inter*national solidarity amongst all workers, can be found quietly wearing the tartan and wiping a tear from the corner of the eye whenever they proudly experience their country's sporting team's defeat of England—'the Auld Enemy'!

Nationalist discourse therefore works to create a deep sense of mutual belonging, and in doing so draws upon images of the historic past of a people. When conveyed vividly and systematically, our belonging to a nation will not only feel historically-based, it will seem thoroughly reasonable and *natural*. Partly through the suggestion of a parallel between one's family and one's nation, our subjective sense of being Scottish, or Irish, or Estonian comes very naturally indeed and its emotive power is hard to deny. As a stark example of the 'naturalization' of nationalism, listen to the philosopher Johann Fichte:

> Our earliest common ancestors, the primordial stock of the new culture, the Germans, as the Romans called them, courageously resisted the world domination of the Romans ... Liberty to them meant this:

persisting to remain Germans and continuing the task ... in consonance with the original spirit of their race ... and propagating this independence in their posterity. We, the inheritors of their soil, their language, and their way of thinking, must thank them for being Germans.

(Fichte, *Addresses to the German Nation*, 1807–8)

Notice that Fichte wrote these addresses in the early nineteenth century; yet such sentiments have found a definite echo many times since, notably in the 1930s, and today in the 1990s when nationalism rapidly revived with the reunification of Germany following the Cold War division of the country into two separate states. In the extract from Fichte, you can see that, through the use of language, both a natural and a historic identity is invoked; one that is inherited and passed on to your children. As a potential German, you are being, in Althusser's term, *interpellated* (that is, *addressed*, in this case quite literally) as in your very heart of hearts one of the true subjects of the nationalist discourse. Whatever else divides Germans, it is implied, should now be ignored for the sake of a higher national unity and identity.

John Bull Guards his Pudding.

John Bull: a symbol of English patriotism, first invented in 1780, and increasingly common in the nineteenth–century press

As Ascherson indicated—and whether the nationalism in question is Estonian, German, Argentinian or Scottish—nationalist ideology is to a great extent the work of the *imagination*. Its effects, of course, are very real and are certainly not to be regarded as fictitious. But a nation is an 'imagined community' all the same. Unlike, for instance, a village community, the vast majority of the members of a nation *cannot* come to know one another in a personal or face-to-face-way. Moreover, Fichte's address to the nation was penned fifty or so years *before* the all-German state was founded, and the Germans that he refers to as resisting the Romans were in fact made up of a great many separate agricultural communities, which made little contact with each other prior to the Roman invasions. Finally, as shown in Unit 8, the language of 'race' is often itself highly charged with imaginative artificial qualities: nations and races involve very few 'natural' properties at all. The 'British' and even 'the Scots' are names for *political* and cultural associations which emerge over time. Research often amply reveals many nations to be composed of peoples who, originally, had very different languages, origins and ways of life. For example, one historian has argued that:

> The whole concept of a distinct Highland culture and tradition is a retrospective invention. Before the later years of the seventeenth century, the Highlanders of Scotland did not form a distinct people. They were simply the overflow of Ireland … the imposition of that new tradition with its outward badges (e.g. clans, kilt tartans, bagpipes … haggis etc.) on the whole Scottish nation, was the work of the later eighteenth and early nineteenth century.

(Trevor-Roper, cited in Hobsbawm and Ranger, 1983)

British nationalism gets much of its force from the performance of impressive symbolic rituals of state

So, in an important way, the nation is an imagined community, and the 'naturalization' and 'interpellation' effects of nationalist ideologies often serve to overcome important social differences which might otherwise separate fellow nationals. Whether or not the young Estonian woman described by Ascherson is poor or wealthy, oppressed or privileged, she is part of an appeal to all Estonians to unite, to be recognized first and foremost *as Estonians*, and not as poor, wealthy, oppressed or privileged people. Such national unity is created through language as we have seen. It is also created through *symbols,* such as the national flag and costume; and *rituals*, such as demonstrating in an orderly collective way and singing the national anthem. These things have a powerful subjective effect. For example, British nationalism gets much of its typical force from the regular performance of impressive symbolic rituals of state. Thus, the annual Opening of Parliament, the Coronation and Royal Weddings symbolize both the historic unity and global superiority of 'these islands'. And as they are all based in London, such rituals also tend to emphasize the *English* flavour of Greater British nationalism.

Such rituals can succeed in generating feelings of national loyalty even though global dominance may now be a thing of the past, and even though those who line the streets to catch a glimpse of Her Majesty may have virtually nothing else in common with her *apart* from that feeling of national identification: she is 'our' Queen. The fact that few people know more than the first and last lines of 'Land of Hope and Glory' does not prevent them stirring to it as if they jointly, proudly, composed that hymn to the greatness of Britain!

The language, rituals and symbols of ideology also tend to be 'packaged' into whole chains of association, reflecting another of our components of ideology from Section 1. Think, for example, of Scottish identity. One familiar 'imagined community' of Scotland arises from the whole string of popular images which links together visions of 'grannie's hielan hame' and Rabbie Burns, the Scott Monument and 'Auld Lang Syne', Doctor Finlay and 'A Scottish Soldier', haggis and kilts, bottles of whisky and bottles of 'Irn Bru' (a popular soft drink). Some items in this chain have a 'real' basis, others are pure inventions. *All* of them in a sense are dependent upon their continual re-enactment in the popular imagination. One influential writer has dubbed this phenomenon the 'vast tartan monster' of Scottish popular culture: 'that prodigious array of *kitsch* symbols, slogans, ornaments, banners, war cries, knick-knacks, music hall heroes, icons, sayings and sentiments (not a few of them "pithy") which have for so long defended the name of "Scotland" to the world ... what unbearable, crass, mindless philistinism!' And yet, even this stern critic concedes: 'Ridiculous or not, it is obviously extremely strong ... it is something else to be with it (e.g.) in a London pub on International night, or in the crowd at the annual Military Tattoo in front of Edinburgh Castle' (Nairn, 1981).

As pointed out in Section 1, such ideological chains of association, however strong, can nevertheless sometimes be *ambiguous* and open to amendment. Scottish socialists and radical Scottish nationalists, for example, have long attempted to pull something more 'progressive' and to their tastes out of the 'tartan monster'. The latter is regarded in part by those radical nationalists as being something of an insult to the intellectual traditions and democratic aspirations of Scotland. Without denying elements of the sentimentality (since sentiment is necessary for all subjective identification), Scottish political radicals try nevertheless to build a slightly different chain of association, highlighting different images, such as the struggles of the 'Red Clydesiders' of the 1916–26 period, or the Scottish Enlightenment of the eighteenth century, or the democratic, collective and educative ethos of much Scottish public life. It can thus be seen how different political perspectives on nationalism can compete or overlap around a string of emotive linguistic connections aimed at

'Local heroes' or 'vast tartan monster'?

fixing the 'true' nature of 'the Scottish people'. Nationalist language is therefore always to a degree open to contestation and susceptible to reinterpretation along various lines.

3.2   NATIONALISM AND SOCIAL INTERESTS

In outlining the power of nationalist discourse, we see at the same time how it fulfils three of the four social roles of ideology as introduced in Section 1.3. Nationalism 'makes sense' of society in terms of relations between national peoples and political states. It offers a powerful sense of belonging and identity. And in achieving a passionate sense of cultural identification, it can promote social integration and overcome sources of conflict in a society, such as class division or individual competition.

The question of which *interests* are served by nationalism is not so easy to answer unequivocally. Some would argue that nationalism serves the interests of the whole of modern industrial society. This is because the growth of nationalism, in spite of its tendency to hark back to the misty golden past of its people, is intimately bound up with the process of industrialization and the rise of modern centralized states. Prior to these conditions, social interaction was more directly of a face-to-face nature and socio-economic life was rather more static or stable than in modern times. Belief systems thus tended also to be somewhat static and imbued with a sense of people's 'fixed' position in the natural hierarchy of things.

Over time, and with increasing momentum, industrialization changed much of this ideological climate. Industrial societies, as compared with traditional societies, require intensive technological change. This in turn creates a need for the systematic storage and exchange of information, general communication media, a literate scientific culture, and a substantial degree of social *mobility* in order that knowledge and wealth are widely generated, growth sustained, and incentives for innovation made available. These changes in fact decisively broke up the fabric of traditional societies. In pre-industrial epochs, there was no such driving rationale for a centralized nation-state or for a common literate culture. Only with the consciousness of time passing, of social *change* being the rule rather than the exception, did a true sense of *history* develop. And nationalism itself was arguably just this awareness of a nation as having definite historical roots and as having a kind of historical mission or destiny.

A further point is that the emergence of industrial society and the state in a nationalist climate, once established in some 'leading' countries, inevitably set off a chain reaction of *uneven development* between national peoples. Thus, 'backward' societies began to develop institutions and ideologies which might enable them to 'catch up' with the leading states in order to achieve whatever gains modern society had to offer. Nationalism's great ideological power to mobilize the populace, to create a new dynamic sense of history and cultural identity, therefore became harnessed either to the attempt to 'stay ahead' *or* to 'catch up' economically and politically speaking (Gellner, 1983).

Under certain conditions, however, nationalism can serve as a powerful force of *resistance* against both political expansion and industrial modernization. For example, in the late 1980s a bitter series of nationalist disputes broke out in the southern peripheral republics of the Soviet Union (see Figure 3). Sometimes the targets of this enmity were *other* ethnic minorities, and sometimes it was the Russian majority nation within the USSR (which remarkably contained over a hundred distinct 'nationalities'). In the Trans-Caucasian and Central Asian republics especially, ethnic violence seemed mainly religious, racial and cultural rather than social. Yet such a systematic series of disturbances can also be understood as having an important social and political rationale. When founded after the 1917 revolution, the USSR was mainly a *peasant* society. Its Russian heartlands underwent rapid industrialization during the next few decades. But it had only been in recent years that *all* of the former Soviet Union had been drawn into this process of transformation from a rural to an urban society. This caused tremendous social dislocation amongst the peripheral ethnic communities, especially since it is they who were most exposed to the inefficiency and uncertainty of Soviet industrial society—unemployment, forced geographical and social mobility, an 'anonymous' physical urban environment, etc. And yet many of these regions provided the mineral resources which fuelled Russian growth. Moreover, whilst these only-until-recently peasant societies were culturally broken up by the urbanization process, the new city life offered little which could provide a similarly stable and positive subjective identity with which to replace the rural and religious bearings in these people's experience (Lewin, 1988). Varying with economic ups and downs, both defensive and aggressive displays of country traditions, ethnic loyalties and religious bigotry have occurred as a result.

On the more political side, we should remember that the USSR, like most confederations, is an artificial geographical entity. Moscow rule was politically *imposed* on the minority nations during the Stalinist period, and Communist policy at that time was one of cultural assimilation, sometimes moving large populations wholesale from one ethnic setting to another (usually to serve economic purposes). This political experience, like industrial change, hardly modernizes *attitudes* at all, but only *heightens and revives* older loyalties, putting nothing very local and tangible in their place. The result once again is a resurgence of antagonistic nationalist passions as people cling desperately to what is fast disappearing into a dynamic but 'random' social fabric being imposed by outside interests. The point of this illustration is to show that nationalism cannot be said unilaterally to serve the interests of industrial modernization and political expansion. This is true only under certain conditions (e.g. nineteenth-century Europe). In other conditions (e.g. the Trans-Caucasian Soviet nationalities in recent times) nationalism provides a means of resisting economic 'progress' and gives considerable impetus to political *secession*.

Finally, as in the Baltic republics of the USSR, nationalist movements for secession may express a continued desire for modernization but in a more manageable and ideologically sensitive setting than mega-nations are prepared to allow. 'Small is beautiful' is one important implication of this type of modern drive towards national autonomy.

These background features of industrial dislocation and the formation of the centralized state within society are indispensable in analysing nationalism,

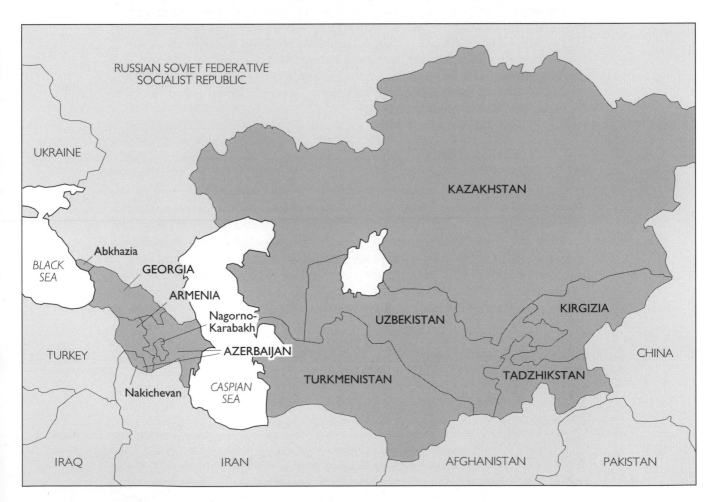

Figure 3   Map highlighting those southern peripheral republics of the Soviet Union in which nationalist disputes broke out in the late 1980s

but, beyond this, how we explain the social role of nationalism depends considerably upon which *tradition* of social thought we are inclined to draw upon. For example, part of our understanding of nationalism's social role is to do with our sense of the chief social *interests* that it serves, and each tradition usually highlights a *different* set of interests. Historically, marxists treated the original growth of nationalism not as the ideological partner of industrialization *per se* but of specifically *capitalist* industrialization. Today, marxists would probably be more equivocal. In some cases, nationalism would be seen as a way of distracting the working class of a capitalist nation from its own sense of identity as a class. In other cases, nationalism would be regarded by marxists much more progressively as a form of national liberation, with the working class and its allies, rather than the bourgeoisie, in the ascendancy. Generally though, marxists see the role of nationalism (like all ideologies) as being to either sustain or challenge *class* power.

Liberals, by contrast, would emphasize how nationhood first emerged intertwined with the establishment of liberal democracy and market society. Nationalism for them has provided a suitable context for a balance between a people's common aspirations and the claims of private interests. The social reformist position would strike a similar balance, but with more emphasis than in liberalism on the collective 'national interest'.

Conservatives for their part see nationalism as giving *all* individuals and families a proper and ever-needed sense of social harmony and order. Indeed, nationalism is seen by conservatives as the modern form of an older, time-honoured sentiment, namely patriotism. Love of one's nation, in the conservative view, is a powerful way of securing the chief political virtue: allegiance to established authority (Scruton, 1980). However, you should remember that there may well be variants *within* each tradition. Other conservatives would argue that allegiance and authority can be readily generated by *international* institutions as well as national ones. In that kind of setting conservatives should be able to declare themselves 'country-lovers' without being rampant 'hyper-nationalists' (Mount, 1989).

3.3   THE TRANSMISSION AND IMPACT OF NATIONALISM

In the case where nationalism has *already* been established as part of the ideological basis of the state, and if it is conducive to the dominant socio-economic interests, then nationalist themes will tend to be transmitted through the major institutions of socialization. The education system, for example, will probably focus on the geographical and historical centrality of the home country. Television programmes and newspaper features will in all likelihood and in innumerable forms generate a sense of patriotic allegiance. Those perceived as deviants and subversives will probably be caricatured as 'alien' elements. The legal system (e.g. immigration procedures) may reinforce this bias. To challenge the dominant form of economy or to express discontent with the mainstream political machinery will generally be presented as being disloyal to the national interest. Families will bring up children, by and large, in the image of the good citizen, with appropriate values for getting on in, and contributing to, the life of the nation 'as we know it'. International competitions (from sporting events to warfare) will heighten a passionate identification with the 'home' country.

Where the nationalism in question has *not* been able to acquire its own state, and if it continues to operate within a wider political unit, then nationalist currents may act as *counter*-ideologies. They will seek to challenge the legitimacy of the reigning (in their view) pseudo-nationalism and perhaps advocate an alternative basis for national identity and sovereignty. Such an alternative will claim to be more *democratic* than the federalist status quo, since the issue of self-determination and autonomy lies at the very heart of the meaning of democracy (see Unit 16). Through political parties, in the dissemination of alternative literature and cultural events, by word of mouth and through some (usually limited) presence in the mass media, separatist nationalist sentiments will be advanced in order to undermine the ruling nationalist or federalist norms. Separatist national movements will perhaps advocate a physical as well as ideological pattern of resistance, since they often lack access to the media and to the armed might of the central state.

Other than in these general terms, the transmission and impact of nationalism need to be studied very carefully in particular cases, and this is a task which would take us well beyond the space allotted to this unit. So it is very important that *you* give some thought to the precise way in which nationalist ideological themes are disseminated. Think of the nationalism 'closest' to you. Following the guidelines set by Section 1.6 of this unit, you should ask yourself how that brand of nationalism is conveyed:

* in workplaces, neighbourhoods and families;
* by the mass media;
* through the legal and education system;
* by the activities of political parties and interest groups.

In considering these forms of ideological dissemination, you also need to ask yourself: is nationalism transmitted in an indirect and 'accidental' sort of way, or is it rather the product of a deliberate ideological strategy? Many people, for example, regard the British monarchy as stretching back into the mists of time in a homely but glorious sort of way. Yet many of the pageants, ceremonies and traditions which foster this image have been literally *invented* in the fairly recent past. The very name of the monarchy—Windsor—was invented during the early years of the First World War to replace the suspiciously foreign-sounding Saxe-Coburg-Gotha.

The combination of deliberation and opportunism in the creation of ceremonies and stereotypes is illustrated for the British (English?) case in the following way:

> The public image of the British monarchy was fundamentally
> transformed in the years before the First World War, as the old
> ceremonial was successfully adapted in response to the changed
> domestic and international situation, and new ceremonial was invented
> and added. And such changes are well reflected in the unprecedented
> manner in which these royal occasions were commercially exploited …
> In mugs and medals, as in music and munificence, the last quarter of
> the nineteenth century and the first decade of the twentieth was a
> golden age of 'invented traditions', as the appeal of the monarchy to the
> mass of the people in an industrialized society was broadened in a
> manner unattainable only half a century before.
>
> (Cannadine, in Hobsbawm and Ranger, 1983)

As well as assessing the balance of accident and strategy in the transmission of nationalist ideology, it is also necessary to make a careful estimate of the *impact* of nationalism. As stressed in Section 1, the impact of nationalist ideology is seldom so strong as to completely brainwash its recipients in a one-way fashion. For one thing, the mass media are seldom wholly successful at this job. Secondly, there may be more than one 'message'. There are competing evaluations of nationalism, depending on how it is combined with other ideological discourses, such as those of democracy, socialism, conservatism and fascism. There are often *rival* nationalisms within a larger federation. There are dominant images of the national culture, but also oppositional and subversive versions of the nature of the 'true' people of a country. Nationalism is thus, like all ideology, shot through with ambiguities and dilemmas. Many modern nationalists, for example, would argue that popular self-determination is of the essence of nationalism. Nationalism, therefore, is intrinsically democratic. Critics of nationalism would respond by saying that the powerful sense of 'self' that nationalism brings to politics is still often a reactionary one, encouraging the citizens of a state to ignore differences amongst themselves and inciting unjustified hostility to other national peoples.

A further factor affecting the impact of nationalism is that, as individuals, we may feel torn between *different* places and groups which appear to be our natural 'home'. The people of Shetland may be more concerned with their own autonomy within Scotland than with Scotland's autonomy within Britain, for instance. And the working-class Mancunian may not feel part of the same 'people' as the person from Salisbury, Wiltshire. Or again, this time broadening out more, a Scottish woman may certainly feel part of a Scottish culture, but she may *also* feel herself to be British in at least some positive sense, and indeed she may also see herself as *European*. Powerful humanitarian campaigns go even further, emphasizing that in an insecure world of famine, pollution and danger, we should be encouraged to feel jointly responsible for 'our common home'—the only planet or world we have. It follows that, as with most ideologies, nationalist identities frequently cross-cut one another, leaving significant space for argument about the nature of nationalist 'belonging' and its relation to democratic or conservative instincts or policies.

As you will see later, in Unit 25, it is important to place nationalism in a setting that is both local and global, for there are signs that, in spite of the continuing power of nationalist sentiment, the political form that is most relevant to nationalist ambitions—the nation-state itself—may be on the decline, historically speaking. Instead, a more complicated picture of strong regional autonomy and loose federal cooperation is possible. The ambiguities within nationalist ideologies as well as their power to mobilize thus look set to continue, particularly in a global order where the level of information and communications is arguably breaking down the parochial cultures of 'separate' peoples.

ACTIVITY 5

As a closing activity, which brings together all the main concepts I have used in this unit, let us examine the different aspects of nationalism and ideology by reading critically the following *Observer* article on Japanese nationalism, by Ian Buruma. As you read the article, jot down in note form some provisional answers to the following questions:

1   Does the author use the 'restricted' or 'relaxed' sense of ideology?

2   What are the main ideological features and functions of Japanese nationalism that he highlights?

3   What forms of ideological transmission does he refer to?

4   How successful is the impact of the new Japanese nationalism?

5   Does Buruma reveal an ideological or theoretical standpoint of his own? What label does he use that best describes his standpoint?

Japan's myth of harmony

IAN BURUMA, examining the temper of the Japanese on the accession of their new, liberal-minded Emperor, finds that the cult of aggressive imperialism still flourishes among intellectuals.

PEACE was central to the picture of imperial benevolence presented for two days on all Japanese television channels immediately after the Emperor's death last week.

Hirohito was a peace-loving man who had opposed the war all along. Only his sense of duty as a constitutional monarch prevented him from acting more forcefully against his bureaucrats and generals. He alone was responsible for ending the war and he it was who presided over and personified postwar Japan's ceaseless promotion of peace. The war, it is suggested, was an aberration in Japanese history. Peace is what Japan is really about.

To some of us who also switched on, there was something disturbing about the combination of continual incantations for peace and the evasion of responsibility for keeping it. The war, like the present trade conflicts, is much discussed in Japan, but rarely is it clearly shown where the responsibility lies for such conflicts.

The Emperor could not have been responsible for the war, for he was a man of peace. The Japanese, being peace-loving people, cannot be blamed either. 'Militarists', to be sure, were carried away by their fanaticism. But they can't be wholly blamed. So, what one got from the Japanese mass media was the tragic view of history: war simply happened, like an earthquake, or, according to the more chauvinist commentators, it was forced upon a peaceful nation by aggressive foreigners who did not understand Japanese intentions.

That this is not everyone's view in Japan is proven by the many letters of support sent to the Mayor of Nagasaki, who is currently under attack for refusing to go along with the tragic view; he believes that the Emperor was at least partly responsible for the war.

The combination of peacenikery and irresponsibility has coloured much of the postwar Japanese rhetoric. A young woman scholar called Michiko Hasegawa wrote some years ago that the uniquely peaceful Japanese people had been forced into international conflict once by belligerent foreign powers, but that it should never happen again. It was highly regrettable, therefore, that America had compelled Japan to go against its peaceful nature and support the US in the Cold War. It

should surprise nobody, then, that American demands for Japan to play a more responsible international role would sometimes elicit the comment from Japanese officials that America failed to appreciate Japan's untiring efforts to promote world peace.

There is more to the Japanese mantra of peace, however. Peace and the unique national propensity — so it is claimed — for social harmony not only fudge political responsibility, but the propagation of such values often has a political purpose.

After the collapse of the authoritarian Tokugawa Government in the middle of the last century, Japan, ruled by an energetic oligarchy of upstart samurai, set out to become a modern state. One thing the new rulers feared more than anything else, more even than conflict abroad, for which they showed a marked taste, was conflict at home. Political pluralism was seen as a threat to the new order and had to be contained, by force if necessary, but more usually through subtle coercion.

Archaic forms

A mythology was literally created out of a mishmash of modern and archaic forms which, against all historical evidence, ascribed a unique harmony and homogeneity to Japanese culture and society. Conflict was not just socially undesirable, but positively un-Japanese. The Meiji Emperor, brought to Tokyo from his traditional quarters in Kyoto, to serve as a figurehead for the new oligarchy, was made to embody the superiority of the Japanese race — superior because of the purity of the one unbroken imperial bloodline and the unique harmony and homogeneity of Japanese culture as defined by the rulers.

Nationalist philosophers extolled the virtues of the family state, where, as the slogan had it, 'one hundred million hearts beat as one'. The will of the Emperor could, in its benevolence, not but be the will of the people. Dissidents were not only un-Japanese, but in danger of committing *lèse majesté*. Politicians and businessmen, regarded as selfish and greedy, were clearly less suited to represent the imperial will than military men and bureaucrats who were above political conflict, though often paralysed by internal strife.

Containing conflict on the home front meant that Japanese energies had to be deflected elsewhere, to the new colonies of Formosa, Korea, Manchuria and, later, all the way to Burma. In the rhetoric of the time, all the world had to be brought under one roof to benefit from the divine benevolence of the Emperor.

The world, as we know, refused to be brought under one roof. Japan was instead brought to heel; the top generals were prosecuted and in some cases hanged; the Emperor renounced his divinity and became the peace-loving symbol of a country which the Americans tried to turn into a functioning democracy by handing down a so-called Peace Constitution.

The likelihood of Japan unleashing World War III is now slim. There is no sign of a renascent Japanese militarism. But, just as many of the wartime bureaucrats simply carried on expanding Japanese power more peacefully after the war, some of the prewar myths have stuck.

The idea that all Japanese are tied by a spiritual bond of cultural, racial and social harmony, is still widely believed and sometimes innocently, sometimes for political reasons, promoted. Such propaganda, even when prewar blood-and-soil terminology is carefully avoided, helps keep Japanese society closed to outsiders and oppressive to those within.

The myth of harmony and consensus is also a useful justification for authoritarian bureaucrats and the ruling Liberal Democratic Party to behave as if they naturally represent the will of the people because of their benevolent stewardship of national harmony. The imperial institution does not inspire enormous enthusiasm among the Japanese people, but that is not its function. It does add symbolic value to the myth

of unique national consensus and racial purity.

Although no Japanese is forced, as people were during the war, to jump to attention at the mere mention of the word Emperor, a growing number of chauvinist intellectuals is actively promoting the prewar mythology, sometimes reviving even the old terminology.

One such thinker, a philosopher called Takeshi Umehara, argued recently that one way of saving the world from ecological disaster brought on by Western materialism is to turn to the 'Japanese Emperor system, which is rooted in the principles of nature'.

Christian barbarism

Another writer contrasted the spiritual benevolence of the imperial line with the barbarism of Christianity, and blamed the aberration of militarist imperialism partly on Christian influence. What matters is not whether every Japanese believes this kind of thing, but that such ideas are starting to dominate some of the most influential intellectual journals, where they find little resistance.

It is often pointed out that the younger generation of Japanese, the so-called 'new species', is largely apathetic and apolitical, more interested in fancy clothes and pop music than in imperial bloodlines. This, it is usually said, would lessen the risk of political manipulation. The contrary seems more plausible. In a nation of apolitical people, with sordid financial scandals degrading the political process at regular intervals, and with an ever more vociferous outside world baying at the door for Japan to open up, spiritual ideals of natural harmony and xenophobic paranoia about foreign threats to the unique Japanese spirit of peace, might have considerable attraction.

If being Japanese is being likened by nationalist writers to membership of a tribal cult, the high priest of this cult is still the Emperor. And it does not really make much difference whether the high priest is a possible war criminal studying the habits of sea-anemones, or a liberal-minded gentleman who used to play tennis with foreign correspondents; as long as the cult is alive, the institution could serve as an added obstacle to political pluralism in Japan and internationalism abroad.

The Observer, 15 January 1989

My own response to these questions was as follows:

1   Buruma is operating with a restricted conception of ideology, not a relaxed one. His overall tone is condemnatory, and he is definitely *not* saying: this is just one way of making sense of society. He uses phrases which suggest that Japanese nationalism is about the deliberate propagation of myths for particular political ends.

2   The ideological myth in question is that the Japanese are essentially peace-loving. This myth is said to work by yoking together 'modern and archaic'

references. A 'spiritual bond' of both 'racial and social' harmony is thus created. So strong is this bond that a particular political system—'the Japanese Emperor System'—is not regarded as a political arrangement at all, but rather comes over as 'rooted in the principles of nature' itself. The peace myth works so well, it is implied, that dissidence and social 'conflict at home' are regarded as unnatural, as 'positively un-Japanese'. The naturalness of these sentiments is strengthened by the portrayal of the state as 'the family state' and the nation itself as one big family, in which 'one hundred million hearts beat as one'. The power of language—'rhetoric'—is noted as central to the dominance of these images. In these various ways each Japanese citizen is powerfully interpellated—their 'hearts' are addressed, not necessarily their heads—as the subject of the nationalist discourse. 'Subject' here means both an essential subjective part of the myth, but also literally a political *subject* of the Emperor and a highly structured belief system. You can see then how all our main features of ideology—naturalization, interpellation, playing down conflict, universality, and chains of association—are highlighted in this case.

As to the roles or *functions* of ideology, Buruma mentions how the ancient myth served to facilitate a transition from feudal society to the 'modern state', under the leadership of a particular élite group—'an energetic oligarchy of upstart samurai'. The particular culture or aura of nationalism was 'defined by' these new rulers for their own ends, though today it is the interests of another dominant group—the 'authoritarian bureaucrats'—that the ideology supports. Apart from particular groups, the myth furthers the interests of the Japanese as a whole, cementing their common sense of 'superiority' as they seek greater national advantage in an inferior world. The dominant ideology also serves to de-legitimize a *counter*-ideology, namely what the author calls 'pluralism'. This is seen as a 'threat' to Japan's authoritarian system, to be 'contained' mainly by 'subtle coercion' (i.e. propaganda).

3   Buruma asserts that a number of specific groups and institutions transmit the national myth: 'all television channels', 'Japanese officials', 'the rulers', and 'a growing number of chauvinist intellectuals'. He also regards the transmission as quite *deliberate*, speaking of the 'continual incantations' of the 'mantra of peace', of Japan's 'untiring efforts' to make the 'propaganda' work.

4   But does such propaganda wholly succeed? Well not entirely, for in spite of its power the myth is only 'widely believed' rather than completely accepted. Indeed, perhaps its *mass* acceptance is not so important. 'What matters is not whether every Japanese believes this kind of thing' but rather that 'influential intellectual' élites subscribe to it. As it happens, many ordinary Japanese, especially nowadays, are decidedly 'apathetic and apolitical'. This is *perhaps* a sign of conscious cultural opposition, but more likely, in the author's view, it is possible that this kind of cynical and 'sordid' sub-culture might instead lead to a further escalation of 'xenophobic paranoia' as the absence of meaningful values comes to be pervasively felt. In this part of the argument the author is saying that the myth is dominant amongst élites, and has great potential attraction for the masses (even the apathetic); but this does not rule out contradictory impulses towards disbelief or cynicism amongst the Japanese people. This message reflects many of our earlier themes in Sections 1.7 and 3.3.

5   The author clearly regards the Japanese myth as distorting and dangerous. Overall, I would say he has a *liberal* outlook, or perhaps the kind of variant of the social reformist outlook which tilts towards the liberal end of that spectrum. His favoured term, however, is 'pluralism'—which roughly means the existence of free and equal competition between political parties and ideas. Unlike conservatives, who believe in the virtues of nationalism as a form of allegiance, Buruma regards nationalism as bordering on irrational mass hys-

teria, leaving no room for the thinking individual. Japan is characterized by authoritarianism, since it throws up profound 'obstacles' to pluralism. In that sense, the Japanese myth is ideological in the pejorative sense because it is a totalitarian 'cult', a blinkered and even fanatical set of images. This account is therefore on balance a liberal one. It is not a *marxist* one, because in the end the interests that are served by the ideology are not those of a socio-economic class as such. And the system it defends is seen as mainly political not economic. (Marxists would see the Japanese system primarily as an example of highly organized corporate capitalism.)

This liberal-pluralist standpoint certainly provides sharp critical insights into Japanese nationalism, and into ideology generally. Many marxists and conservatives would agree with part of the writer's analysis. But the passion of the article is notable, and the picture of Japan which emerges is surely likely to be challenged by less hostile observers. And notice how 'pluralism' is merely *assumed* to be an altogether better system, one which is *naturally* taken to be both freer and more rational. However, this perspective seems rather blinkered to the fact that the liberal West has *its own* ideological myths of the nation and freedom, myths which could be subjected to equally serious criticism. Indeed, whether genuine pluralism actually exists in the West is open to doubt. Even if we assume it does exist, what right does the author have to take it for granted that pluralism alone represents progress, and that other belief systems are so backward that they must jump over 'obstacles' in the scramble to attain that pluralist goal? And finally, of course, we may want ultimately to question the firmly 'conspiratorial' useage of ideology in Buruma's analysis. Perhaps if the writer himself had been more aware of the very distinction between restricted and relaxed interpretations of ideology, he might have given more space to the *indirect* and subtler mechanisms of ideological discourse.

In sum, the kind of 'reading' exercise that we have been engaging in is very valuable for training ourselves to think analytically about the concept of ideology. The author takes one ideological theme as his object of concern and discussion, but then he himself, perhaps unconsciously, sets in motion a number of ideological preferences of his own. Although the article is a newspaper feature, many social science discussions of ideologies operate in a similar sort of way.

4 CONCLUSION

We have covered a lot of ground in this unit. Partly, this is because the topic of ideology is undeniably complex at times, and so it is always desirable to break it up into more manageable sub-topics. Thus, we found that the question 'What is ideology?' led quickly to others: 'What are the social roles of ideology?'; 'How does ideology work?'; 'How is it transmitted?'; and 'What is the nature of its impact?' The unit could not cover these questions in great detail, but I trust you will by now be entirely familiar with this *sequence* of questioning, and will be able to say something under each heading.

Much depends, of course, on the particular examples we put in ideological focus. I tried to show, at each stage, how the theoretical questions could be concretely illustrated. But two main sorts of ideological framework emerged as central cases. The first was the various traditions of social thought. The second was nationalism. Once again, neither of these central cases was dealt with in full detail. But, as with the general theoretical issues of the unit, the key thing here is that you should now have a general *grasp* of the major characteristics and debates around such ideological frameworks as these. Finally, let me remind you that this is certainly not the last time you will meet the topics of this unit, so there will be ample opportunity in the near future to further rehearse and consolidate your work here. In Unit 20, for example, many of my general themes are taken up again, in a slightly different way. And through the link with Unit 20, the question of 'social identities' is developed in the D103 Summer School. The traditions, regarded both as ideologies themselves and as resources for the analysis of ideology, will also figure prominently in your summer school work. TV 09 asks whether the mass media is a vehicle of dominant ideologies, whilst nationalism reappears in TV 10 as a key source of ideological affiliation. It is also relevant to the discussion of relations between regions, nations and Europe in Unit 25. In all these contexts you will find the concerns of this unit cropping up regularly.

=== AUDIO CASSETTE ===

Now is an appropriate time to listen to the review of course themes on the second segment of side B of the audio cassette for Block IV.

REFERENCES

Althusser, L. (1972) 'Ideology and the Ideological State Apparatuses', in *Lenin and Philosophy and other Essays*, London, New Left Books.

Anderson, B. (1983) *Imagined Communities: Reflections on the Origins and Spread of Nationalism*, London, Verso.

Ascherson, N. (1988) 'The Religion of Nationalism', *The Observer*, 4 December.

Billig, M. *et al.* (1988) *Ideological Dilemmas*, London, Sage.

Chomsky, N. (1989) *Necessary Illusions*, London, Pluto Press.

Gellner, E. (1983) *Nations and Nationalism*, Oxford, Blackwell.

Hobsbawm, E.J. and Ranger, T. (1983) *The Invention of Tradition*, Cambridge, Cambridge University Press.

Kamenka, E. (ed.) (1976) *Nationalism*, London, Edward Arnold.

Lewin, M. (1986) *The Gorbachev Phenomenon: A Historical Interpretation*, London, Radius.

Marshall, G. *et al.* (1989) *Social Class in Modern Britain*, London, Unwin Hyman.

Mount, F. (1989) 'Hypernats and Country-Lovers', *The Spectator*, 18 February.

Nairn, T. (1981) *The Break-up of Britain* (2nd edn), London, Verso.

Scruton, R. (1980) *The Meaning of Conservatism*, Harmondsworth, Penguin Books.

ACKNOWLEDGEMENTS

Grateful acknowledgement is made to the following sources for permission to reproduce material in this unit:

Text

B. Silk, G. Jones and J. Weeks, 'Rioters kill policeman', *Daily Telegraph*, 7 October 1985, copyright © The Daily Telegraph plc; B. Hitchen, 'Red butchers', *Daily Star*, 8 October 1985, copyright © Express Newspapers plc; I. Buruma, 'Japan's myth of harmony', *The Observer*, 15 January 1989, copyright © The Observer, London, 1989.

Figures

Figures 2 and 3: Redrawn maps from an article in the *Guardian*, 19 September 1989.

Illustrations

p.127 (bottom left): Copyright International Wool Secretariat/Courtesy of the London College of Fashion; *p.127 (bottom centre):* Liverpool Daily Post and Echo Ltd; *p.135:* Mansell Collection; *p.138 (top left):* Glasgow University Media Group (1982) *Really Bad News*, London, Writers and Readers; *p.138 (bottom left):* Glasgow University Media Group (1982) *Really Bad News*, London, Writers and Readers/Colin Wheeler; *p.138 (top and bottom right):* Szymon Kobylinski/*Polityka*, 17 November 1982 and 19 March 1983; *p.148:* Mary Evans Picture Library; *p. 149 (all three photographs):* Popperfoto.

UNIT 18   THEORIES AND EVIDENCE

Prepared for the Course Team by David Coates

CONTENTS

This block has covered a lot of ground. We have asked you to move the focus of your concerns from questions of international politics to issues of domestic agenda setting, and from questions of democracy to issues of ideology. What has united this movement has been a concern with the *state*. We hope that you now have at your disposal a far larger body of information than before on what the UK state does, what forces operate upon it, and on the character of your relationship to it as citizen and subject.

We have also, at various points, raised questions of theory. We have tried not simply to document what the state has been doing. We have also tried to provide you with different ways of *explaining* what it has been doing. There has been a rhythm to the material in the block: at times a focus on *facts* and documentation, at other times a focus on *theories* and explanation. The purpose of this half-unit is to review the major concerns of Block IV by looking specifically at the interplay of facts and theories.

1 THE STORY SO FAR

We have already touched on the interplay of facts and theories — and on related questions of social science methodology and knowledge — at the end of each of the last three blocks; and indeed we will continue to touch on similar issues at the end of each block to come. In doing this, as we explained in Unit 4, we are hoping to add to your understanding of the exercise on which you are engaged as practising social scientists. So what is the story of the review half-units so far?

The main story line of these half-units, to this point, is that social analysis is a far more complicated business than it at first appears. It is not enough to treat the analysis of society in what Unit 5 called a 'positivist' and Unit 9 an 'empiricist' way. The terms are daunting, but the broad approach being criticized is not. For what we are rejecting is a view of social analysis that says: 'What's all the fuss about? Just go out and look. Faced with the complexity of social life, open your eyes, drop any preconceptions and prejudices, have an open mind, get detached, and let the truth flow in to your mind through your senses'. This is a view of social science that ultimately sees the job as one of building a picture inside your head of what you see, feel, and hear actually going on about you. It's a view of social science that sees its task as one of gathering the facts; see Figure 1.

What the half-units in D103 are arguing is that doing social science — indeed doing any science — is just not that simple. In Unit 9 we suggested to you that the 'movement' of social science knowledge isn't so much linear as circular. You don't accumulate knowledge by letting it flow straight into your head through your senses. Rather it accumulates through what Unit 9 called 'a cycle of social science enquiry'.

——————————————— ACTIVITY 1 ———————————————

Re-read the first paragraph of Unit 9, to see what is meant by 'the cycle of social science enquiry'.

This concept of cyclical enquiry is quite tough to grasp, isn't it? But its meaning and significance for us should begin to become clearer if we rehearse the three reasons already given in the half-units for the inadequacy of a positivist/empiricist view of social science. These are:

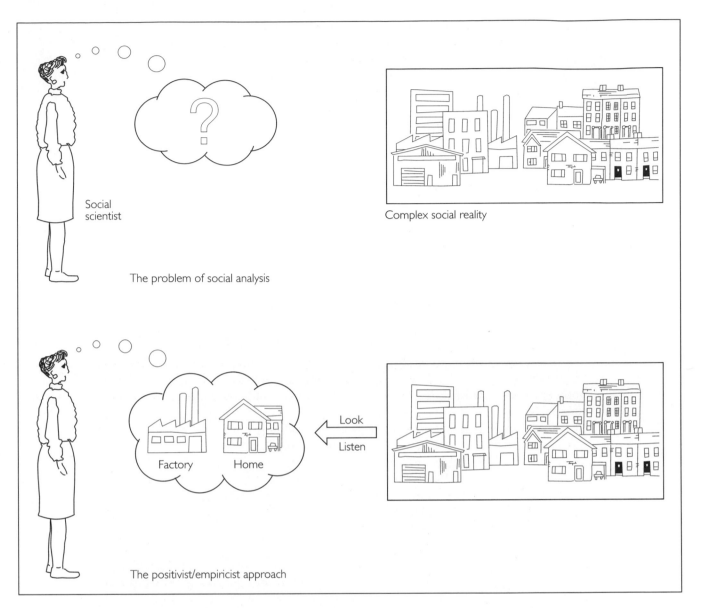

The problem of social analysis

Social scientist

Complex social reality

The positivist/empiricist approach

Look

Listen

Factory   Home

Figure 1

1   that to establish 'facts' we need concepts;

2   that to analyse 'facts' we need models and theories; and

3   that there is an important set of connections between concepts and models/theories.

Let's look at each of these reasons in turn.

1   Having read Unit 9 it should be clear that 'facts' don't speak for themselves in any simple and direct way. We saw that — in something as apparently self-defining as a picture — in the examples of the duck and the stairs in Unit 9. It wasn't possible for us to stand passively before even those pictures and allow them to define their message for us. Rather, we had to engage actively with them, and put our interpretation upon each. In social analysis, the grasping of what is actually going on 'out there', beyond and around us requires active work by us, inside our heads. It requires, amongst other things, the act of *conceptualization*.

To get any purchase on the workings of the world in which we live, and to be able to talk to other people about the world and our place in it, we have to group things, put them into mental boxes, and give those boxes names. As Unit 9 says, 'there is always more to perception than meets the eye. … Observations are dependent upon concepts, … conceptualization is the principle element in all human knowledge'. Alan Bennett's mother used concepts. We all use them. Both social action and social science are impossible without them. We need what Units 9 and 13 calls 'linguistic representations of reality', conceptual tools, 'glasses', to put a sense of clarity on the complex reality we face. As Unit 9 put it, 'our direct observations are always patterned, shaped or organized by the concepts and theories at our disposal. What we *see* is strongly conditioned by our general cultural stock of concepts, values and expectations'. There is a real sense in which we can't actually 'get to that reality' except through the concepts with which we begin to appropriate it. What we can do, however, is to be very clear and precise about the concepts we use, and very aware too that the way we see the world will be affected by the conceptual spectacles that we choose to put on; see Figure 2.

2   Unit 9 made clear how active a process conceptualization is. We bring our own concepts to bear on the world we analyse. And we are active in another way too. Analysis involves more than conceptualization. It also involves probing for explanation and understanding. Such probing is invariably a long and drawn out business. It involves a range of activities: the construction of systematic description, the pursuit of possible clusters and patterns in our data, the probing for particular sets of interconnections between and within the things we are looking at, and the formulation and testing of initially tentative hypotheses about why those interconnections should exist. At many of these stages, as we saw in Unit 13, progress can only be made by building and using models — that is, by abstracting parts of what is under view, and looking at how they might interact in isolation from the rest. It is then sometimes possible to carry those models back towards the complexity from which they were extracted and reconstitute them as theories of what is actually going on. So the pursuit of understanding requires a second form of active involvement by the analyst. It is not just that we bring concepts to bear on the world we are analysing. It is also that that world can only be grasped, assessed and interpreted through the models and theories brought to bear upon it by the particular analyst concerned; see Figure 3.

3 We have seen too, in the earlier half-units, that there is an intimate connection between conceptualization and model building/theorizing. Models are built out of concepts: 'it is helpful to think of a model or theory as a structured set of concepts' (Unit 13). We go beyond concepts by building models: concepts are only the individual building blocks of theories and models in social science,

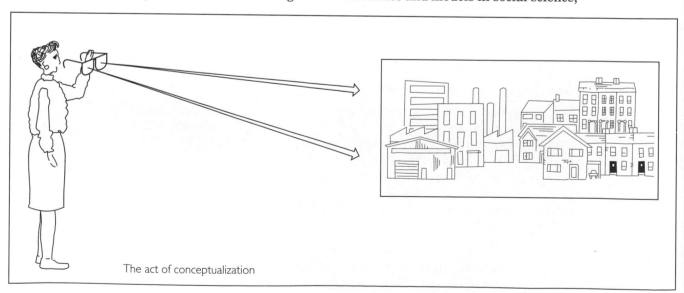

The act of conceptualization

Figure 2

and it is the theories or models, not the concepts, which do the explaining (Unit 9). We learnt too that concepts partly reflect and partly construct the 'reality' they capture. The words we use to analyse the world, and the theories we develop to explain it, have what Unit 9 called 'a dual character': 'On the one hand they are mental or linguistic representations of reality. On the other hand they are the means by which people effectively communicate with each other in language'.

Unit 9 called the first part of this dual character the *representational* aspect of social science knowledge, the second the *communicative* aspect. We develop concepts, build models, construct theories, to give us at least a provisional grasp/representation of social reality. But our grasp is always a provisional one — subject to debate and change — and the change comes through communicating our concepts and theories to other social scientists, and by entering into debate with them.

As Unit 9 made clear, there is always something of a difference of emphasis between social scientists on the relative importance of the representational and communicative aspects of concepts and theories. Some social scientists seem happier treating their arguments as more or less direct representations of social reality — as a pretty straightforward capturing of 'the facts' of social life. Others seem more content to treat models and theories as devices they construct themselves to enable them to discuss with other social scientists the character of social reality and how best to understand it. The first group (and I know that on a bad day I tend to drift their way) tend to be quickly impatient with all this worrying about the status of knowledge, and just want to get on chasing 'the facts'. The others, quite properly, are forever questioning what we mean by 'facts', and forever pointing out how hard they are to isolate and determine.

But wherever particular social scientists stand in this debate about the status of social science knowledge, one thing seems common to them all. There seems to be a shared recognition that we do need some way of examining the 'fit' between the concepts, models and theories we use to analyse the world, and the character of the world so analysed. There does seem to be a general recognition that 'theories' and 'facts' do interrelate in social analysis, and that the nature of their interrelationship is critical to the evaluation of social science arguments and explanations. So, as the next stage of the story, let us look at the interplay of 'facts' and 'theories' in more detail.

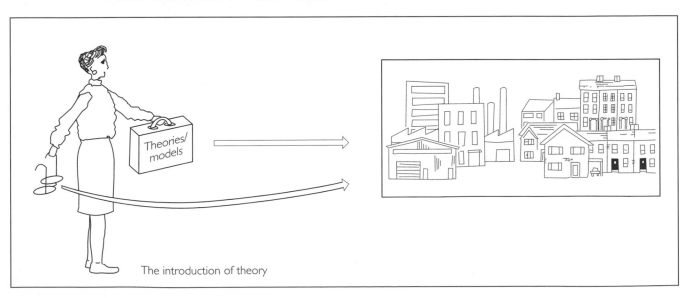

The introduction of theory

Figure 3

SUMMARY

- We need to be cautious about any simple view of 'facts' speaking for themselves. What is 'true', what is 'real' in the realm of the social is very problematic, and there is no easy and direct route to it.

- Social analysis is necessarily an active process, involving conceptualization and the building of models/theories. How the world is defined and understood will turn on the concepts and theories adopted to do so.

- However, it is still possible to evaluate the relative merits of particular models/theories by exploring their relationship to the 'facts' captured by particular conceptualizations.

2   FACTS

You have probably noticed that I keep putting the word *fact* in inverted commas to indicate that there is something problematic about it. Perhaps you have noticed too that there were no inverted commas around the term when positivism was being discussed. If you hold to the view that reality can be understood simply by observing it, then facts are the things that you see. But once you start talking about conceptualization and the building of models — not to mention the way in which our knowledge is socially constructed and contingent on the culture in which we live — then it is easy to end up feeling that nothing is solid any more, that everything depends on the concepts chosen, and that facts are things you invent to bolster your own particular point of view.

That is a very understandable reaction to any theory of knowledge in the social sciences that attempts to go beyond a simple empiricism. But it is also too extreme a response. Concepts do indeed partly reflect and partly construct the reality they purport to capture, but there is a reality out there to be reflected and captured in this way. It isn't all in the mind. What a sensitivity to the nature of conceptualization and theorizing ought to do is to encourage caution about the status of facts. I am sure that most of us live quite happily with the notion that there are things called 'facts', that they are things that are true and verifiable, things that exist whether we like it or not. And why not: after all, life is too short to be forever wondering about the theoretical underpinnings and conceptual choices locked into everything we say and do. But though life is short, there are times when such a wondering is particularly valuable. Now for instance!

─────────────────── ACTIVITY 2 ───────────────────

Pause for a moment and ask yourself — what is a fact? Write down an example of something you think of as a fact.

───

How did you get on? Defining a fact can be tricky. On a day-to-day basis I'm sure we often say: 'It's a fact that ... this is a table ... the English are generally a tolerant people ... famine is caused by overpopulation ...'. In other words, we often treat as 'facts' statements of very different kinds, with very different origins and justifications. Some of the things we hold on to as 'facts' we treat in that way because of their fit with our own direct experience (of what, for example, constitutes a table in this culture). Some we hold on to because they are received wisdoms, preached at us by the media and so on (that the English are tolerant, the French perfidious…); and some because we think it is so (it is our opinion, belief, even theory) and we've never seen much evidence to set against it (that famine is caused by overpopulation, crime by broken homes, economic decline by strong trade unions). In other words, some of the things we regularly treat as facts derive from our direct perceptions, some from the cultural forces that operate on us, and some from the battery of opinion and unexamined beliefs on which we necessarily build our everyday lives.

That's OK for living, but it's not quite good enough for analysis. Somehow we have to get a tighter grip on this notion of 'facts' if we are to approach the study of society as social scientists rather than merely as participant members. We can do this in two ways. We can do it first by realizing that we have to *construct* facts, that it is part of our job as social scientists to gather as much reliable information as we can, not least by using proper scientific methods of enquiry. (We will discuss these, and the status of the information they yield, in Unit 22.) The other thing we can do (our task in this half-unit) is to realize that not all statements that purport to be factual are as unproblematic as they would claim. We have to recognize the importance of *interrogating* statements in order to establish the extent to which the propositions they contain are factual in the common-sense meaning of that term (that is, the extent to which they are somehow true, verifiable, things that exist whether we like it or not).

——————————— ACTIVITY 3 ———————————

Consider the following seven statements. Are they true, real, verifiable? Are they all facts?

1   The Conservatives won the general election of 1987.

2   In the UK most adults over the age of 18 have the right to vote in general elections.

3   Prime Ministers in the UK have almost always been men.

4   More skilled manual workers voted Conservative in 1983 than voted Labour.

5   The United Kingdom is a democracy.

6   The Labour Party is more responsive to working-class interests than the Conservative Party.

7   Affluence and radicalism are incompatible.

What did you decide? My reaction to these statements was that they can all be presented as facts, and may well come to you in that form in the literature that you read. But, though they can be presented as equally factual in character, they actually differ in the degree to which they can be said to be verifiable.

Every one of these seven statements contains concepts. None are concept free. In each case, you (the reader) have to be already armed with a shared understanding (with me, the writer) of what those concepts mean — what a general election is, what a Prime Minister is, how you recognize a Conservative. Moreover, there is just no way in which you could simply wake up in the morning, open your eyes, go to the polling booth, and see skilled manual workers voting. You have to be able to spot a skilled manual worker; and spotting him or her involves the activities of conceptualization and categorization discussed in Units 4 and 9.

And yet the necessary presence of concepts in all seven statements doesn't stop me feeling that it is worth splitting the list in two, differentiating statements

1–4 from the final three. The first four look much more factual to me than the last three. Why? Because (a) the concepts with which they are put together look pretty uncontentious, and (b) the way each can be verified looks reasonably straightforward and likely to be convincing to most of us. This is clear if we look at each of the four in turn.

Have we any doubt about the meaning of any of the concepts in the first four statements? I take it we all agree on our understanding of terms like adult, men, general election, Prime Minister, Conservative, Labour, UK — and that if we don't, a quick chat should produce such an agreement without much bother. No ideological brainwashing or arm-twisting needed here?

Then the verification?

- The first and second are very specific statements about one election result and about electoral rules: they can be checked by looking at polling statistics and voting regulations.

- The third and fourth statements are less specific. They are generalizations: about a trend in the filling of one office over time, and about group behaviour in one election. Each would take some time to check, using primary sources to do the first, polling statistics to do the second. But in each case there are no insurmountable obstacles to establishing their accuracy — their 'fit with reality' — and once checked it is likely that all of us will accept them as data too solid to ignore or discount in the analyses that we make.

There are lots of propositions of this kind awaiting you in the social sciences: pieces of information about specific individuals or events, or social/historical generalizations about the behaviour of groups or institutions. Much of this you will have to take on trust. But even as you accept such propositions as 'facts' you would do well to keep two caveats at the back of your mind.

1   Reality and the measurement of reality are never the same thing. Take, for example, unemployment and unemployment figures. There is unemployment. That is not in dispute. People are without jobs. But the 'fact' of the existence of unemployment does not give us the data on unemployment that we need, and that we will be obliged to work with as social scientists. The figures on unemployment have to be constructed — by statisticians using certain definitions and certain procedures for the collection of the numbers. Neither the definitions nor the procedures are entirely innocent in their effects on the figures. This is particularly true with unemployment figures, which depend on registering for unemployment benefit, and depend on a government definition of who is to be counted. That keeps changing, as perhaps you know. So you always need — particularly with statistical material — to ask yourself how much of the impression they give is a product of what is actually going on, and how much a consequence of how it is counted.

2   With both quantitative and qualitative data, their acceptance as reliable is always in the end a matter of trust. Some of the propositions we meet can be checked off against our own immediate daily experience. That's a pretty tough test — though not water-tight of course. We might be the odd ones — with the atypical experience. The fact that our experience doesn't fit may tell us more about ourselves than about the social science data we are given. But anyway most of what we have to take on trust we can't check in that way. We accept it because we have faith in the scholarship and integrity of those generating it. That too isn't always reliable. Scholars used to tell us the earth was flat. You can't believe everything you're told. So again, you just need to be alert to the possibility of inadequacies of scholarship, defects in research design, and sloppiness in thought and execution by the social scientists whose work you are taking on trust.

Even so, for most of the time — bearing in mind these caveats — propositions of the 1–4 variety must constitute as near to a universally accepted factual base for the study of society that we can get. But that is not something you can say with as much ease of propositions 5, 6 and 7.

———————————— ACTIVITY 4 ————————————

Why not? Have a look at propositions 5, 6 and 7 again. Look for things they are asking you to take on trust if you are to accept them as somehow unambiguously true.

What did you find? In my notes I came up with the following:

- Whether the UK is a democracy depends on how we define 'democracy' as well as on the information we have about the voting rights of 18-year-olds.

- The statement on the relative responsiveness of the two parties to working-class interests will only be true to the degree that we can adequately measure responsiveness and specify working-class interests.

- Whether affluence and radicalism go together will be even harder to establish since the statement is one without qualification, and so will have to apply everywhere and at all times. It will in fact be quite easy to *dis*prove Statement 7. One counter-factual piece of evidence would do, one example of affluent radicalism. But it will still be extraordinarily difficult to establish conclusively the statement's veracity for all time, even in the absence of damning evidence of this kind.

When we stand back from the detail of statements 5, 6 and 7, and ask 'what is it about them as statements that stops us treating them as facts?', two issues come into view.

1   To begin with, they are too impregnated with particular understandings of certain central concepts in political science (democracy, interests etc.) to enjoy the unambiguous status of facts. They are only true if, and to the degree that, the concepts on which they are built are defined as we would define them. But definitional consensus is not something readily available in the social sciences. On the contrary, as Lukes has observed, 'there are probably few terms in social science whose expunging from the lexicon has not been advocated by someone, on the grounds of persistent disagreement and confusion over definition and application' (Lukes, 1981, p.398). His list of contentious terms came out as: '*social system, class, deviance* and *role* in sociology; *political system, state, political culture* and *power* in political science; *religion, symbol, culture, kinship* in anthropology; *capital, value, utility* and *consumer surplus* in economics' (ibid.).

But Lukes could have come up with all sorts of other terms that are equally contentious. Certainly 'democracy', 'interests', 'affluence' and 'radicalism' are, and their presence in statements 5–7 reminds us that the truth of propositions in social science is often a truth dependent on consensus. Statements have a chance of being accepted as true only if everyone participating in the communication shares a common understanding of the terms they contain. Not that this should really surprise us. For, as we saw earlier, concepts (and the models/theories built upon them) have a communicative as well as a representational role; and only if there is consensus on the terms of the communication can there hope to be consensus on the adequacy of the representation.

2   Statements 6 and 7 differ from the other four (and indeed in this respect from Statement 5 as well) in another way. It is not simply that they contain contentious terms. It is also that they are heavily impregnated with particular

presuppositions — with particular models or theories about how the world actually works. They assert the existence of relationships which are difficult to isolate and measure: relationships of policy and interests, wealth and political attitudes. Taking them as true requires taking on board the presuppositions each contains.

- Statement 6 implies that classes exist, that they have recognizable and different political interests, and that political parties differ in the classes they represent.
- Statement 7 implies that radicalism and poverty go together, that it is economic interest that stimulates political action, and so on.

This impregnation of factual statements with presuppositions is also a very common feature of the propositions of social science. And because it is, it is very often the case that 'apparently factual statements are dependent upon theoretical suppositions. What at first look like straightforward descriptions can, on closer inspection, be seen as more complex and controversial' (Walton, 1982, p.12). So statements 5–7 turn out to be much more contentious than statements 1–4 and as such, much less 'hard'.

This examination of seven propositions helps to remind us that 'facts' in social science come in different degrees of 'hardness'. In the case of some statements, the degree of consensus on meaning, and the ease of verification, is so total that no one queries them. We just take them on trust, and get on with struggling to explain their occurrence. In the case of others — at the other end of the spectrum — the degree of impregnation by contentious concepts and presuppositions is so high that virtually no one accepts them as unambiguously true. At that end of the spectrum, facts slide away into hypotheses masquerading as facts — that is, they slide away into statements which need to be demonstrated, pretending that they have been. Statement 7 in the list above is near that end of the spectrum, just as Statement 1 is at the 'factual' end. But the crucial thing is that propositions all along the spectrum are important. The 'hard' facts are often the least exciting ones, and the least illuminating. OK, we know the Conservative Party won the 1987 general election. That is a fact. But so what? What is going on in Britain in the 1990s? Is affluence destroying radicalism? Are workers deserting Labour? These seem to me to be the big issues. 'Hard' facts on their own are not enough if we want to explain what is going on as well as to document it. We therefore need something else. We need some statements impregnated with contentious concepts and presuppositions. In other words we need some *theory*.

SUMMARY

- All factual statements contain concepts. But they vary in the degree to which the concepts they contain are contentious. They also vary in the ease with which they can be verified.
- Factual statements vary too in the extent to which they are impregnated with theoretical presuppositions.
- Even factual statements that lack contentious concepts and are low on theoretical presuppositions still need to be treated with caution. They are still representations of reality constructed by particular academics. But they are the nearest to individual social facts that we are likely to get, and in the main they can be treated — for the purpose of social analysis — as in some rough-and-ready sense 'true'.

3 THEORIES

So we come to the question of theory. We need theory to help us make the move from documentation to explanation. We need therefore to know what we mean by the term 'theory'.

=== READER ===

Please read the 'Introduction' to the essay on traditions of thought in Section 1, Chapter 22 of the Course Reader.

The traditions essay argues that theoretical material comes in different but related shapes. It comes as conceptual schemas, particular hypotheses, specific theories and general theoretical frameworks (what the chapter calls grand theory or traditions of thought). We can develop that observation here in three ways.

1   By observing the presence of all four of these kinds of theoretical material in this block:

- We made great play of *conceptual distinctions* — for instance, between three levels of power in Unit 15.

- We offered *particular hypotheses* by way of explanation of particular events — we explained the equal opportunities legislation in Unit 15 as, partly, the product of pressure from women's groups.

- We offered different *theories* of the state at the end of Unit 15 and we returned to these at several points in Unit 16, Sections 3 and 4.

- We related those theories to particular *traditions of thought*.

2   We saw too that there was an intimate connection between the four kinds of theoretical material: that, in particular, grand theories spawn specific theories and use particular conceptual schemas, and specific theories spawn particular hypotheses. As we will see later in this half-unit, there is actually a complex two-way relationship between the various kinds of theory — with the adequacy of a grand theory often having to be reassessed in the light of the fate of the hypotheses and specific theories it characteristically generates. But the initial movement is invariably from grand theory to specific theory; and in Unit 15 we made quite a point of that — introducing specific theories of the state as the application in this area of thinking from broader traditions of thought. We linked pluralist state theory to social reformism and we linked marxist state theory to marxism (of course!). We also said that liberalism and conservatism have generated theories of the modern state.

=== ACTIVITY 5 ===

Go back and read what is said about the state in the 'power and the state' sections of the *liberalism* and *conservatism* parts of the traditions essay in Chapter 22 of the Reader. Then complete Table 1, overleaf, on theories of the state. I think you will find that neither liberalism nor conservatism offer you as detailed a specification of the contemporary state as do marxism and social reformism; and that in consequence it will be difficult to fill in all the boxes. So don't force the material. If it is hard to fill in a box, say so. The *gaps* in theories are as important a guide to their quality as is their *content*. To make this less painful, let me add that you will find the table repeated — with my answers filled in — at the end of this half-unit.

Table 1

	Liberalism	Marxism	Social Reformism	Conservatism
Society		capitalist nature of economy dominates society and state	society immensely complex individuals play many roles, have many interests	
Democracy		capitalist economy generates inequalities of economic power which rob democratic rights of much of their significance	lot of groups lobby state in a democracy strong electoral relationship exists	
Agenda setting		capital interests prevail public opinion moulded by mainly capitalist media revolutionary groups suppressed if dangerous	insider groups and political parties setpolitical agenda	
Determinants of policy		state responds to group and electoral pressures only within limits set by health of capitalist economy and interests of capitalist class	state responds to intensity and volume of group lobbying and electoral demands ultimately voters decide policy	

3   Activity 5 serves to remind us that theories come in packages, and that using one particular theory involves taking on board lots of other theoretical assertions too. It involves adopting a characteristic way of conceptualizing the world, and a particular way of analysing the world as a whole, and not just the state itself.

- So, to accept a marxist theory of the state involves using distinctions between modes of production, and between classes, as the characteristic framework within which to analyse the state. More particularly it involves accepting that the economy over which the state presides is a *capitalist* one, as Marx argued, and that the key political actors and interests involved are *class* actors and *class* interests.

- To use a pluralist theory implies a different reading of economy and society — with a more reformist view of economic practices and a sense of the non-class factors at work in society. It involves a set of conceptual distinctions between *managed* and *unmanaged* economies (rather than between capitalist and non-capitalist ones) and it adds categories of *status* and *gender* to those of class.

—————— ACTIVITY 6 ——————

From what you read earlier about liberal and conservative views of the state, try to fill in the empty boxes in Table 2. Once more my answers are reproduced at the end of this half-unit — though, as you will see, there are matters of judgement here, and you may have included things that I did not.

Table 2

Characteristic categories of analysis

Liberalism	Marxism	Social Reformism	Conservatism
	modes of production capitalism classes ruling class hegemony revolution	mixed economy status groups dominant elites pluralism reform	

Characteristic statements about the world

	life dominated by contradictions and instabilities of capitalism requires revolutionary change	modern society is immensely complex, but open to incremental reform and democratic management	

We are then left with the problem of choosing between these theories, of deciding which — if any — is good enough to accept as an adequate account of how the contemporary state behaves and why. And this in its turn brings us back to where we began — to the question of facts. We need to consider how far we can resolve our choice of theory by some reference to 'the facts'.

SUMMARY

- Theories help to illuminate facts. Theoretical statements come in different forms. They come as conceptual schemas, hypotheses, specific theories and traditions of thought (grand theories).

- These different kinds of theoretical statement are intimately connected. Traditions of thought spawn their own characteristic range of specific theories, particular hypotheses and characteristic conceptual schemas.

- Using a particular theory (of the state, for instance) involves taking on board a lot of related propositions from within the particular tradition of thought from which the theory derives.

4   FACTS AND THEORIES

There are lots of things we could say about the relationship between facts and theories; but let's restrict ourselves to two broad propositions: about the vulnerability of theory to facts, and about the degree to which theories can escape the control of facts. To see how far we can use facts to test theories, let's look at these questions of vulnerability and escape.

4.1 VULNERABILITY: CERTAIN KINDS OF THEORETICAL STATEMENTS ARE TESTABLE AGAINST FACTUAL DATA, OTHERS ARE NOT

We have just seen that theoretical propositions come in different forms. They come as:

- conceptual schemas;
- individual hypotheses;
- specific theories; and
- traditions of thought.

There is a movement here from the specific to the general. Some theoretical propositions (specific hypotheses) cover a little territory. Some (theories of something as specific as the state) cover more ground. Others (broad traditions of thought) have things to say about all sorts of areas (about states, economies, social structures and cultures). In general it is the theoretical statements which cover only a limited area that are most open to being tested against facts. Broad theoretical statements are much less vulnerable to testing against facts than are the specific hypotheses to which they give rise.

To illustrate this, let's look at marxism again: at marxism as a broad tradition of thought, at marxist state theory, and at particular marxist hypotheses about individual states. Marxism as a broad tradition of thought covers a vast agenda; and that agenda includes a view of the state. There are a number of marxist state theories. They are all marxist — that is, they all accept basic marxist specifications of capitalism, its classes and its contradictions. But they each posit slightly different consequences of all that for the state.

- There is a quite simple marxist theory of the state, which says that the modern state is the *agent of* the ruling class (i.e. of the capitalists). This theory derives from the things Marx (and Engels) wrote in *The Communist Manifesto* about the state being the executive of the whole bourgeoisie.

- There is a more sophisticated marxist theory of the state which sees the modern state as acting in the long-term interests of the capitalist class but enjoying a degree of autonomy from its everyday direct control. This theory derives its view — of the 'relative autonomy' of the state from the control of capital — from other things Marx wrote (and from the writings of later marxists, such as Gramsci).

So marxism as a broad tradition of thought is capable of generating at least two theories of the state. Each of these in its turn can then generate a series of discrete hypotheses. Figure 4 illustrates this.

See how the simple theory of the state might generate a hypothesis about the influence of the CBI on government policy. This hypothesis *can* be tested against propositions that sit near the 'hard' factual end of the fact–hypothesis spectrum discussed in Section 2. It is this level of theory which is most open to testing in this way. Political scientists can talk to ministers, CBI representatives, trade unionists, bankers and so on. They can read policy statements and minutes of meetings. They can gather a lot of pretty hard information to prove/disprove this particular hypothesis.

Yet though this hypothesis is directly vulnerable to 'facts' gathered in this way, the theory that spawned it is not. For, even if the particular hypothesis about the CBI is disproved to everyone's satisfaction — which wouldn't be too hard to do — the facts surrounding it would not by themselves disprove the state theory which had generated that hypothesis. All they would do is weaken the credibility of the theory to the extent that it had generated a hypothesis which

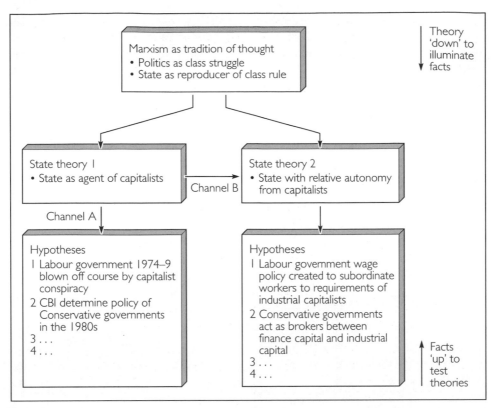

Figure 4

was subsequently disproved. If, time and again, the flow of hypotheses along channel A proved easy to refute, then you might begin to wonder about the adequacy of the source generating them.

Can you see that? If a simple marxist state theory kept on generating rotten hypotheses, then eventually you might be tempted to give it up as a bad job. But you might equally be tempted to redesign a marxist theory to make it more sophisticated. You might shift over, along channel B, to a new marxist state theory, rather than out of marxism altogether.

What facts do (as testers of theories) is therefore threefold: they

1   disprove specific hypotheses,

2   weaken the credibility of certain theories, and

3   encourage the refinement of others.

4.2   ESCAPE: FACTS 'UNDERDETERMINE' THEORETICAL STATEMENTS OF A MORE GENERAL KIND

Traditions of thought, and the more general theoretical statements generated by them, are not so easily proved/disproved by facts. They are more capable of escaping from the control of facts. This is because they can normally accommodate a range of facts. The same factual information can be used to support different theories. As Lukes puts it 'theories may be incompatible with each other and yet compatible with all possible data' (Lukes, 1981).

If that sounds daft, look at state theory again. A pluralist, for example, takes the existence of political parties, general elections and the usual activities associated with democratic politics as evidence of responsive and neutral government. A marxist, on the other hand, treats the political process of

democratic capitalist societies as evidence of the effectiveness of the dominant class in creating the illusion of genuine, free and effective political activity. So the same facts can be interpreted in completely contradictory ways: and the facts themselves don't help us much to distinguish which broad approach is the one we prefer. Figure 5 illustrates the ability of incompatible theories to cope with common data.

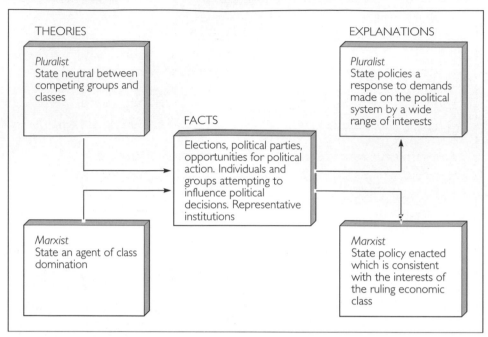

Figure 5
Source: Walton 1982

Yet this ability of incompatible theories to cope with common data does not make the facts irrelevant. 'Grand theory' cannot escape from the control of facts altogether. Facts don't determine which theory of the state is right or wrong. But they do constrain our choice of theories, and they do this in two ways:

- They block out any theory that denies the possibility of democracy in capitalism — any theory which says that elites always rule, or that democratic politicians always fall to the military, for example. Facts oblige theories to deal with the 'truths' they contain, and destroy the credibility of theories which deny the existence of the facts we have established as 'true'.

- Facts also give us a benchmark against which to judge the adequacy of particular theories. If, time and again, the hypotheses generated by a particular theory fall foul of the facts, then the credibility of that theory must begin to wane. If a theory only survives by forever explaining away exceptions, then its general credibility must begin to diminish.

Facts, that is, rarely enable us to dismiss all the theoretical contenders but one. But they do offer us a way of checking the credibility of theories. So facts partly determine, partly constrain theories. That is what we mean by *underdetermination*.

SUMMARY

- Facts do enable us to test the adequacy of particular hypotheses, and to spot the weaknesses of unsophisticated theories.

- Facts on their own do not enable us to resolve the choice between sophisticated theories, or the traditions of thought from which they come. But they help us to make that choice, by setting constraints on the theories that we can recognize as viable.

5 CONCLUSION

The analysis suggests a particular strategy for assessing the adequacy of particular theories — in this case theories of the state. It suggests a strategy with four stages.

1 Clarify the content of the theory — locate its component elements.

2 Situate the theory between the tradition of thought from which it derives and the characteristic hypotheses it generates.

3 Seek out as much hard, reliable evidence as you can find, to throw against the theory's characteristic hypotheses — to see if they stand up — to see if so many of them fall that the general credibility of the theory generating them is seriously dented.

4 Think about the general adequacy of the broad tradition of thought inspiring the theory. Does it help you to make sense of the world you know — the facts you live. Does it accord with your understanding of human nature, and of an ideal society? Does it tie in, that is, with your values?

This fourth stage will occupy us in the half-unit at the end of Block VI, and throughout Block VII. But what we need to do next is to examine the methods available for the pursuit and creation of hard data. That is the topic which awaits us in the next half-unit, Unit 22.

———————————————— ACTIVITY 7 ————————————————

For your last activity in in this block, note down which of the four theories of the state considered in Activity 5 seems the most credible for you. And do it by checking through the first three of the four stages listed above: that is,

- think of its component elements;
- think of how it fits in to a wider tradition of thought and to specific hypotheses; and
- think of which bodies of evidence uncovered in Block IV seem to fit best with its argument.

Then, note down a fact or two that you would find difficult to fit to your chosen theory. It is as well never to relax your guard. Always be sceptical of theories. Always make your acceptance of them provisional on their capacity to handle the 'facts' that you have managed to find!

REFERENCES

Lukes, S. (1981) 'Fact and theory in the social sciences', in D. Potter *et al.* (eds) *Society and the Social Sciences*, London, Routledge and Kegan Paul.

Walton, T. (1982) *Why do Social Scientists Disagree?* Unit 18 in D102: Social Sciences: a Foundation Course, Milton Keynes, The Open University.

POSSIBLE SET OF ANSWERS TO TABLE 1

	Liberalism	Marxism	Social Reformism	Conservatism
Society	society made up of rational self-interested individuals	capitalist nature of economy dominates society and state	society immensely complex individuals play many roles, have many interests	society an organic unit headed by the state society composed of different, unequal but functionally-related parts
Democracy	consent, representation both vital dangers of too much democracy	capitalist economy generates inequalities of economic power which rob democratic rights of much of their significance	lot of groups lobby state in a democracy strong electoral relationship exists	not hostile to democracy, but emphasizes importance of strong, high-quality political leadership
Agenda setting	agenda set by contract between individuals and the state	capital interests prevail public opinion moulded by mainly capitalist media revolutionary groups suppressed if dangerous	insider groups and political parties set political agenda	agenda of state needs to be restricted sticks to maintenance of basic rules avoids radical change
Determinants of policy	government must answer to the people; and if it doesn't, it can be replaced	state responds to group and electoral pressures only within limits set by health of capitalist economy and interests of capitalist class	state responds to intensity and volume of group lobbying and electoral demands ultimately voters decide policy	not clear leaders themselves (people of superior background or training)

POSSIBLE ANSWERS TO TABLE 2

Characteristic categories of analysis

Liberalism	Marxism	Social Reformism	Conservatism
individuals rationality markets rights liberty contract	modes of production capitalism classes ruling class hegemony revolution	mixed economy status groups dominant elites pluralism reform	human imperfection organic society tradition and custom partnership social order inequality leadership

Characteristic statements about the world

society a sum of self-interested individuals in the rational pursuit of private goals	life dominated by contradictions and instabilities of capitalism requires revolutionary change	modern society is immensely complex, but open to incremental reform and democratic management	society a complex interlocking organic unity beyond the capacity of people radically to transform